DisOrganization

THE HANDBOOK OF CREATIVE ORGANIZATIONAL CHANGE

Brian Clegg and Paul Birch

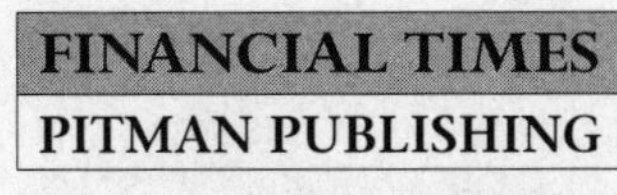

LONDON · HONG KONG · JOHANNESBURG
MELBOURNE · SINGAPORE · WASHINGTON DC

FINANCIAL TIMES MANAGEMENT
128 Long Acre, London WC2E 9AN
Tel: +44 (0)171 447 2000
Fax: +44 (0)171 240 5771
Website: www.ftmanagement.com

A Division of Financial Times Professional Limited

First published in Great Britain 1998

ISBN 0 273 63107 1

British Library Cataloguing in Publication Data
A CIP catalogue record for this book can be obtained from the British Library.

1 3 5 7 9 10 8 6 4 2

Typeset by Northern Phototypesetting Co Ltd, Bolton
Printed and bound in Great Britain by Redwood Books, Trowbridge

The Publishers' policy is to use paper manufactured from sustainable forests.

FINANCIAL TIMES
MANAGEMENT

Knowledge Skills Understanding

Financial Times Management is a new business created to deliver the knowledge, skills and understanding that will enable students, managers and organizations to achieve their ambitions, whatever their needs, wherever they are.

Financial Times Pitman Publishing, part of Financial Times Management, is the leading publisher of books for practitioners and students in business and finance, bringing cutting-edge thinking and best practice to a global market.

To find out more about Financial Times Management and Financial Times Pitman Publishing, visit our website at:

www.ftmanagement.com

About the authors

Brian Clegg

Born in Rochdale, Lancs, and educated at the Manchester Grammar School before getting MAs from Cambridge (Natural Sciences) and Lancaster (Operational Research). Spent 17 years with British Airways in a range of jobs, including Information Centre Manager, Business Support and Operational Research Manager and manager responsible for all personal computing. Promoted creativity within British Airways before becoming an independent business creativity consultant. Author of a number of novels and regular columnist with *PC Week* and *Personal Computer World* magazines, Brian is co-author of two successful books on business creativity, and has recently written *The Chameleon Manager*, a guide to flourishing in a dynamic business environment. Lives in a country village with his wife and two daughters.

Paul Birch

Born in Chalfont St. Giles, Bucks, and educated at Dr. Challoner's Grammar School, Amersham before getting a degree at Newcastle Polytechnic, DMS at East Berkshire Management School, and MBA at Lancaster University. Worked with British Airways for 18 years in a range of roles covering Operational Research, Information Technology, Marketing, Finance, Strategy and even Corporate Jester. Left British Airways to set up a creativity consultancy and as well as working on that is creating a children's problem solving centre at his farm on the Welsh borders.

To Frances, Gillian, Rebecca and
Chelsea, Joanna and Katy –
the long-suffering women in our lives.

Contents

PART THREE: Inward channels

Preface

Traditional organizational structures are failing in a world of frantic change, instant communication and information overload. The truly effective business of the future will have to be responsive and flexible, yet this seems incompatible with the typical corporate hierarchy. Faced with a choice between management and leadership, innovation and reaction, centralization and fragmentation, most have opted for a weak compromise.

DisOrganization offers an original alternative. Don't compromise. Go for both extremes at once. Have inspirational leadership, *and* manage the detail. React to your customers *and* innovate wildly. Break up your business into small units *and* have mechanisms in place to provide superb centralized communication.

A DisOrganized company will be split into units of no more than 50 or 100, to all intents autonomous. These mini companies will be coordinated by a net company, providing overall direction and the fast, effective communications needed to survive. The whole – a hypercompany – will be comprised of a net company and a range of mini companies, some of which are likely to be entirely independent. What were partners now become part of the hypercompany network. This structure combines the flexibility of small business with the power of the big players.

Equipped with the weapons of clarity and direction, fun and empowerment, creativity and innovation, the new organizations will leave the old dinosaurs standing, wondering where the business went.

DisOrganization covers some uncomfortable areas, but is presented in plain language. We want you to be able to take the messages from this book and act on them. If you have been looking for a business book that has something essential to say about your business but is readable, you have just found it.

Key to margin symbols

Throughout the book, notes appear in the margin that expand on the main text.

Interesting facts and figures

A book reference

An exercise

A reference to another relevant section of the book

An interview or biographical information

A quotation

Time out – examples of DisOrganization in action

PART ONE

Direction

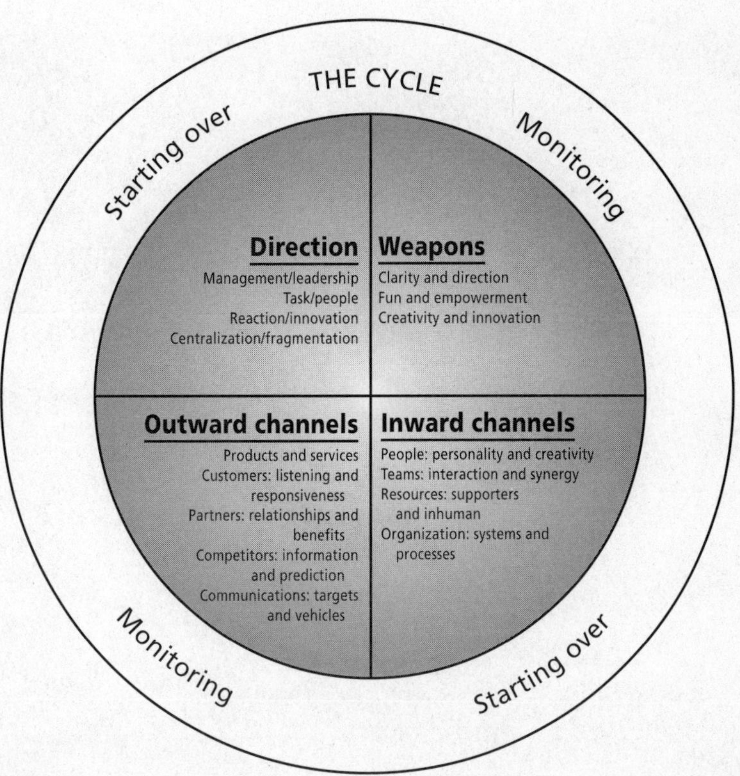

1

Reformation

- Explaining the need for reformation
- Simultaneous opposites, not mushy compromise
- DisOrganization – direction, weapons, inward channels, outward channels, the cycle
- Introducing the DisOrganization map

Why bother?

Change is frightening, exciting, challenging, stimulating – take your pick. Most significantly, though, change is here to stay, and if you don't cope with it, it's going to walk all over you.

Unless you have been living in a monastery, you will have come across books on organizational change before. It's time for a fresh approach, though. Traditional management techniques are becoming increasingly weak when faced with the new world of ultrarapid transformation. In a bewilderingly flexible marketplace with new challenges emerging all the time, the whole concept of strategy begins to fail. There may not be an obvious business route forward, yet to keep things as they are is not acceptable. Stay still and you will perish.

DisOrganization provides a guide to recreating your organization, using creativity techniques and business skills to give the company a new sense of direction and purpose.

REORGANIZING

'I was to learn later in life that we tend to meet any new situation by reorganizing; and a wonderful method it can be for creating the illusion of progress while producing confusion, inefficiency, and demoralization.'

Petronius Arbiter, c. AD 60

This isn't an exercise to undertake lightly. As Petronius noted 1900 years ago, reorganization is a dangerous business. Yet so is any life-saving operation. We won't have the exact answers you require. Like any good consultant (though at a fraction of the cost), we can guide you on where to look, what to consider, what makes sense, but you make the decisions. If you're looking for easy answers and a check-list for success, you are heading down a dangerous route that we can't endorse.

DisOrganization will guide you through establishing a new direction, checking out your weapons for change, examining your inward and outward channels and establishing a cycle of change.

The DisOrganization map (see Figure 1.1) will be used as a reminder of this process throughout the book.

'It's not my job'

We're in the business of radical change; reformation is not for wimps. Chances are you will have to take your organization by the

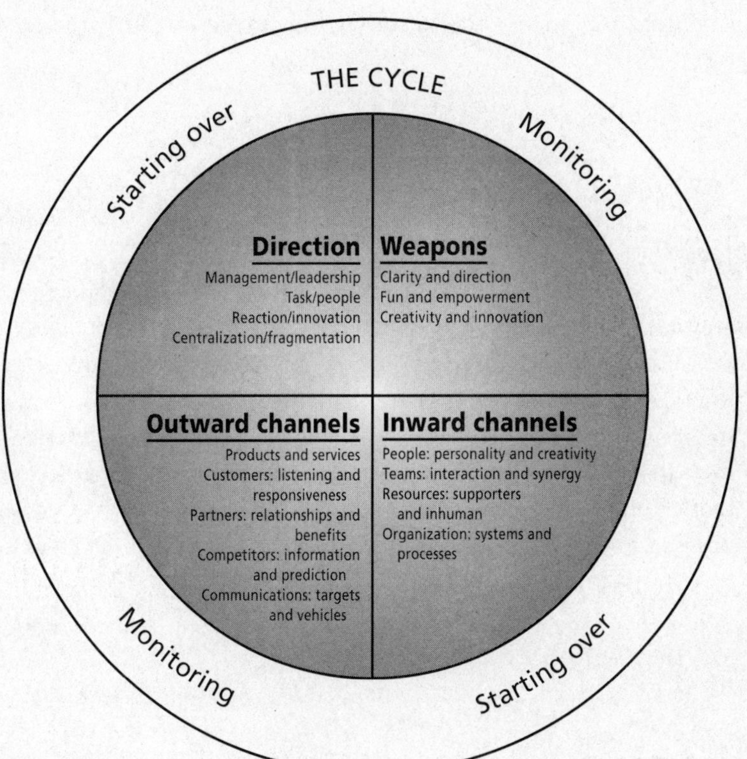

Figure 1.1
DisOrganization map

scruff of the neck, turn it upside down and give it a good shake. This is all very well if you are the CEO or on the Board, but what if you aren't? Make it happen in your department or team, as if it was your own company. Does that mean breaking company rules? It certainly does. There are two possible outcomes. Either the big boys will love you for it, and maybe you'll influence the way the whole enterprise develops (let's hope so for all your sakes), or they'll hate you.

So, you're in a fix. Maybe you've had time to make your company-in-a-company work. If you have, you'll be hard to fire. Your external contacts and influence will be too important to your parent company, but you will still need to think about moving on. If your top management can only recognize gold when they're threatened, you ought to be elsewhere. If it's still early days and you've no protection, all the more reason to walk.

What about the small business? You've already got all the advantages fragmentation can bring, so make sure you pay attention to the other areas. Your centralization imperative is with your external partners – make it work. And there's plenty of leverage still to be had from the other dimensions. Get on with it – and remember to resist the temptation to become another big, faceless company as you grow.

> Many chapters contain a short interview with a business figure. We aren't endorsing the views shown or countering them: we simply present them as a viewpoint. A number are from the information technology (IT) industry, because DisOrganization needs IT and, increasingly, IT companies need DisOrganization. This doesn't make the message any less applicable to other markets, but sometimes it is necessary to look for advice from the young industries. Just as children tend to be more creative than adults, because they haven't been indoctrinated with what is possible, young industries are less hide-bound. It means they make more mistakes, but come up with some fresh answers.

Direction

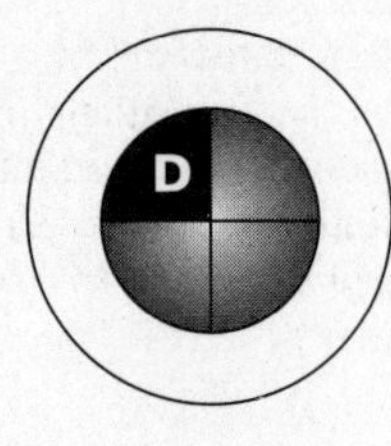

Without a direction, your enterprise is rudderless, drifting in the sea of business possibilities to strike land if you're lucky. To make matters worse, you are in the middle of a sea of icebergs, and the currents are ever-changing. Before this metaphor gets strained beyond breaking point, two considerations emerge.

The first is the need to have a clear target, a set of goals, a purpose for your existence as an organization. The second is not to set your goals in concrete. Don't forget those changing currents. We can't repeat enough how fluid the business world has become. This is a world where a company like Netscape can move from little more than a garage-based outfit to the producer of the world's most popular applications software in a handful of years, selling (or even giving away) software that meets a need that wasn't even envisaged a decade earlier. What's more, that same changeable world could drop Netscape on the scrap heap tomorrow.

Post-modernist sociologists see a world in backlash against the rationalist, science-loving, stable Victorian views that drove early business theory.

It is this post-modern world that makes the ability to change and adapt an essential. This isn't a comfortable situation. You only have to look at the scorn heaped on politicians who make U-turns to see that managers are expected to present a consistent line. Yet the post-modern world will demand a responsiveness that makes last week's right answer into this week's failure. The concept of the learning organization, described in the Weapons section, is one way to help you cope, but, also, there is a need for a dynamic method for establishing and maintaining the direction of the company, rather than pointing one way and going that way evermore.

THE LEARNING ORGANIZATION

See page 76.

POST-MODERNISM

'Clearly the post-modern world has enormous implications for business management. Deregulation, advances in information technology, the globalization of markets, the rise of consumerism and environmentalism, alterations in organizational culture and other transformations of business situations generate the need for firms that are flexible and responsive to change.'

***Roger Bennett, Organizational Behaviour* (Pitman Publishing, 1997)**

In the Direction section of the book, we examine four dimensions that, together, set the overall destination of the company. By making these dimensions explicit and known to the whole company, there is an opportunity to go beyond the rigid mission statement into a comprehensible navigation of the company through the iceberg-laden sea. The dimensions are defined by their extremes, such as centralization or fragmentation, and management or leadership. Most of your companies will be at a certain position on each dimension. We'll be checking out where. Chances are it is not ideal, so we need to find a more ideal location. That will probably be in the middle, a balanced approach, right?

This seems eminently reasonable. The trouble is, being reasonable does not win the day. Do you know what's in the middle? A weak, mushy compromise. It just isn't good enough. Does this mean we're advocating extremism? Yes and no. Not a politician's answer, but the exact truth. Yes, you must aim for the extremes, but no, not in the sense that is generally understood. You shouldn't be a pure management fanatic or a leadership buff. You have to be both. The target is not the middle, but both ends of the spectrum simultaneously. Difficult? Yes. Impossible? No.

Taking such an extremist view, you will need to have pure leadership setting the vision, mission, principles and so on, and micro-management ensuring the best is delivered in meeting them. Then you've got to put your people first and empower them, but always in order to help them focus on the task. At the same time, you must innovate wildly while always listening to the market, not to mention totally fragmenting into small companies, while establishing a mechanism that pulls them all together.

Weapons

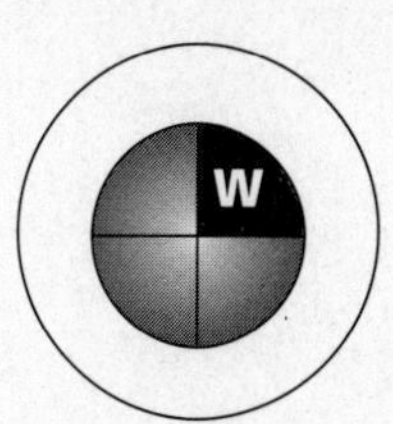

If establishing a new direction is hard, providing the means to get there is even harder. (Don't think, by the way, that the need to be positioned at both extremes of each dimension makes finding an initial direction any easier. Remember, there are no easy prescriptions. You can't DisOrganize off the peg; each company will have its own extremes, its own scale, its own universe.) We can no longer rely on weaponry of change that was designed for the twentieth century. In stable times there is less need for innovation, but in a fast-changing world that shows no sign of slowing down, creativity becomes an essential for survival. Accordingly, we need creative means to achieve change.

Our first concern will be weapons of clarity and direction. Once these would have been driven uniquely by the conservative ends of the directional dimensions: management, task, reaction and centralization. They still play their part, but there is also need for vision, mission, and principles. Support for communication and the free dissemination of information will matter every bit as much as control systems and project planning.

Next are the weapons of fun and empowerment. Most talk of fun and empowerment in business has been just that: talk. It makes great theory on a planning session in an expensive hotel. It sounds good when talking to the staff. But when the day-to-day circus of problems and decisions strikes, fun goes out of the window to be replaced by the miserable countenance that is considered the only context for 'real business', and empowerment is replaced by the chains of tight budgetary control. We'll look at why very few businesses have done anything to make these concepts real, why they can slip under pressure with disastrous results, and how to take fun and empowerment as seriously as the more traditional tools of management.

Finally, we will be looking at the weapons of creativity and innovation. In fact, creativity will be important throughout the process of change, but here we focus on the explicit application of creativity. Again, there is an overwhelming temptation for creativity to go to the wall when things are most critical, yet it is when problems seem insuperable that creativity is most needed. Obviously hitting the innovation target on the reaction/innovation continuum will require some creativity. Paradoxically, reaction also requires innovation – the innovation of problem solving, rather than idea generation, but innovation none the less.

Inward channels

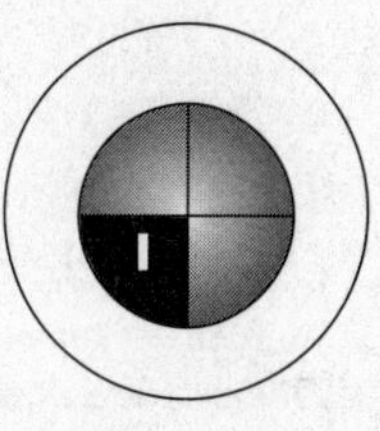

You don't apply your weapons of change to your direction – the direction is the outcome you hope to bring about. Instead, the weapons are focused through a number of channels. In the next section of the book, we look at the inward channels, the targets for change within your direct control – your people and teams; your organization as a whole.

The main vehicle we're going to use is the 'how to'. Rather than spout endless theory on applying particular weapons to particular channels, and ending up with a creed that's about as readable as a railway timetable, we're going to take a series of key questions that arise from our fundamental assumption that your organization needs to take the radical step of moving to both extremes of each dimension simultaneously. By addressing these questions, we will bring out the lessons, without a boring list-every-combination structure.

Your inward channels are the starting point. It's no good saying the customer comes first; your people, your resources have to be the initial focus, with the understanding that they're there for the sole reason of making the customer's life joyful. That's why we'll be looking at your people, your teams (whether small project teams or whole departments and divisions), your resources and your organization.

Outward channels

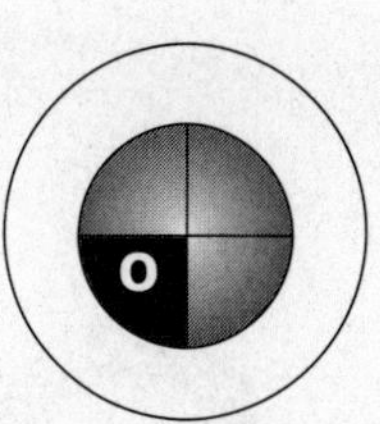

Next, it's time to bridge the gap to the outside world. We start with products and services. They could arguably appear as both inward and outward channels; we put them here as they are worthless without an eye to the market. After all, apart from subsistence farming, it's hard to think of any business activity that isn't dependent for its survival on external factors just as much as internal ones.

We also apply the 'how to's' to your customers, partners, competitors and broad communications. Don't be put off by the 'partner' word. It's another management buzz word that has become meaningless as a result of brainless repetition. Traditionally, a company dealt with suppliers, other companies used to provide the needs of your business, in a strict relationship of 'take them for all they're worth'. From the buyer's viewpoint, the aim was to minimize cost; from the supplier's to maximize profit. You can't afford that outlook any more. What's more, if you've achieved a split down to small

HERBERT MARSHALL McLUHAN

Born in Canada (1911–80), McLuhan developed the pop 1960s tag 'the medium is the message'. His theory that the electronic media were becoming more important than the information they carried predated the popularity of the Internet by a couple of decades, but is ideally suited to the wired world. McLuhan's awareness of the ability of the media to change society is paralleled in the changes that new vehicles of communication are working on contemporary business.

units, their relations with external partners are likely to be more important than with many other units in the original corporation. Remember, too, that innovation can provide new opportunities for supplier partnerships. After all, every supplier is also somebody's customer.

All channels – inward or outward – are about communication, so why give it a chapter of its own? Some communication is indirect – it will slip through the cracks unless it is explicitly dealt with. Use of the media, and now the Internet, requires a quite different approach to that conventionally used for dealings with staff or customers. In such circumstances, creativity is often left to an outside agency, but is this the right approach in a new world where advertising can be changed daily in direct response to customer comment? Marshall McLuhan's observation that the medium is the message may not be entirely true, but it reflects the need to be more aware than ever of how you are putting across your message internally and to the wider world.

The cycle

Surrounding our DisOrganization map is a ring labelled 'the cycle'. The cycle is pure chicken and egg. It comprises monitoring and starting over. Monitoring, because what gets measured gets done. When you measure the right things, you are taking a big step towards success. Not an easy step, though. Measurement can become an obsession that gets in the way of action. How do you know what to measure? How do you measure it effectively? How do you minimize the cost of measurement on the bottom line and yet maximize its impact? Creativity keeps the measurement towing the line.

Starting over is more insidious. The world does not stand still. The days of a successful idea or a single static structure that offers sustainable competitive advantage are long gone. What a business needs for long-term success is fast-paced innovation that is never-ending. This not only means changes in products and services, but an organization that itself is ever searching for a better form. DisOrganization is not satisfied with a major upheaval that is supposed to result in stability for the next ten years – this is a fiction. DisOrganization requires not a big bang followed by stagnation, but continuous creative development.

DisOrganization

Each section of this book ends with a summary mini chapter that pulls together the section and points on to the next. It's a reminder that whatever directions we are setting, whatever weapons we establish, whatever channels we attack and cycle we follow, DisOrganization is about more than simple creativity techniques, more than organizational change, but about a reformation into a new, more flexible entity.

Thanks, Tom

With many others, Tom Peters has already recognized the need to fragment. In *Crazy Times Call for Crazy Organizations*, Peters comments on the need for decentralization and how, in most cases, where this has occurred that it hasn't been enough to bring in the small company feel. In fact, he observes that companies need to go beyond decentralization to disorganization.

DISORGANIZATION

Tom Peters, *The Tom Peters Seminar: Crazy Times Call for Crazy Organizations* (Random House, 1994).

We hadn't realized when deciding on the title for this book that we were hitting on the same word as Peters uses for a book chapter on fragmentation. It doesn't really matter; we might not always agree, but our approaches are complementary. If you like what you read here, check out *Crazy Times* … and thanks, Tom.

Moving on

It's time to move on to establishing your direction. We begin with the management/leadership dimension. Without a change here, nothing else can follow.

2

Management or leadership, task or people?

- Management – getting results through others by instruction
- Leadership – getting others to achieve results by setting a direction
- Achieving management and leadership
- A focus on people and unreasonable requests
- Where do you sit now?

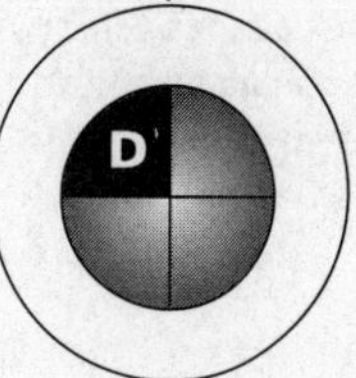

Hard man or touchy feely?

To generalize painfully, there are two models on which management can be based: the army and the family. The first relies on absolute focus on task. The individual simply doesn't matter; the soldier (worker) is just another resource. Such a management approach assumes that the workforce needs detailed instructions to carry out any task and a complicated bureaucracy to support management activity. The prime motivator is the stick – get something wrong and you are in serious trouble.

The second approach is driven entirely by people. Instead of prescriptive management, we see inspirational leadership, setting an example and broad principles, but not attempting to give detailed instructions. Individuals are considered to be just that, and are given considerable freedom to find their own way of working and to make best use of their talents. The prime motivator is the carrot – get it wrong and you learn from your mistake; get it right and enjoy the praise.

Continuing with our gross generalization, the task-driven army model was the basis for business management for the first half of the twentieth century and for much of the second. The Henry Ford style of organization, where people were just additional machines on the production line, carried far beyond manufacturing industry. Workers were expected to perform their specified tasks – no less and no more.

ARMIES AND IDEAS

'A stand can be made against an invasion by an army; no stand can be made against an invasion by an idea.'

Victor Hugo

In the 1970s and 1980s, this approach was breaking down. Many influences were conspiring to encourage the family model. Words like 'empowerment' and concepts like 'Management by Walking About' were the vogue in large corporations that could afford expensive consultants. There were some improvements, yet all did not become rosy. Something was amiss. Could it be that the pendulum swung too far the other way? That a total obsession with people resulted in loss of focus on the task? That the real business imperatives of profitability and competition got lost in the fuzzy warmth of people being 'our most important asset'? Or could it be that an awful lot of lip-service was paid to putting people first, with very little actually happening to back it up. A manager we know once remarked, 'the secret of management is fooling them into thinking you care about them'. Was this the obstacle to success?

Dimensional drift

This chapter is something of a fake. It is covering not one dimension, but two. As well as the continuum from management to leadership, there is the parallel span of task to people. However, when you get down to detail, the two dimensions are practically inseparable. Leadership achieves its breadth of vision by concentrating on people. Management tends to home in on the detail of task. Although it is possible for a leader to be task-focused, the tasks are always achieved by people. Because of this tight interlinking, we have not tried to separate the two.

Michael J. Skok is Chairman and CEO of AlphaBlox Corporation, formed in 1996 in Mountain View, California. Actively involved in the software industry for more than 18 years, both as an entrepreneur and an investor, in 1988, Skok founded European Software Publishing (ESP), which acquired the publishing rights for Symantec UK. This organization has been built into one of the most successful parts of the group and, as such, it was subsequently reacquired by Symantec Corporation. ESP has gone on to become the leading independent software publisher in Europe. Skok served three terms as President of the Software Publishers Association (SPA) Europe and was a member of the Board of Directors of the Federation Against Software Theft (FAST).

What comes first, tasks or people?

The greatest inhibiting factor for companies is communications bandwidth. My role changes each time we add a person to the company. With six people, you've got a natural grouping. One office, one water cooler, one meeting. You don't need to formalize anything. The speed with which things are done is incredible.

If you look from there, between 6 and 36 you can do things in 2s, with say 6 departmental and 1 group meeting. Informally there's a lot can still go on between the groups. But the next scale up there's a dramatic shift. Every new person has to build their own interpersonal links and cross-departmental knowledge. You get to a stage where there are more people than we have human capacity to deal with, and have to resort to systems and processes. A really smart company thinks about the principles for communication and collaboration long before they've got a problem with it.

SPHERES OF INFLUENCE

Spend five minutes jotting down the names of everyone within your company you have regular, significant interactions with. Classify them by the organizational structure: are there any gaps? Do you really understand what's going on in all those areas?

So how do you get big and remain fast and flexible?

One thing that doesn't work is setting rules. Rules are set at a specific point in time. You can't rely on rules, because they'll be out of date as soon as they're set. Rely instead on principles – principles based on fundamental values with a strong underlying culture. When you need guidance, the question ought to be 'What does the culture say here?'

For example, lots of companies say 'the customer comes first'. Is that really the case? What happens when an employee calls in sick? A principle is something derived from the culture. Ours is that happy people make for happy customers. If you are looking after your people, then you are providing the underpinning for them to look after your customers. Sure, the only reason the staff are here is to serve the customer, but the underlying principle of health first is key. So when someone calls in sick, they'll let us know what needs to be done – but keeping the staff happy is our aim. You don't have to worry about how big you grow if you have this kind of underlying approach based on principles and values, and fundamental to it is building the right corporate culture. At AlphaBlox we spend one to two days with a new employee just working through the culture.

Culture becomes critically important as you scale up, because there comes a point where I can't even set the principles. Say you've got a field service organization. Someone in the field is going to see the realities faster. The right person to sort out the principle is the person in the field. The person closest to the customer should have empowerment to do the right thing; they don't need to refer back up the hierarchy. This principle is backed by a cultural belief – that we're hiring the right people for the job. Let's trust them to refer to the culture, accept they're going to make mistakes and let them learn from them and get on with it. Working from culture to values to principles and then to actions is the way to build an enduring company.

So what's gone wrong in some large companies?

It's incredibly hard to turn around a large, lumbering firm. For instance, IBM built a fabulous company, but perhaps it was built on rules. They got in the habit of doing things particular ways that crystallized into rules. Then they can't respond quickly to changes. It might be controversial saying this – I've spoken to many great industry leaders and ultimately culture has to be something that senior management don't delegate. I delegate everything *except* culture. If the principles of management differ from the principles of action, then there's a mismatch. You've got to set the culture and build trust for your people to go and live it.

The fundamental thing is that management know that setting culture is their role and know that it's the single most important thing. They've got to walk the talk. In practice I might break more of my principles than anyone in the company, but I don't find it acceptable. I have to be accountable for it, and anyone in the business should be able to come up to me and tell me.

There has to be more than just culture?

You can't do all this based just on culture. Your company has to be based on a single, clear compelling vision, mission and goals. The vision might come from many different sources, such as the customers and market, but the key is to make sure that everyone's energies are clearly pointed in a single, unified direction. By clarifying and focusing on what your unique differentiators are, you harness the energies of your people. The speed of change now means that the vision has to be an understanding. If it is just words, you've got a problem. Although the objective might say we want to build *N* new customer relationships, what's important is why. If it turns out we can't get the number we set, then the principle of building the business should serve, not the words. Objectives should be a series of understandings, and clearly set expectations. You are saying here's the map. To say we'll travel down this specific road is the wrong way to operate. You are setting a destination, a direction, but not a road.

When we established Symantec in Europe, one of the challenges was to make our quarterly returns. Customers don't operate neatly by quarter. Do you blow the deal to try to make the numbers or do you stand back and make it clear what you are doing? One country went for the numbers; another recognized that the smart thing to do was to establish the core root of the problem. It wasn't in the objectives, but it turned out that the need was to train the field sales force to sell the product differently. Fortunately, the country manager knew that he wanted to build business. He couldn't fix things in time for that quarter, but the outcome was much greater ultimate revenues against short-term meetings of objectives by 'stuffing' the channel.

It's all about maps and training people to navigate for themselves. Don't get me wrong – it's very hard to implement this. But very necessary.

DIFFERENTIATE

1 constitute a difference between or in.
2 find differences (between); discriminate.
3 make or become different in the process of growth or development (species, word-forms, etc.)

***Concise Oxford Dictionary* (9th Edition, Oxford University Press, 1996; all extracts appear by permission of Oxford University Press).**

Management

Management has been described as the art of getting things done via others. This definition is, of itself, inadequate for our needs because leadership could be seen in the same terms. To be more specific, management is about organizing people and other resources to achieve the aims of the company. Management focuses on the detail, the intimate mechanics of making things happen. Management is largely based on the authority of position rather than the authority of the individual. People do what a manager tells them (or not) because of the job role, not because of the individual filling the role.

There's nothing wrong with any of that. Management is neither better nor worse than leadership. It is simply different, more or less appropriate in different circumstances. The reason that pure management is sometimes derided is that it can also be about making sure that things get done today the way they've always been done. Management can be a huge block to change. That's because management is a rules-based approach. In a managed culture, when an employee encounters a situation that's not covered by the rules – an increasingly common occurrence in a frantically changing world – they are stuck until management can issue a new rule.

Leadership

Leadership is about causing other people to follow a direction you set or a vision you lay out for them. Unlike management it need have no resources, no projects, no tangible outcome. It is about direction more than goal. Leadership has little concern for detail, it is much more about painting the broad picture and letting individuals and circumstance dictate the detail. More often than not, a leader is also a manager. That is, there is usually a need to ensure that the detail is falling into place if the aims of the company are to be met.

We have spent a significant part of our careers trying to understand leadership. It is one of those rare commodities that, if bottled, would make the vendor a fortune. So far we have been unable to bottle it and have found it equally difficult to buy elsewhere. The closest we can come is in identifying a couple of simple principles that delineate leadership. First, leadership is about people and, second, leadership is about unreasonable requests. A gross oversimplification? Absolutely. When did you ever read a management book that wasn't? Yet, such simplification is justified when we are talking about leadership. After all, leadership is about setting broad principles and letting you fill in the details yourself.

People

So, what about people? It's a truism that's so obvious, so basic that it's almost always ignored: the thing that makes your organization work is its people. How many times have you read in a company's report and accounts, 'Our most important asset is our people'? How many times have you seen companies that really act as though it were true? Most of us have seen hundreds of companies that claim to be people-focused and, if we are lucky, have seen one or two that really act that way. Leadership has to be about the way you relate to other people.

There are individuals who are uncomfortable with this. They may be painfully shy or just unable to relate to others. This is certainly an obstacle to leadership, but not insurmountable. We have seen shy people who really hate to be seen in public who have realized that this is their only road to success. They have forced themselves to be more able to cope in public. Those who are genuinely unable to relate to others have a harder time. They may be able to fake leadership for a time, but will say or do things that are at odds with their created persona. These are the leaders who end up being distrusted by those they lead. We can all think of examples of politicians who fit this image. People who have been voted in because they were good at faking it and who have then been unable to retain the faked sincerity. Usually they will look after people only so long as it suits them. This is not enough. The key to the people element of leadership is not that you are liked; this is nice for the ego, but unnecessary for leadership success. What is essential is that you are *trusted* by your people. Without trust you cannot lead.

Unreasonable requests

When you find a company, a department or a team that really looks after its people, look at the person in charge. The chances are, you will find a leader. This seems to have an uncomfortable fit with our 'unreasonable requests' requirement for leadership. How can you care for your people and then make unreasonable requests of them? Yet there must be a way to join these seemingly opposite approaches, as leaders have demonstrated this mix since the dawn of time. Generals, politicians, captains of industry have put their people through hell and still muster a degree of loyalty that few of us will ever achieve. The issue here appears to be fairness. That is, if you demand much of your people, you should demand more of yourself, and what you demand should be done in a consistent and equitable manner. Together, trust and fairness will move mountains.

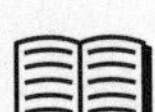

MORE FISHY TALES

For more information on Sea World's work in training marine mammals, visit its web site: http://www.seaworld.org

Training a killer whale

One of us recently went on holiday to Florida and made the obligatory visit to Sea World. Like most of the audience, we were overawed at the sight of killer whales leaping so high out of the water, at times propelling their trainers ahead of them like missiles.

So, how *do* you persuade a few tons of killer whale to leap out of the water at your request? By asking it nicely. The trainers deliver positive reinforcement to the animals every time they perform in a desired way. For instance, you don't get them to leap over a rope hung way up in the air by putting it up there and waiting for them to jump over it. Instead, the rope is placed low in the water and the whale is rewarded every time it passes across. The reward can be food, a back scratch, a toy, even squirting with a hose. The whale just needs to know it is being told 'Well done'. Once the animal establishes a relationship between passing over the rope and reward, you raise the level. When it approaches the surface they must jump to pass over. Ultimately the rope will be raised to the desired height and you have one small part of an amazing show.

What about punishment when they fail? There is none. To quote from the Sea World web site, 'If we request a particular behavior and the animal does not respond, or the animal responds with undesired behavior, we remain motionless for three seconds ... We never force a situation and we never punish an animal.'

Wouldn't that be a wonderful way for us to learn at work? We would set targets and would provide (or be provided with) huge amounts of praise for achieving them and no punishment for failing. Yet most companies we work with have performance appraisal systems that emphasize failures and effectively punish at times when things go wrong while ignoring the huge number of times things go right. Next time you are working with a colleague, how about catching them passing over ropes and letting them know they're doing it. You'll soon have them leaping in the air.

So what did you do today?

It seems that a key differentiator between leadership and management could be that leadership is about making things happen that would not have happened without the leader, and management is about facilitating those things that might have happened anyway. Most of your staff probably believe that, at best, you make happen what would have happened anyway and, at worst, you get in the way. Put less judgmentally, managers achieve goals and leaders create them.

But don't make the mistake of seeing leadership purely in simplistic terms. It is a continual, never-ending process. It is not a series of high-profile events. The balance between looking after people and making unreasonable requests of them is only one of the seemingly irreconcilable conflicts faced by a leader.

Where does your organization sit right now?

The chances are that your organization exhibits more of the characteristics of a *managed* company than a *led* company. This would not be surprising as it is true of almost every large organization (and most small ones) anywhere. In order to establish where your organization sits, we've devised a short test. This is wholly unscientific, untested and gives no more than indicative results, but we think that you'll identify with the answers it provides. If you don't, then by all means come up with a better one and send it to us.

If you decide that the test has no value in positioning your understanding, try thinking through task versus people. How task-focused is your company? How people-focused is it? If you are managing or leading a team of people, how much of your effort is spent on making sure that results are delivered and how much is spent on looking after the people doing the delivery?

MANAGED OR LED?

Score each of the following statements out of 10 (0 if the statement is wholly untrue and 10 if it is wholly true).

My organization...

1	is clear about direction	______
2	tolerates mistakes	______
3	has a sense of humour	______
4	buzzes with energy	______
5	is truly effective	______
6	supports me in what I do	______
7	provides more than just a job for pay	______
8	helps me to develop myself	______
9	is able to change course and approach swiftly	______
10	challenges and stretches me continually	______
	Total	______

Your test results
The higher the score (the maximum is 100), the greater the tendency towards leadership in the company.

Where do you want your organization to sit?

When looking at the dimension of leadership and management, most organizations would say that they wanted to be at the leadership end. It's not surprising. You have only to look at our previous paragraphs to see all the admirable, hero-type qualities that relate to leaders, while poor old managers just make the everyday happen. Yet it's worth remembering that an obsession with task management still has its place. There are industries where labour supplies are plentiful and turnover is not an issue. However, these industries are dwindling and, over time, even they must expand their focus to include people along with task.

It is not enough, though, to aspire to the sexy option. We believe that you must excel at both leadership and management to be truly successful. You must take on both extremes of the task/people continuum in parallel. If you accept this, you need to find tools that will allow you to become better at both styles. The chances are that you will need to work more on leadership than management because you will probably have found by now that you lack this quality more.

Before you do decide this, take a look at the management skills in your organization. Even if you decide that you are lacking in leadership, you may still need to work on your managerial skills. Being poor in the one does not automatically make you strong in the other. Whatever you decide, you will find some useful hints in the Weapons section. This is where we focus on the things you can do to move yourself and your organization towards the ends of the continua we describe.

Where are you going?

One final observation about this dimension that is fundamental, obvious and often overlooked. Neither leadership nor management is an end in itself; they are means to ends. Being entirely successful at spanning both ends of our continuum, yet pointing the organization in the wrong direction is to guarantee success in leadership and management terms, and failure of the business. Remember that we are talking about ways of getting things done. Nothing more and nothing less. Selecting what is done is certainly one of the roles of a leader, but you can be very successful at the *process* of selecting and entirely wrong in what it is you select.

3

Reaction or innovation?

- The dangers of not being reactive – and of being too reactive
- Achieving real reaction and in-depth innovation
- Innovation by copying
- Where do you sit?

D

What's the opposite of innovative?

When you look at a spectrum that has 'innovative' at one extreme, what do you put at the other? 'Boring', perhaps. If you call someone innovative it will rarely be taken as an insult (except, perhaps in a government department). On the other hand, relying on reaction is often seen as a negative. How many management texts have you read encouraging you to stop being reactive and start being proactive?

Yet, consider your relationship with your customers. Look at the success of a company such as Morgan Cars in Britain, which has been making essentially the same model of sports car for decades, because that's what people want. Remember the ever-present need to listen to the customer. We might admire innovation, but is it desirable to innovate to the extent of ignoring customer requirements? Ignoring customers is a route to disaster, but, sadly, so is slavishly listening to them.

Fawlty business

The classic John Cleese TV series, *Fawlty Towers*, revolves around an autocratic owner to whom customers are simply an irritation. While you would be hard pressed to consider Basil Fawlty an innovator, his only reaction to customers is disdain. It's great fun, but of course no real businesses are like that, are they?

- Pan American Airlines spent the last ten years of its life on the verge of bankruptcy, yet the management still felt it knew what its customers really wanted, and was delivering it, never realizing that it was wrong.
- The Conservative Party in the UK has accepted that it lost the 1997 election because it ignored the messages from grass roots party activists. The Party became so involved in Westminster politics that it thought it knew best what the electorate wanted. The result, its largest landslide defeat ever.
- Royal Dutch Shell lost a huge number of customers when it

ignored the public outcry against its handling of the obsolete Brent Spar drilling platform.

- Kodak has been pretty successful over the years, but it's hard to imagine who Kodak's managers were listening to when they launched PhotoCD as a consumer product. The idea that anyone would get their holiday snaps put onto a CD that needed a special player to view them on the TV is technically exciting, but the fact is, everyone wants to carry their photographs around to show their friends. PhotoCD has achieved some success as a professional format, but has been disastrous commercially.
- British inventor Sir Clive Sinclair had a string of hits from miniature radios and TVs to home computers. However, he is primarily thought of now as the man who introduced the C5, a one-person electric microcar. The trouble is, the public thought it was a joke. Result, that's the way it started to treat the company.

CUSTOMER FOCUS

Got a new product under development? Go to see half a dozen customers with the product yourself. Get some feedback, and do something about it. Trivial? No, because your company has built up systems that get between you and the customer. Go around them.

The customer is hardly ever right

All these businesses suffered by ignoring that time-honoured maxim, 'the customer is always right'. The trouble is, the customer is hardly ever right. What is really intended is 'treat the customer as if they were right, whatever they say'. That's fine for customer service, but it's a dire way to decide on your product range. Generally, customers are less dumb than we believe (you've only got to watch satellite TV to see how dumb some companies think the punters are). But it's a mistake to take this as giving any great value to formal market research. The fact is, important though your business is to *you*, chances are it's pretty peripheral to your customers. They aren't about to put the effort into thinking about what new stuff they'd like, so they'll say they want more of the same. Marketing departments throughout the world suffer from the shared delusion that their product is fundamental to their customers. In reality they would be better assuming that their product has no value and working to change that.

Even if customers were willing to come up with great new ideas, they generally don't have the training in creativity techniques to do it effectively. We aren't saying ignore your customers as they're usually good at telling you what's wrong with what you do, and that is absolutely essential information. Good reaction is crucial when problems are hit. However, there's little point in expecting customers to tell you much about the future. Market research isn't a total waste of time, but you'd be much better having senior executives talk directly to customers than all the market research surveys in the world. When you hear someone praising a market research survey, you're listening to someone who has never been on the receiving end. Who has never rushed through an interview in the street, giving any old answer or ticked boxes at random because there's a prize on offer?

So, reaction to your customers isn't enough, but you knew that. You innovate all the time, just like these companies.

- IBM in the bad old days was a watchword for customer service. The computing giant was built on an intense focus on the customer. In theory, IBM was innovative too, with an immense effort going into research. The trouble is, when it came to products, IBM was conservative. For years, IBM's PCs were underpowered, partly because they didn't want to outshine much more expensive minicomputers, partly because IBM had promised customers that the ageing 80286 chip would be at the centre of its business for years to come. IBM's innovation inertia was a significant contributor to its multibillion dollar losses in the late 1980s.
- There are few product love affairs better documented than that between the American consumer and the automobile. American manufacturers were great at listening to what the public wanted and pushing every possible gadget into huge, gas-guzzling monsters. In came the Japanese, with small, fuel-conscious, flexible models. Thankfully, lacking the invaluable customer knowledge that the American consumer wanted big cars, they ate up a vast chunk of the market.
- The peoplemovers or family vans are another automobile example. Vehicles such as the Plymouth Voyager, Ford Windstar/Galaxy, Renault Espace – everybody seems to make one these days. These were cars that no research indicated a need for.
- The Sony Walkman is another product that nobody wanted until they saw it. Now it seems most people can't even go for a run without one.

John Sculley is a founding partner of Sculley Brothers, a New York-based private investment and strategic advisory firm. Through this he has involvement in a number of high-tech firms, including the role of Chairman of Live Picture Inc. He was CEO of Apple Computers from 1983 to 1993 and President and Chief Executive of the Pepsi-Cola Company for five years previously.

How can a big company be innovative?

By definition, big companies are not organized to be innovative: they are organized to implement in ways that are both strategic and tactical to the well-understood mission of the enterprise. Innovation, on the other hand, is usually about breaking the pattern and looking for new markets and new ways of doing things. Big companies are turning to small companies to do their innovation for them. This is particularly true as the product development cycle shortens and the activity with strategic alliances and acquisitions of small companies by big companies increases. New companies have to be innovative because they are justifying their existence all the time.

How do you balance giving the customer what they want and coming up with original products?

More and more companies have to be very responsive to customers. Fortunately technology is helping us with customer feedback systems, the ability to customize products and services easily and inexpensively and the increasing use of datamining and database marketing tools.

Can you create the excitement and drive of a start-up in a large organization? If so, how?

Start-ups take a leader who can focus the team on a single, important, exciting idea and charge everybody with a lot of passion to do whatever it takes to succeed.

We've heard a lot about empowerment and management by walking about, but it seems rarely to be employed – is it business school theory or a practical approach?

This may be rare in the UK, but it happens every day in Silicon Valley. It is a fundamental characteristic of every successful start-up I know.

Should work be fun? If so, how do you make it happen?

It's easiest to have fun when companies are in their early stages of building a business. This is because everybody feels a part of what needs to be done to be successful.

COSYING UP

Nowhere is the use of acquisitions to generate innovation more obvious than in the IT business. Before takeover by IBM, the only significant application software giant Lotus developed itself was the spreadsheet 1-2-3; the rest were bought in. It's rare for a week to pass without half a dozen headline takeovers and joint ventures in the industry.

So how reactive or innovative is your company?

Use this informal questionnaire to get a feel for your current position.

REACTION OR INNOVATION?

Score each of the following statements out of 10 (0 if the statement is wholly untrue and 10 if it is wholly true).

In my organization...

1	we don't like to be at the bleeding edge	______
2	customer surveys are important	______
3	we aren't driven by technology	______
4	we don't use prototyping	______
5	we launch products/services infrequently, after perfecting them	______
6	we spend very little on R&D	______
7	we let the competition move first, then follow	______
8	we give people what they want	______
9	we try not to anticipate new trends	______
10	if it ain't broken, we don't fix it	______
	Total	______

Your test results
The bigger your score, the more reactive you are.

Where should your company sit?

This is the easiest of the dimensions in which to understand the need to sit at both ends of the spectrum simultaneously. It seems natural that a company should be prepared to listen to its customers and react to customer needs. Equally, in a dynamic, uncomfortably unstable world, it is inevitable that innovation is an important force in staying ahead of the game. Such reassurance does not mean, though, that many companies are achieving both goals. At best, they are liable to aim for a compromise. We'll generally listen to what our customers ask for, water it down, mix in a little innovation to make sure that we have new(ish) products in the pipeline and sit back, happy. That's cloud cuckoo land.

In fact, there does appear to be one way to cheat with this dimension. At first glance there is an excellent way to succeed by being totally reactive. Listen to your customers to fix what's wrong, and listen to your competitors to achieve new products. Don't bother with being innovative. Let the rest do all the hard work and piggyback on their research. This is an entirely legitimate argument, yet it doesn't damage our premise. Admittedly, the reasoning is wrong, as being innovative doesn't have to be hard work (see Chapter 8, our Weapons of creativity and innovation chapter, if you need convincing), yet the conclusion is legitimate. You can succeed by watching what successful companies do and reacting to them. Our argument isn't damaged because this approach requires innovation, too, just pointed a different way. To adopt this strategy and succeed demands innovative production, design and marketing.

WEAPONS OF CREATIVITY AND INNOVATION

See page 79.

A copycat reactor must be able to manufacture a product in half the time of the competition, because the others have a head start. They've already got something to market, and you are starting from scratch. There's also a need for innovation because it's not enough to make a carbon copy (except with a totally commoditized product, and it is arguable that any product in the world can be differentiated if we are imaginative enough). You have to make your design seem like version 2, the product the other people would have made if they hadn't been first on the scene.

Some of the greatest business successes of this century have involved taking an existing product, giving it a twist and improving on it no end. There is even a flourishing trade in brushing off and rebuilding obsolete patents, ideas whose time had not yet come. Yet, whichever path you choose, the need is the same: reaction and innovation in partnership.

'Innovation's not what we do'

Like the rest of the media, the publishing trade is notoriously reactive. Just as Hollywood will imitate any successful film to death, fiction publishers will cling onto a format that has been a success until someone manages, by an accidental step into novelty, to start a new trend. There has never been a worse time for new fiction authors, as publishers spend fortunes on promoting established names and spend so much effort avoiding risk that they wouldn't recognize it if it punched them on the nose.

We have a personal example here. Check out these remarks: 'this is an intriguing and imaginative idea', 'I find this a fascinating idea', 'this a very diverting idea', 'we like this idea very much', 'this is an ingenious idea' ... quotes from great reviews? No, from rejection letters. Each from a different publisher, each saying 'this is an effective business proposition, but we don't do books like this'. The trouble is, the proposal was for a kind of book that no one does yet. In the IT industry, publishers would be falling over themselves to develop a product that addressed an as yet untapped market, but to book publishers the response was pure reaction. We can't do this because we don't do this. Some business sectors go out of their way to make every opportunity a problem.

Great reaction

We've majored on how not to be a good reactor. As usual, it's easier to say how to do something wrong than how to do it right. In later chapters we'll be looking at the channels by means of which reaction and innovation can be furthered. Here, though, it's enough to consider what it's all about. Reaction has two benefits beyond simple market tracking: positive responsiveness and intelligence. When customers get a warm glow because you've reacted to their request, they will go away and tell the world. When you acknowledge the value of intelligence, you turn your competitors into a research arm. Many companies have suffered by assuming that there was nothing to learn from the competition.

It's arguable, for example, that Apple Computer's uncertain position in the late 1990s was down to the way that the company (and particularly its customers) looked down on IBM-compatible PCs. This position was maintained long after the Intel-based machines had caught up, much to Apple's detriment. Intelligence-gathering about competitors, objective comparison of products and services, and effective stealing of ideas (then improving on them) are just as essential as listening to customers.

As we've already seen, you can't rely on your customers to tell you what the next blockbuster concept should be. Yet, there is a lot that they can tell you. They can tell you when things have gone wrong. They can tell you what incremental changes they would like. And you can ignore them. In fact, you can either ignore them completely because you know better or you can give them the impression they're being ignored by not telling them what you are doing about their suggestions. Forget about knowing better. OK, the customer isn't an expert in leather craft/running a supermarket/financial services/your business. They won't understand the problems you've got, but they do understand the problems they've got, and your contribution to them.

Great innovation

We've already seen how some innovation can come from watching the opposition. Piggybacking on others' great ideas and improving on them is often valuable, yet real breakthrough successes come from true innovation. As Mark Ralf, Group Purchasing and Property Director of health insurer BUPA says, 'The greatest opportunities come from discontinuities in trends, not from following and predicting trends. Imagination is the real scarce resource, not money. There's no limit to the investment you can get if you show the returns.' The trouble is, you can't quantify and forecast imagination in a way that will keep the financial team happy. It doesn't mean that innovation can't be systematized, though. As we'll see in Chapter 8, Weapons of creativity and innovation, there are techniques that can build creativity, enhancing the natural innovative ability we all have. Beyond that, there's a need to nurture innovation. Almost all innovative concepts are laughable in the early stages. It's frighteningly easy to stamp on the next great thing because it doesn't seem sensible now. Of course it doesn't. If it did, it would already have been done. Innovation is about taking risks. You don't risk the whole company, but you need a systematic programme of risk-taking, investing an appropriate amount of money in making new things happen.

Going for the double

Hopefully, by now you are convinced of the need to hit both ends of the reaction/innovation dimension. We're not pretending it's easy (though it's easier than many of the requirements of DisOrganization), but it is essential.

The great divide

The final dimension covered in our next chapter is the most significant for the achievement of DisOrganization. Without taking on board the dual challenge of centralization and fragmentation, companies with more than 100 staff will have little chance of reaping the benefits of DisOrganization.

4

Centralization or fragmentation?

- Centralization should bring consistency, departmental specialization, market domination and the best allocation of resources
- Fragmentation should bring speed, energy, enthusiasm, flexibility and focus
- Achieving both – the benefits of fragmentation without anarchy
- The mini company, hypercompany and net company
- Where do you stand at the moment?

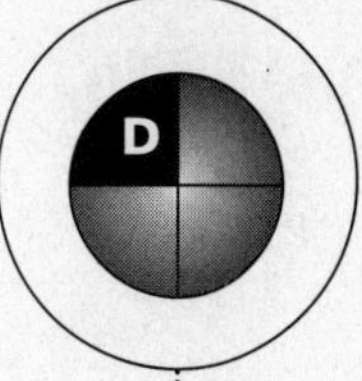

Centralization to fragmentation is the dimension at the heart of Dis-Organization. The issue here is not only the structure of your company, but also the location of the seat of power. A centralized organization concentrates power at its heart. Things happen, or do not happen, because of this central powerhouse. A fragmented organization has its power base spread throughout the structure with a high degree of local autonomy. As with the other dimensions we have discussed, there is not a single right place to be on this dimension: there are two right places to be simultaneously, at both extremes.

At the heart

A centralized organization is structured to direct flows to and from its seat of power at the centre. These flows will be information, instructions and even resources. Different parts of the organization must be prepared to give way to others. In principle, centralization can generate strong benefits: consistency, specialization, market domination, drive and best allocation of resources.

Consistency

The most obvious advantage of the centralized organization is consistency. A company that is led from one point and works with one philosophy should be in a good position to ensure that at every point of interaction its customers get consistent products and services. When things go wrong, a centralized organization should handle the problems or complaints in a uniform way. In general, you should know where you stand with a centralized company, no matter where you interact with it.

Naturally, this model of a centralized company falls down from time to time. Indeed, you could argue that it falls down more often than it stands up. We have all come across organizations that are very centralized but fail to deliver consistency across different units of the company. It is tempting to blame this failure on the application of the organizational model rather than the model itself. However, it is equally likely that this reflects an inherent impracticality in the hub-and-spoke corporation.

Specialization

Centralization should allow parts of the organizational structure to be specialized and focused on one sub-issue of the whole production problem. This should provide the most efficient production within each operating unit. A company with a number of factories that manufactures a range of electronic products does not need to produce the full range in all those factories. It could decide to make a single product in each location. This would mean that the supply of resources to each factory could be similarly specialized and the whole range of subcomponents need not be spread across the whole organization.

Where the organization manufactures dissimilar products, specialization becomes even more useful. Each factory can specialize to a degree that allows excellence in its own product, or product range, to be developed. This sounds quite similar to a fragmented organization, but supporters of centralization point out that the centralized structure allows the factories to concentrate on exactly what is necessary – production – without worrying about development, marketing and finance, which can be left to the centre.

Market domination

The benefit of centralization that is most real and hardest to achieve in a collection of fragmented companies is market domination. Most of the money that large organizations lose through their inherent inefficiency they make up for in their domination of markets. Take a look at any organization that measures its employees by the thousand and you will find that their inputs are less efficient than organizations that measure their employees individually. How, then, do they make money? By cornering entire markets. Small companies, unless they are tightly tucked into a niche, do not tend to measure their market share. The number would be so small as to be meaningless. Large companies measure their market share because it is an effective measure of their monopoly power.

We can already hear the cries of protest from those who work in large organizations: 'ours is not a monopoly; we don't dominate their market'. We don't believe you. Just take a look at the choice offered to your customers and look at the price range of that choice. You will often find a very limited number of real options at very similar prices. Those markets that do not exhibit conformity of pricing often have market domination by virtue of customer confusion. This is a great tactic for the large company. You and your competitors offer apparently dissimilar functionality with an overwhelming range of price/functionality combinations. This ensures that you will take a cut at some point in the operation no matter how inefficient you are. High-tech fields are a great example of this latter tactic, typified by the home computer and mobile phone vendors.

Allocating the best resources

Large companies have the ability to move resources to where they will be most effective. The skills of their employees are one of those resources. The effect of this could be that where a company has a need for, say, retail skills, it can find those skills internally rather than by going outside. As internal recruitment is invariably cheaper than external, and as those recruited internally already know the ropes, this is a much cheaper and more effective option.

It is surprising, when you look closely at large organizations, that they do not make more use of this option. Many big companies have a permanent staff assigned to external recruitment, and this recruitment is not just at the bottom of the pyramid as seed corn. It happens at all levels. There appears to be an organizational inferiority complex at work. Many organizations develop the notion that there are more skilled and able people working in other industries than there are working in their own. There must be some better individuals around, but the notion that the average of these people is better than the internal average does not make immediate sense. This inferiority complex, then, means that many large companies are willing to pay more (often much more) for people they recruit externally than those they recruit internally. This limits the benefit achievable from resource allocation.

Rod Lynch is Chief Executive of the Resources Directorate of the British Broadcasting Corporation (BBC). He has been leading much of the BBC's organizational change that has received so much press coverage over the last few years. Before working for the BBC, he was a senior manager at British Airways.

John Birt arrived as Director General of the BBC five or six years ago and was faced with an organization that was extremely inefficient. The BBC is funded by licence fees, so its stakeholders are people in the UK at large and it has a very specific brief to supply broadcasting to the whole nation. It's a public service organization and not fully commercial. For the BBC's permit to operate to be renewed, they have to demonstrate that they represent good value for money and a real public service. That puts real pressure on it to improve efficiencies. The response to this was to find ways to behave with the financial responsibility that had hitherto been lacking.

There were two studies. One to identify all those service functions which could be outsourced, and secondly an internal economy where producers were free to buy the resources they needed to make programmes. The so-called, 'producer choice' system. If someone is holding a programme budget, then they can go to the BBC studios and say, 'How much will you charge me to make this?', and then go along to Granada or Thames and say, 'How much would you charge me?' They go for whichever suits the purposes best. This caused a significant drop in the amount of work coming through the BBC studios, which already had over capacity.

By introducing the internal market, there was a fairly ruthless exposing of the costs. If the programme maker came back and said, 'Well, I can't use your studios because they're too expensive' we would tell the staff this. So the staff were not only told in management propaganda style but by the evidence of their own eyes that they were not competitive. Surplus facilities became self-evident. By going through this with staff in their own units you could say, 'Look, we have ten studios on this site. We only ever use five of them. It is grotesquely inefficient. Half of this is surplus. We're going to shut it.' And, with that goes 200 jobs. Whilst this went down like a rattlesnake in a lucky dip, it was pretty indicative to the people involved that the place was chronically inefficient.

What's now left is an organization that is efficient relative to market price and in terms of utilization of facilities and staff, and which is now starting, as much as the BBC Charter allows it to do, to trade externally. A crossroads is now apparent to decide where to go next. The financial needs of the business are at least in part met by the ability to take in external work.

There are no real dangers in allowing competitors access to the skill base of the BBC because studio time can be bought anywhere. The fact that our studios are good is neither here nor there. If they're standing idle the programmes that our competitors make would still get made. Our competitors now make programmes for us as well and the BBC buys about 25 to 30 per cent of its output from independent programme makers.

A lot of people at the BBC absolutely loathe and abhor the whole process – hence the vilification of John Birt and others as the wreckers of the BBC. It should have been left as it was, shouldn't it? Two successive governments have thought not and have put real pressure on to make it change. Having joined the BBC four years back, the level of waste and inefficiency was absolutely mindboggling. The fact that I've been able to cut my staffing from a peak of around 12,000 to under 7,000 tells you just how lush things were.

Our communication programme with staff was not particularly well-handled. It wasn't done as well as British Airways, for example, with its handling of the same situations in the 1980s. But it was done well enough for people to understand what the issues were and accept the inevitability of substantial change.

I think that combination of carrot and stick is particularly effective. Realpolitik combined with loads and loads of communication. Communication on the stump being the most effective – getting up and talking to staff groups up and down the country. I've done I don't know how many hundreds of meetings. Backing that up with briefings from unit heads. Backing that up with a magazine we introduced to Resources. Communicating heavily with people through every medium at our disposal from the intranet through to staff meetings.

The British Airways experience spanned ten years and had several distinct phases to it. With the BBC the phases have had to be concertinaed and in, some cases, run in parallel.

If you're not careful, you end up spending far too much time on process. The BBC is guilty of this. You agonize so much about how you're going to measure the output. I see great value in service businesses and media businesses cutting people as much slack as you can. Allow them freedom to express themselves through the job. There are rules, but they form a template. I'm not at one with the traditional BBC culture on this. John Birt has a strong leaning towards process whereas I tend to delegate more and, on occasion, I will wing it if I believe that the individual manager is capable of achievement without overt supervision. This can make me appear cavalier against the BBC background, but then I regard the conventions of the organization as being a bit stuffy. At the end of the day, there is a need for all of us to find a degree of conformity with the organization, although this doesn't stop my wish to open up the culture perhaps more than some of my colleagues.

I think organizations respond much better to leadership models than they do to management models. Management models are control-based and have as their central flaw the premise that they are there to stop people from doing things. Leadership models have the premise that people are capable of almost anything if you give them the chance and enough motivation. The leadership's role is not controlling (equals stopping), but enabling, therefore helping achieve. The leadership model opens up far more fun, far more scope and also a lot more risk.

The BBC is adequate at leadership. It's still not good enough, and for the next stage of improvements we'll have to get better. What it has done is the combination of stripping cost, the refocus of the business and the turnaround. What it hasn't done is win the hearts and minds of its staff to the new way of doing things.

You do need to be good at both ends of the leadership, management continuum but you also need a balance and that can shift according to the point you're at on organizational change. The Beeb has got where it is light on leadership. It's still very much a command structure. We've moved from a command economy to a trading economy and that's been successful and has driven the values of the marketplace into the BBC and has left the place better run. But the communications style is still that of the Soviet. You still have the non-accountability of managers to their staff and the feeling that responsibilities aren't truly shared. It is a blame culture. There is a real need to get in and shift the culture of the organization forward, but shifting the culture of something like the BBC without breaking it can be difficult.

Spread all over

A fragmented organization minimizes the flows to and from the centre and maximizes local control. Direction comes primarily from the fragmented unit of operation with only occasional involvement from the centre. Local interests will often outweigh those of other parts of the organization. Information is kept within the local unit with only very summarized flows elsewhere. Resources are supplied and consumed locally. This approach gives rise to a whole new list of benefits. By being fleet of foot, channelling energy and enthusiasm and having appropriate focus, the fragmented organization has plenty of potential.

Being fleet of foot

Because of their size, dinosaurs had to develop a central nervous system that was able to react without waiting for messages to travel all the way to and from the brain. In order to be successful, a large organization should need to make a similar adaptation. Few, if any seem to possess this. Fragmented organizations, on the other hand, have no need for this because they keep their brains where they are needed – at the centre of each of the parts of the operation. The fragmented company has no need to wait for corporate headquarters to sanction a response to a competitor or to agree to a new product being developed. It just goes and does what is necessary.

Channelling energy and enthusiasm

A key reason for breaking up monoliths is the energy and enthusiasm generated by a feeling of ownership. This comes because every employee knows that they make a real difference within a smaller company. A fragmented company will have operating units that are able to generate higher levels of energy than those of a centralized company because they will have higher levels of ownership.

This effect is equally valuable in front-line and support units. Customer contact staff will be able to provide a better service by having more autonomy, not needing to consult central policy. Support units traditionally have low morale because they are not considered to be a key part of the business. In a fragmented organization, their role *is* their business, building a culture where things get done.

Focus pocus

A well-run fragmented organization will exhibit a high degree of focus within each of the operating units. Perversely, this is very similar to the specialization advantage of centralized organizations. The part of the company that takes care of a particular function will know exactly what is required of it and will be left alone by the centre to get on with it.

So, how centralized or fragmented are you?

Use this informal questionnaire to get a feel for your current position, by awarding each item a mark out of ten.

CENTRALIZED OR FRAGMENTED?

Score each of the following statements out of 10 (0 if the statement is wholly untrue and 10 if it is wholly true).

In my organization...

1	decisions are referred to a central committee	______
2	big is beautiful	______
3	there is a big, glossy head office	______
4	budgets are controlled at a high level	______
5	there are no autonomous operating units	______
6	the finance department pulls the strings	______
7	salaries are set centrally	______
8	there are departmental organization charts	______
9	generalists are valued more than specialists	______
10	there are this many levels from Chief Executive to worker	______
	Total	______

Your test results
The higher the result, the more centralized is your company.

Note how a number of these measures are finance driven – the way finance is organized in a company is usually a convenient measure of just how centralized or fragmented it is.

How can you span the extremes?

Neither of the ends of this continuum is ideal, but we aren't looking for a wishy washy compromise. You need to straddle the dimensions like the Colossus at Rhodes straddling the harbour entrance. This is hard - not because it is conceptually difficult nor because it is difficult to operate in practice, but because it is difficult to get from here to there. Establishing the centralized/fragmented mix is much easier in a start-up company – whatever its size – than in an existing company.

If your company is already fragmented, the move will be relatively easy. The missing component is the strong communications that will allow you to be centralized when that makes sense. If your company is centralized, and most will be, your journey will be much more difficult.

The hypercompany structure

The picture we have of the successful outcome of embracing centralization and fragmentation is key to the rest of the book. We don't like using fancy terms for the sake of it, but we have been forced to introduce four as shorthand for the way the new breed of company works. Three of the terms are illustrated in Figure 4.1.

We are calling the fragmented units mini companies. A mini company is a small entity – between 1 and maybe 50 people in size. The mini company is small enough for everyone to know everyone else and to understand just what the mini company is about. Other num-

Figure 4.1
The DisOrganized company

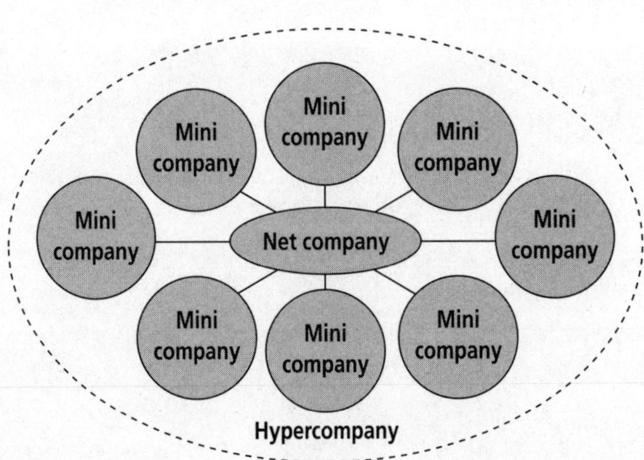

bers have been proposed, running to three figures, but we like Michael Skok's assertion that the maximum realistic team size is around seven, and the maximum easily manageable unit is a team of teams. This isn't a prescriptive number, but we believe that to go beyond 100 begins to stretch small company flexibility beyond breaking point. By this time you are already beginning to see bureaucratic rigidity set in.

Each mini company has its own goals, its own purpose for existence. It can be a wholly owned part of the overall corporation or exist in its own right. Independent mini companies might once have been part of the parent and spun off or might simply have been brought in as partners.

Left to themselves, mini companies will rapidly degenerate into anarchy. While independent action is essential to gain the benefits of fragmentation, mini companies need extremely good communications ties and to understand the broad direction of the parent.

The second term we use is the net company. The net company combines senior executives with a powerful communications role. The net company is not the traditional head office, though. It does not control the mini companies: it sets broad directions and decides which mini companies to interact with. No mini company is forced to adopt the direction of the net company – it can always work with someone else. In practice, to begin with, the net company will probably own most of the mini companies on paper, but to have an effective working relationship, it must act as if it doesn't or at least as if it is simply a holding company.

The spanning term we use is hypercompany. The hypercompany contains a net company and those mini companies the net company links. The mini companies could be owned by the net company, totally separate businesses or owned by another net company: the hypercompany spans the whole business entity. The hypercompany has no staff or facilities. It is a useful descriptive term, but has no legal, financial or visible basis.

A final label is sometimes necessary to cover the net company and all the mini companies that are legally part of the same entity. While less important internally, this metacompany is a necessary concept for legal and financial reasons.

Of course, a hypercompany does not exist in isolation: it interacts with other companies. The mini companies that form the hypercompany may also have links into other hypercompanies (see Figure 4.2).

Figure 4.2
More complicated DisOrganization

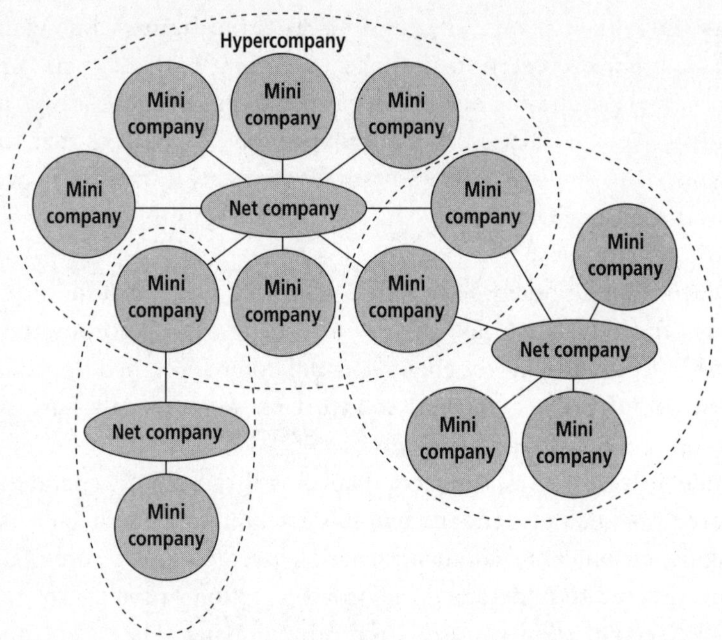

In praise of size

The concept of breaking up any organization into small units is certainly not universally accepted. While we are sure about its validity, here is a counter-view from Rod Lynch at the BBC. We would argue that this picture does not take into account the whole DisOrganization approach, but the choice is yours.

'Around about 50 is too arbitrary for me. It's too doctrinaire. I don't want to run 6800 staff in a flat structure of pockets of 50 or fewer. I have functional groupings that, for example, run Television Centre in London, which is an organic structure. We're probably talking about some several hundred people. And, indeed, a very very high emphasis and reliance on teamworking. People have to do things blind without seeing the end output but knowing its relevance and being content with that. The people who drive satellite up-links, for example, to carry the news, know that they're feeding straight through into the Newsroom where journalists are making stuff up for screening on an edit and putting that together with a graphics artist sitting alongside them who is putting together charts and graphs and animations and so on. All of them can feel a relevance and pride in what they're doing, but inside a structure that goes way beyond 50 people working as some sort of nucleus.'

Providing centralized benefits

The net company is there to ensure centralized benefits. By concentrating on extremely good information flows, it provides the opportunity for consistency. In fact, imposed consistency isn't a great benefit. Even where the trademark of companies is consistency, such as McDonald's, they operate with a large amount of regional variation. The net company ensures that the mini companies understand the key elements of consistency that are required for the benefit of the hypercompany; the mini company employs those elements that make sense locally.

Similarly, the net company will ensure that the mini companies it links cover the required span of specializations. It will not be able to enforce a unique specialization on a mini company – the span of work covered is for the mini company to decide – but it can require all the benefits of specialization and leave it up to the mini company to establish how they will be delivered.

Most of all, the net company provides the scale of corporation that is necessary for the sort of large projects that it is not practical to take on with a small group of people. In theory, there will also be the traditional economies of scale, but, as we examine elsewhere, these may be more illusory than actual.

ECONOMIES OF SCALE

See page 232, in Chapter 21, Monitoring.

Reaping fragmentation rewards

The small size of a mini company brings many of the rewards of fragmentation automatically. That is not to say that you can simply split a company into small chunks and instantly have functional mini companies. A lot of effort will have to be put into bringing the people involved round to a new way of working. Yet, this is achievable with a mini company in a way that simply was not possible in a large company, even for a department or team.

The degree of autonomy that mini companies have should not be forgotten in the rush to ensure that centralized benefits are gained. While the net company decides which mini companies it works with, a mini company is free to work with several net companies or with none of them at all. What is to stop a key mini company from abandoning the net company and dropping it in the mire? The net company has the responsibility to keep things together. This requires a huge change of mind-set for senior executives. Before becoming a hypercompany, it was possible to order operating units about. Organizational charts that put the workers at the top and the executives at the bottom, supporting the inverted pyramid, were a joke. In a hypercompany, though, this is deadly serious. The key mini companies will stay in place because the net company supports them well – gives them good servicc – not out of feudal loyalty.

Tools and techniques for moving on the continuum

Achieving the move on this continuum is particularly difficult. It will be necessary to employ all the weapons we will cover in the following chapters:

- clarity and direction, to ensure that the splits are made effectively and that communication between the mini companies is effective;
- fun and empowerment, to ensure that the mini companies operate effectively;
- creativity and innovation to overcome the barriers that inertia and conservatism will place in the way of this development.

5

DisOrganization: direction

Each major section of *DisOrganization* is summarized in one of these mini chapters.

Changing the unchangeable

There's a real sense in which DisOrganization is about changing the unchangeable. The whole field of business creativity and lateral thinking is concerned with challenging the assumptions we constantly hold in our heads, which fix in place a blinkered vision of what is possible. Just as creativity techniques are about breaking out of this tunnel vision, DisOrganization is about breaking the company out of its rut. Generally, business decisions are made based on an awful lot of givens and assumptions. To make as big a change as DisOrganization suggests for most companies requires the questioning of all and the changing of many aspects of the company that have been assumed to be unchangeable.

Determining the direction of the company into DisOrganization is primarily based on three axes:

- managing or leading
- reacting or innovating
- centralizing or fragmenting.

As you will already have seen, our assertion is that you need to embrace both ends of each spectrum simultaneously.

Managing and leading

Running a company was easy once: you told the workers what to do; they did it – simple as that. Setting aside the fact that this rosy view of the past is entirely fictional, such a model is all very well when things stay the same from day to day, but rapid change makes it impossible to always be on top of your staff, telling them what to do. There has been an increasing need for leadership – setting broad principles, leading by example and stretching your staff – rather than the giving of rigid rules. Yet, leadership alone isn't enough. You do need to be able to handle the fine detail sometimes. Even so, despite the popularity of people-led management as a theory, most companies are a lot weaker on leadership than on management.

Reacting and innovating

While it seems reasonably natural that a company should both react to customer requests and innovate to produce new and exciting products, all too often the reality is a mushy compromise with very limited reaction to customers and very little innovation. This is the dimension where sitting at both ends simultaneously is least painful. However, remember that, while it's essential to listen to your customers about what's wrong with your products and services (and equally essential to fix the problems to their satisfaction), don't expect your customers to lead you when it comes to innovation. They are unlikely to take the leaps you'll need. Turn, instead to your creativity tools and be prepared to fail fast and frequently on the way to superb new products.

Centralizing and fragmenting

Crucial to DisOrganization is the notion of fragmentation, of breaking a company up into self-sufficient units no bigger than 50 to 100 people (they can be as small as you like). This is a painful concept to accept. It means reduced power for the centre. And everyone knows that their company is different, is a special case where our arguments don't apply. The fact is, though, that the only way to achieve the sort of responsiveness, flexibility and ownership that is required to boost a company enough to make it superb is to introduce the small company ethos that is only possible by means of fragmentation.

We don't stop with mini companies, though. The centralization end of the spectrum has plenty of benefits, too. So, the net company is there to pull together the efforts of the mini companies and ensure that there is excellent communication between them. The overall hypercompany is liable to include mini companies that are part of the original structure and other, partner mini companies that never were.

Stocking the armoury

With the direction established, we move on to the weapons that will help you to achieve DisOrganization:

- clarity and direction
- fun and empowerment
- creativity and innovation.

PART TWO

Weapons

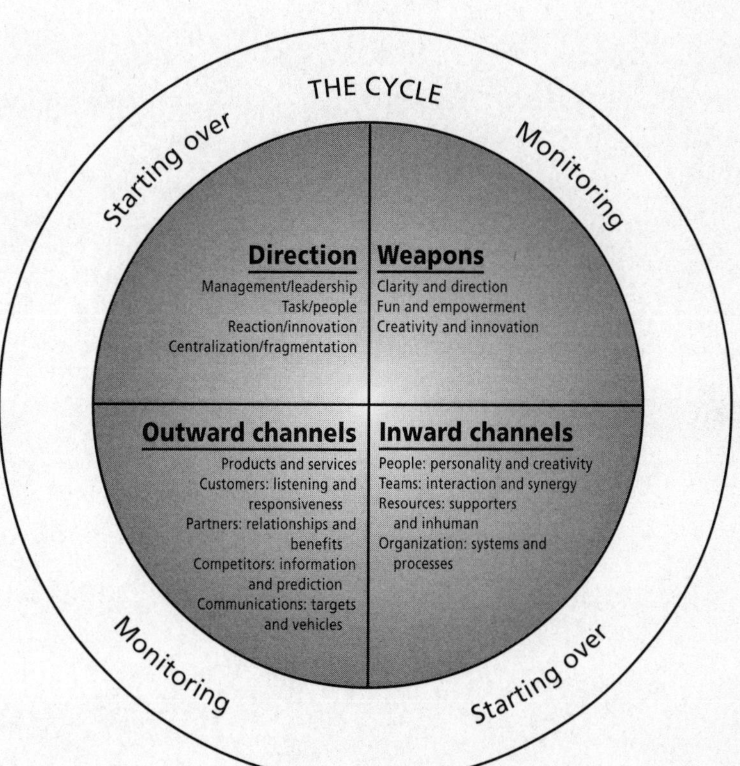

6

Weapons of clarity and direction

- Practical steps towards your direction
- Developing a clear message
- Ensuring that your message is heard in the way you intend
- Right message, right timing
- Living your messages
- Providing direction and drive

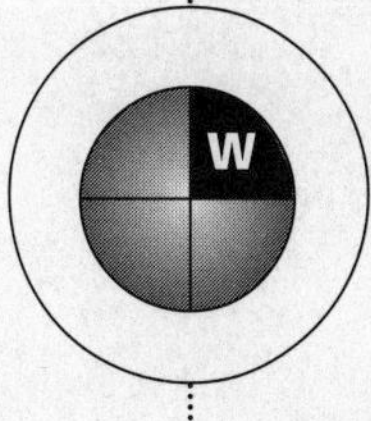

So this is what you mean

There comes a time in the career of every leader or manager when they realize that those working for them don't always do as they are told. At first this seems to be wilful disobedience, but the more experience you gain, the more you see that it is often misunderstanding and miscommunication rather than mischief. Our mythical manager then goes through a period of soul-searching where they ask themselves how they can be getting it so wrong and what they can do about it. Fortunately, help is at hand in the form of thousands of textbooks on communication skills. And if communication skills were really the problem, this is where we could leave it.

The better leaders develop an understanding that the fault lies not only in the communication between themselves and those working for them, but also within themselves. The need for clarity and direction starts within the leader and then moves outside. Unless you are clear in your own mind what it is you want to achieve, how you will make it happen, and what part others play in this objective, you cannot possibly communicate your requirements clearly. Once you are clear in your own mind, you need to become clear in the minds of others. This is a much more difficult task.

This chapter will help you improve the clarity of your own thinking about where you are going and then the clarity of the message you pass to others. This will go some of the way to removing the misunderstanding and miscommunication from your leadership.

Nick Spooner is Managing Director and co-founder of Internet commerce specialists Entranet. He began his career as an engineer on the Exocet weapons system at Sperry Gyroscope, going on to work for Digital in hardware and software engineering roles around the world. In the early 1980s, his career developed through project management, new business and financial sales before he left Digital to join Steve Jobs at the start-up company NeXT. Nick successfully led NeXT European sales to capture major contracts for Linklaters and Paine, British Telecom and Mitsubishi. Nick was educated at MIT and Harvard, USA.

For companies larger than around 50, knowing all your staff must become a problem?

That's my problem. I was fortunate at Digital. DECPark had the Street; like a terraced street, it gave you the opportunity to get to know people. It could be distractive, but only with too much exposure. In Entranet I keep the organization flat. There's no reason why the most junior employee can't come and sit at my desk and share views. But at the same time, I can educate them – culture is about education to a great extent. I know of one organization that puts its executives on the front line for a week a year. When they come back, they've got the opportunity to make changes from what they've learned. It's heading to subsidiarity, which is very different from empowerment. It's a partnership.

Decision times here are short. I'm able to quickly walk around everyone and consolidate our position on the issue; building on all that knowledge. That's supportive of the brand. That's how you get a business to work, by getting everyone in the organization able to articulate what the business stands for.

That's easy in a start-up, but what about a corporation?

My example comes from Mike Wilson, Chief Executive of Jacob Rothschild. His view is examine what we do and see how much we really need to do. He's adopted Charles Handy's model of the inverted doughnut, concentrating on the core functions. Farm out as much as possible, with tightly coupled people in the centre. Generally, in corporations there are too many people fighting for one position. I really like the Hewlett-Packard model – each group is a profit and loss centre. You can get a load from the mother company, but you can't carry on if you aren't worth while. The other thing is small teams – give them subsidiarity. If the staff aren't behind what you are doing, you've either got the wrong people or you've not done enough setting of direction. So many directors don't set direction.

The other thing that works well is proper profit-related pay. We have a baseline salary with extras for the overall business performance, individual performance and team performance.

Direction versus dictatorship

I talked one week about how I managed – I gave them my top ten. Now everyone has one. It wasn't a matter of telling them what to do, dictatorial, but leading by example. By making them visible, everyone can see what everyone else is working on. It helps me to pull it all together.

How do you make your presence felt in a large organization?

I think one of the things is being seen. At Digital, one of Olsen's greatest attributes was memory. He remembered who he spoke to about what, and came out among the staff a lot. I've been examining my work pattern and seeing what can be handed on to a good assistant. I've thought through how repetitive the tasks are – a hell of a lot of them – you keep doing them because you're the decision maker. It's not that they're hard to make, so you can move more to your assistant, and spend time on what you enjoy doing. The assistants are not managers, but they have my authority and represent me. You have to infuse your analysis framework into someone else. If you've got someone you're really close to, you can make it work. Perhaps I'd have a club of five assistants to become more effective.

What makes a good manager?

You've got to be interested. So many managers just push back and say give me something easy. It's a paradox. You want to grow analysis skills in your people, but the manager still needs to understand the details. That's one of Steve Jobs' greatest strengths. He really did understand. It went further than that. You know *Stranger in a Strange Land*? The term 'grok' – Steve grokked it and was able to go into engineering and discuss things at their level, drag it to the surface and then turn it into something understandable. It's nothing to do with vision. Steve's vision comes from taking everyone else's ideas and swilling them around.

STEVE JOBS

Co-founder (in his garage), with Steve Wozniak, of Apple Computer, Jobs always had a tendency to plunge in, never more so than with the development of the Macintosh, which he took under his direct control. When John Sculley forced Jobs out of his position, he went on to set up NeXT Computer. Like the Xerox GUI products Jobs had seen and learned from, this proved to be a great idea without any market penetration. Towards the end of the 1990s Jobs went full circle, returning to head up Apple.

Know what is happening

A natural response to a demand for a clearer message is to try to tell it more clearly. That is why, for us, the first weapon has to be listening, not telling. Communication is always a two-way street. Even if you really are just telling others a fact, you must ensure that they have understood what you have said and why you have said it. More often, you need to listen far more than that.

Most direction setting is grounded in the here and now and is aimed at moving into the future. Without a firm grasp of what is happening now, you will not be able to develop robust plans for moving forward. You will also be unable to communicate the process or progression of events that will be required in order to achieve movement.

What listening posts do you have in the area or company you manage? 'Listening posts', as the name suggests, are places or methods of collecting information. If there is an in-house magazine in your company, that might provide information, but only if it is free from editorial bias. What about allowing, or even encouraging, the creation of an underground newsletter that will criticize the status quo?

LISTEN

'Give every man thy ear but few thy voice'
William Shakespeare

How do you collect customer input? Most companies see complaints as a negative and success as minimizing them. However, one way to gain input from your customers is to encourage complaints. See them as a source of data and a direct communication with the purchasers of your products or services. If you were to measure the performance of front-line staff or outlets in terms of the number of customer comments they collected, you would find a marked upswing. Naturally, before doing this you would have put in place mechanisms to process the comments to the satisfaction of the customers. As a customer, there is nothing more frustrating than feeling that your opinions are being ignored. A company that listens well is halfway to success. A company that has a track record of doing something about what they have heard is much further forward.

What do you know of your competitors and how will you learn more? There is an alarming amount of data available in public sources that you never look at. In some work with a team of management consultants and merchant bankers, we looked at various potential partner companies. We needed to know all we could about them and started with a description of what our ideal (but unachievable) data pack would look like. By the end of the study we had 90 per cent of the data for all of the companies. At the outset, we would have said that anything more than 10 per cent was impossible. Since this experience we now work on the assumption that what we need to know is available if only we are able to ask the right questions in the right places. It used to be that a complete set of data involved extensive searching of library resources, but these days the Internet can be a superb source of timely information.

COMPETITORS

Read Chapter 18 from page 199 for some tips on how to find out more about competitors.

THE INTERNET

Read Chapter 18 from page 204 for some tips on how to glean information from the Internet.

How do you communicate with your suppliers? Most companies, even the most enlightened, still have an 'us and them' attitude to their suppliers. They tolerate the relationship as a business necessity but do not move towards partnership with them. We have come across a number of organizations that say all the right things about partnership and win–win relationships but, when push comes to shove, they try to screw as much out of their suppliers as possible. Do you share information with your suppliers? Do they share information with you? If you did, what could you learn? If you did, what would you risk? Would the risk be worth the additional information?

The chances are that you will end up answering 'no' to that last question. Most businesses would. The chances are, however, that you would be wrong and you have just turned your back on a very fruitful business partnership. As you move through the DisOrganization process, you will find that more and more of your contacts are with suppliers. Your company will become a network of suppliers. If you do not develop strategies for working with them rather than against them, this process will fail.

Know what you want and what you need

Having listened, we must consider our requirements. Setting the direction of companies is a subject that has filled almost as many textbooks as communication. Read some by all means, but knowing what you want is a relatively simple task. Knowing what you need is harder. It proves to be difficult, or even impossible, for many companies, not because of any inherent complexity, but because of the massive inertia that surrounds business direction.

Often, what the leaders of a business want is not what the business needs. What they want is usually more of the same. This is not necessarily because they are inherently conservative (though they might well be), it is because they have steered the business through success and they know what is needed to be successful. Unfortunately, what they know is not true. It is usually out of date and inappropriate. As Charles Handy points out in *The Empty Raincoat*, businesses have to launch themselves into a new way of thinking and a new approach to their business at the very point that the old approach seems most successful. This is a difficult, often terrifying, leap to make. It is far easier to stick with an existing, successful formula until it is no longer successful and the business does not have the energy or resources to meet the challenge effectively.

THE EMPTY RAINCOAT

Charles Handy, *The Empty Raincoat* (Arrow Business Books, 1994)

The setting of direction is a job that cannot be delegated. Leaders of a business must do this together and without interruptions. This will require a significant chunk of time to be set aside (maybe two or three week-long sessions) and employing some external help. Management consultants often deserve their poor image, but there is a role for them in helping a business to see itself more objectively. The setting of direction is a time that that role is most effective. This thinking needs to be done at least every five years, especially when it seems that you are so successful you don't need it.

Raise the game and change the game

Another direction-setting issue is closely linked to leadership. The direction of a company must have in-built challenges. The unreasonable requests of a leader are built around the need to push the business harder and further than it would go without them. These unreasonable requests may take the form of raising the game – doing what is done now but more so. They may, as the previous section described, take the form of changing the game – doing something new and demanding.

Whenever challenges take the form of raising the game, you must check that you are not being trapped by inertia. Whenever they take the form of changing the game, you must check that you are not changing just to be different. We never said it would be easy and obvious did we? This is also an area where some external help might be useful. Spending time imagining worlds where your success will diminish and finding ways of being successful in those worlds is a challenging task. The creativity techniques used elsewhere in the book will be useful, but a skilled facilitator, able to guide you through their use, will be more useful still.

CREATIVITY

Read Chapter 8 from page 80 for weapons of creativity and innovation.

Create a process for communication

Having established where you are and decided where you want to be, you must communicate that with the rest of your company. However small the company, it is not enough to assume that communication will happen by osmosis. It is certainly easier in small companies, but it is still necessary to think through the process.

A communication process need not be a huge affair with laser shows and dry ice. It often needs to be nothing more than a series of prompts and reminders. Communication is such an integral part of the job of any manager or leader that it cannot be left to whim and chance.

Certainly there will be impromptu opportunities to communicate a part of the message and these should be leapt on. In addition to these, regular and systematic opportunities must be created. These might take the form of newsletters, memos or group meetings, but by far the most effective are the one-to-one, face-to-face occurrences that can only happen if you get out of your office and walk around. They are doomed if you leave them to your spare time. This form of communication is a primary role. It should be scheduled in your diary as systematically as Board meetings or other formal events; it is not a nice-to-have.

So, how can you do your job if you are tied up with all of this communication? This *is* your job! Until you realize and accept that, you are going to fail at communication.

Finally, do not allow communication to dwindle as you move from the start to the end of an initiative. Your focus will be interpreted as a measure of its importance and you could easily fail by letting things slip at the last minute. It is frightening the number of times managers have lamented their people not sticking with an initiative they have started when their own focus has already moved on to the next project.

RETAIN YOUR FOCUS

'Some men give up their designs when they have almost reached the goal, while others, on the contrary, obtain a victory by exerting at the last moment more vigorous efforts than before.'
Polybius

Right message

What you communicate is a vital part of the mix. By now, you know what you want to say, but that will not be the same as what is heard. You assume a series of links in your message that may not be there for the recipients. If, for instance, you run a supermarket and you want to increase the number of open checkouts, you could just tell the staff that you need a change in shift pattern and an increase in productivity. This message will not be heard in the way that you intended. Indeed, it will probably cause resentment and the interpretations of your motives will be entirely negative. You must make all of the links in the chain explicit and explain that the queues are too long and some of your customers have started shopping elsewhere. Furthermore, once they're lost they are almost impossible to regain. If this continues, then the queues will get shorter of their own accord, but the supermarket will not be able to support its current staff levels. There will be layoffs. Then you will have their attention. There may still be negative interpretations of your motives, but the more open, honest and explicit you are, the less opportunity there is for misunderstanding.

Right time

The next element of communication is when it will be most effective. A general rule of thumb for this is immediately and continually thereafter.

Many managers hold back a message until they have an appropriate time to deliver it. There are huge dangers in this approach, not least if someone finds out the time lag between when you knew and when you chose to speak. Nothing communicates dishonesty more effectively than holding back important information. However honourable your motivation, you will lose trust.

There are circumstances where it is a mistake to communicate immediately, however. Where you only have a partial picture or do not know what the possible impact of an event might be, you may cause unnecessary fear and uncertainty by broadcasting immediately. Often, though, this reason is used long after it has time-expired. It is very easy to take an overly paternalistic approach and try to protect staff from unpleasant truths. Remember that they are adults, not children and that they manage their own lives outside your business perfectly effectively. If you were in their shoes, would you want to be told? Ask yourself whether or not there is a real reason to hold back any information or whether you are either being too paternalistic or chicken in refusing to give a tough message.

Right stuff

You know what you want to say. You have the process, you are saying the right thing for the audience to hear it and you know when you need to say it. So, how are you going to say it? Which media will you use to get the message across?

You already know that we're going to say that the more variety of media you use, the more effective your communication. You do need to consider the appropriateness of the medium to the message, however. For instance, when launching a cost-cutting campaign, a series of glitzy, costly events in a prestigious location will get the message heard, but will simultaneously prove that you don't believe in it. Similarly, if you are launching a marketing campaign, a poster in the canteen might not reach the audience in the way you need.

You can also say the wrong thing by getting the medium only slightly wrong. We once saw a cost-cutting campaign launched with a note to all employees. The fact that the note was on high-quality paper and so cost more than necessary overwhelmed the worthy contents. What's the difference between this and the example in the margin right headed 'Going too far'?

First, the note was communicating a cost-cutting exercise; the banned newsletter wasn't. Second, as it happened, the glossy paper

GOING TOO FAR

An insecure departmental director of our acquaintance was launching a new communications vehicle – a newsletter for his department. Unfortunately, it coincided with a company-wide cost-cutting initiative. The director was worried that the glossy paper the newsletter was printed on would look too expensive. He had it reprinted on plain paper and threw away the glossies. It didn't go down well.

of the newsletter was no more expensive than plain. It might have been necessary to communicate this, but not to double the cost during a period of belt-tightening. Whether it is good news or bad, but particularly when it is bad, you must consider the impact of the smallest element of the message and the media used to convey it.

NLP

Neuro-linguistic programming (NLP) is one of the more controversial of the various business techniques. It was developed in the early 1970s from the work of Richard Bandler and John Grinder. NLP is based on the theory that the ways you decide to behave can have an effect on the ways you perceive the world, and the ways you perceive the world can have an effect on the ways you decide to behave. NLP identifies three basic sensory systems operating: auditory, which deals with verbal communication and other sound messages; kinaesthetic, which deals with feelings, both emotional and physical; and visual, which deals with images and sight stimuli. NLP is about subjective experience – it makes no claims to objective truth. The models that are created are tested against the world and are kept if they are felt to be useful and replaced if they are not.

The range of media is your next consideration. Word of mouth is one of the most effective ways of communicating, so how can you have this issue discussed by everyone? You can start the ball rolling by making it your number one topic of conversation. You also need to make sure that those working for you are discussing it. How can you get customers talking about it? How can you get suppliers talking about it? How can you get investors, shareholders and the Board talking about it? The list is endless.

One way of making a subject the topic of conversation is surprise. Find ways to attach a pleasant surprise to your communication. This will be commented on and will raise the subject. With a marketing campaign, this could be a surprise gift of some sort. With a service campaign, it could be better service than was expected. With a staff communication, it could be as little as you being out there delivering the message personally. Surprise! Your boss is willing to talk with you.

As well as word of mouth, you will often need other avenues. This is partly so that the message is not garbled by repetition, but mainly so that you catch those who have not heard it. Remember the lessons learned from NLP. Some will hear, some will see and some will feel most effectively. How can you reach them all?

Right, have you got that?

Now that you have broadcast the message, you must go back to listening once more. Check that the message has been heard and that what has been heard is what you intended. Check this with each target audience and each medium. Again, the most effective way of checking is to talk directly to people. Get them to play back the messages. For more broadband communications, a survey might be appropriate. Choose the way you check to line up with the way you broadcast, but the more ways you check, the more chance you have of finding the gaps in communication. Do not rely on checking using one channel alone – it will be biased, it will be partial and it will mislead.

The really worrying thing about this advice is that sometimes a range of channels will come back with different results. Is this success or failure? It is a successful check and a partially successful communication. It gives you information about where and how to redouble your efforts. The message again is, do not allow your effort to dwindle as you move through the process; stick with it.

NLP

See David Molden's, *Managing with the Power of NLP* (Pitman Publishing, 1996).

Once more, with variations

Now that you have communicated what you want done and you are sure that it is clearly understood, your job is complete. Oh no it isn't! It has only just started. Communicating direction with clarity is a never-ending task. The more variations you throw into the pot of methods used, the more effective will be the communication. Despite this, the message must be the same, and must be heard as being the same, every time it is communicated. This means repeating the message *ad nauseam* and checking understanding every time.

Read my feet, not my lips

Don't forget your footwork. It doesn't matter what you say if what you do contradicts it. What you do will always be deafening in comparison to what you say. For this reason you should watch your feet. That is, you should be aware of what you do and ensure that it is consistent at all times with your message. The slightest variation will be seen as evidence of dishonesty and your direction setting will suffer.

Even the most convincing orators have learned to their cost that it is tough to lie convincingly all of the time. As one of our college lecturers once said, 'The most important thing in business life is sincerity. Once you can fake that, you've got it made.' Unfortunately, unless you act at all times as though it were true, the faking will get you nowhere, and by the time your act is perfect, you will make the worrying discovery that your sincerity has become real.

Remember, too, even if you don't watch your feet, others will.

ACTIONS WIN

Next time you are in a conversation, try saying 'I agree with you' while shaking your head and frowning. Which part of the mixed message is believed?

The director's chair

Direction is so strongly intertwined with communication that by covering communication we have established much of the requirement for direction. As Mark Ralf, Group Purchasing and Property Director of health insurer BUPA points out, 'The job of the CEO is to turn the conviction of everyone in the company into a plan. This does not work the other way round. You cannot generate conviction from a plan.' Without effective communication to understand that conviction, there can't be effective direction. Footwork, particularly, is key: good direction will only work if you act out your direction – 'do as I say, not as I do' is a dead end.

CLEAR DIRECTION

'The clinching proof of my reasoning is that I will cut anyone who argues further into dogmeat.'

Sir Geoffery de Tourneville, c. AD 1350

Additionally, there are strong elements brought in from the next two chapters. Creativity is an essential to setting a direction. Trust, established through fun and empowerment, is essential to having others buy into your direction. Direction is all about painting a big picture, making sure that others understand it and trusting them enough to let go of the reins and let them get on with progress in your direction.

An easy mistake is to assume that direction setting equates to strategic planning. This might have been the case when the world was relatively predictable (if it ever was), but is certainly no longer true. Mark Ralf again:

> Strategic planning is madness. You cannot see the end from the beginning, but strategic planning assumes that you can. The chances of planning the future when it changes so rapidly are nil. So you'll see extremes of success and failure, and a few companies refusing to play by the rules. These companies will routinely transform themselves and will do a ten-year turnaround every year.

This isn't just rhetoric. Collapsed timescales are happening. 'How far into the future is the future? If you need to re-invent yourself, what timeframe are you looking for? In the USA it took 35 years for 10 million people to get a TV. It took 18 months for 10 million people to get a web browser. It took only 13 months for 100 million people to get Java.'

7

Weapons of fun and empowerment

- Fun at the heart of business success
- Valuing staff
- The uses of power
- You can't fake fun and empowerment
- Putting energy into the business

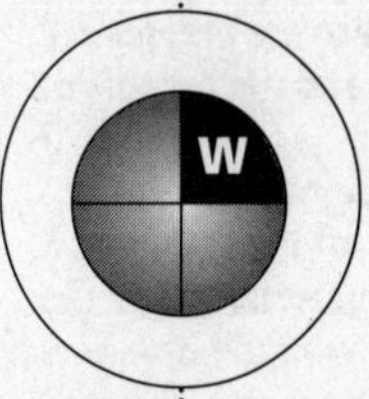

Come work for me

HR MANAGEMENT YEAR BOOK

This chapter is developed from an article written for the *HR Management Year Book 1996* and is reused with the permission of AP Information Services.

THE FUN THING

Uncomfortable with something like fun appearing in a business statement? Worried that thinking about fun will trivialize your business? Remember that the US Declaration of Independence reads, 'We hold these truths to be self-evident, that all men are created equal, that they are endowed by their Creator with certain inalienable rights, that among these are life, liberty and the pursuit of happiness.' If happiness can be one of the three most important rights in the creation of a new independent country, surely fun can be one of your goals.

Why do people work for your company? Why does anyone work for any company? Most of us never get around to asking that question, but in a world where smart people are going to be our scarcest resource and intelligence (in both senses of the word) a decisive weapon for survival, this could be fatal.

There are, of course, a host of explanations for the status quo. If the economy is weak it could be that they're glad of a job, any job. It could be that you pay more than the competition. It could be that you offer challenges that other employers don't. It could simply be inertia – that they've been with you for some time and haven't thought about leaving.

Specific skills frequently move into shortage. When that happens in a discipline you depend on, what can you offer to entice people to continue to work for you? If your answer is money alone, you've as good as lost the battle. In the market for scarce staff – just as is the case in the market for scarce customers – you need a sustainable source of differentiation. Money isn't it. Even in a world without skills shortages, staff are like customers. Retaining a staff member costs a lot less than recruiting a new one. Quite aside from the monetary cost, in a DisOrganized company your staff will be the key that unlocks your business' true potential. Fire them up and you are onto a winner.

A powerful, sustainable source of differentiation in the employment market is fun: provide a workplace that offers employees an enjoyable time. This not only keeps staff but also gets them to give of their best while they're there. So, what is the fun quotient (FQ) of your workplace? Is it one of the most enjoyable firms in the country or in your worldwide market? Is it one of the least enjoyable? Probably it is stuck firmly in the middle of the normal curve. A normal curve with a huge degree of clustering around a soggy, dull average and a few exceptions at the sparkling end.

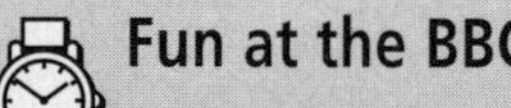

Fun at the BBC

The BBC has sometimes been represented as an overly serious organization, but BBC Resources Chief Executive Rod Lynch is convinced of the importance of fun.

'Fun is absolutely vital. You can't run an organization like this unless people like what they do. They had a situation that was all over the other media – *Private Eye* had a field day of it – about a catering lady who was fired. Amongst her personal habits, she had a belief that her skin would be improved if she washed in her own urine and she didn't believe in washing her hair except when the moon was full. As you can imagine, this lady was handling the sandwiches and the tea off the trolley in the morning. This created something of a stir. In any normal organization, of course, she would have either been fired or would have received counselling from a sympathetic personnel outfit. In the BBC, it being what it is, the journalists had a poll which they released to *Private Eye* and the *Evening Standard*, universally praising this woman and wishing that she would stay because of the general state of the BBC canteen. It was hilarious.'

Scott Sund is Marketing Communications Manager, Lucent Technologies, Bell Labs Innovations, based in Brussels. He looks after Europe, the Middle East and Africa.

It's funny that you should be stressing a business size of 50 people. Only last week I was having a conversation with a friend and we were saying that one person cannot effectively manage more than eight direct reports. If each of them managed 8 people or fewer then we'd end up not much bigger than your 50.

I believe in small companies. My background is in Apple and, even though Lucent may seem to be huge, it is organized and works as a group of small businesses working together. For instance, we don't go after huge market share gains. We will go for a gain of 1 or 2 per cent here and there. If you do this from a group of small companies, pretty soon you'll end up with 10 per cent or more.

It is particularly important that we act this way in Europe because we are so small in this area. We have a 5 per cent share and huge quotas. We aren't going to succeed by behaving in the normal way.

We need to change the paradigm and rely on our creative flair. We need to find new and different ways of doing things. This must involve us in taking risks. One difficulty in this area is that the wide cultural diversity means that some risks may end up unintentionally giving offence. You must be so sensitive to cultural differences and ready to respond appropriately.

Fun can be tough. We didn't have a lot of fun at first, but it's starting to build. There are obstacles, particularly after work when you have a diverse bunch of people, many of whom drive a long way. It makes close contact harder.

We do work at celebrating successes and at playing. Special touches are important, particularly those that recognize the person as an individual. If you have someone who likes fine malt whisky, then a thank you should be fine malt whisky. If it's cigars then you buy cigars. Knowing about people and their preferences makes recognition work. Rewards must be personal and unique.

Passion is vital in business. When I was at Apple, we were absolutely passionate about the company. If you cut us we would bleed the six-colour logo. It was an incredible place. After-work and teambuilding events there were commonplace. Once, for instance we hired a top chef and we cooked a five-course meal in teams. The chef judged the results at the end. We also went white water rafting as a way of pushing people's limits. We also worked a lot with the Covey Institute.

COVEY

See Stephen R. Covey's *The Seven Habits of Highly Effective People* (Simon & Schuster, 1990).

In some ways I am regarded as a little off the wall at Lucent. My office is full of unusual paraphernalia. For instance, I have a white board covered with magnetic poetry pieces and with quotes, I have rubber ducks, boxing gloves and airplanes decorating my walls and ceiling. This goofy stuff helps to get people off on the right foot, to get them relaxed. I am also pushing hard on the idea of dressing down. If someone comes into the office in a collar and tie, we will rib them as a way of getting the point across.

One of the biggest problems we face in this business – and every other business I've come across – is that managers never say thank you enough. We don't let people know how well they have done nearly often enough. Unless we are able to do better at this we will never build passion.

'Nobody expected to enjoy work when I was a boy!'

Surprisingly, this seems to be true. A large number of people today expect work to be satisfying, even fun, but this was probably not the case in our parents' or grandparents' day. What is it that has altered expectations? Are these expectations reasonable; and, if so, what can we do to meet them?

One source of change is school. Since the inception of child-centred teaching in primary education, there has been a trend towards all levels of schoolwork being made more attractive to the child. Children who have gone through school in the last 20 or 30 years and moved into work have carried with them an expectation of enjoyment. Not all of the time, but at least some of the time.

Another change is the trend towards people-centred employment. There have been many periods of momentous change throughout history. The start of job specialization in the early days of human settlements, the agrarian revolution that led to farmers being able to support a larger, non-farming population, and the Industrial Revolution, which, among other things, created massive centralization of the workplace. We seem to be going through a similar upheaval – an information or communications revolution.

The most likely outcome of this revolution is a breaking up of the centralized workplaces created by the Industrial Revolution. We are already seeing a trend towards homeworking and smaller, autonomous businesses. The short-term effect of this on most firms is a move towards more small teamworking, with individuals within those teams becoming more important. To be sure, this is not a wholesale change – some types of work are more affected than others; some firms are further ahead than others. Our intention is to see this trend continue and DisOrganizing your company is a huge step in that direction. One effect of this trend is that individuals will become less tied to single firms. Creating and maintaining the right teams will involve finding ways of attracting skilled and motivated individuals to work for you on a short-term project basis.

In this sort of job market, money may work as a motivation for a short time but it is easily matched – it is an unsustainable form of differentiation. If you accept that fun may be a sustainable form of differentiation, if you accept that fun will encourage your people to give of their best, and if you accept that making work fun may become an important role of the employer, what can you do about it?

AN EQUATION

'If A is a success in life, then A equals x plus y plus z. Work is x; y is play; and z is keeping your mouth shut.'

Albert Einstein

Value your people

The first thing is to value your people. That's easily done. Put the ubiquitous phrase 'our people are our greatest asset' into the report and accounts and you've succeeded. At least you will if all your employees are simpletons who ignore the evidence of their own eyes in favour of propaganda. In that case you have no need to make work fun because you obviously do not need to employ high achievers. If, on the other hand, you don't think that this will fool people, why bother? If your people are your greatest asset and everything that the management team does or says reinforces this fact, do you think they'll need the report and accounts to tell them? If, on the other hand, your people are treated as a fully interchangeable resource with no individual unit value, is a statement in the report and accounts likely to change anything?

Accepting that valuing your people involves more than simply telling them that you do, what action can you take? There are three main weapons in the armoury of the firm that really wants to value its people:

- power
- creativity
- energy.

Power

By this we mean offering your staff choice and power over their destiny. Elsewhere we have called this empowerment, but that term has been so grossly misused in recent years that it is open to many misinterpretations. If you interpret empowerment as giving away power, then use the word. If not, stick with power. There has been some argument that empowerment isn't right, that subsidiarity is a better term because empowerment is given from on high, while subsidiarity is a sort of reverse delegation. Frankly, this seems to be more semantics than useful information. In any traditional firm, the power is at the centre. It needs to be given away before subsidiarity can be achieved. The establishment of subsidiarity requires empowerment. Subsidiarity is the key to the fragmentation aspect of DisOrganization, but don't underrate the need for empowerment to get the ball rolling.

THE EMPTY RAINCOAT

For an impassioned plea for subsidiarity over empowerment, see Charles Handy's book *The Empty Raincoat* (Hutchinson, 1994).

Power takes many forms. The ways in which you can give it away can, similarly, take many forms. One of the simplest is in the structure and organization of the job. Given that many managers have not performed the task they are there to manage, what makes them uniquely qualified to say how it should be structured? Granted, they may have experience of other ways of doing things; they may have academic knowledge that they can bring to bear. Accepting all of this, there is still a huge role for those who are actually performing a task on a day-to-day basis to say how the organization of that task could be improved.

What about the day-to-day activities of your people? Most firms that we have studied put a great deal of effort into measuring the inputs to jobs and almost ignore the outputs. They measure the hours worked. They comment on and notice early arrivals and late departures as if this was all it takes to deliver a high-class result.

In a previous role, one of us once collected together and managed a team of individuals who were generally regarded as mavericks. They were totally unconcerned about the hours they worked. If there was a need to be at work, they would stay at their desk until the job was done. Similarly, they might take work home and continue working at a problem until it was solved. These same individuals had generally been written off by their previous managers because they would also disappear in the middle of the day if there was something they would rather be doing elsewhere or be found racing model cars in the office.

The output of the team they formed was absolutely unbelievable. They would produce high-quality products while others were still conceptualizing. The team's inputs were unpredictable and spasmodic. If the individuals felt that they were needed, they would be there and stay there. If not, they would go away. The single most noticeable feature about this group was the laughter that accompanied any work they did. There was always an atmosphere of fun.

Timeout – What about Microsoft?

Microsoft is one of the greatest success stories of the late twentieth century. Rising from nothing to a market value that beat IBM, Ford, Boeing, General Motors and many other great names, Microsoft was pushed forward by drive. It has been well-documented elsewhere that this success was accompanied by a regime that could push all but the most dedicated to the wall.

HARD DRIVE

For an account of the motivation behind Microsoft, see James Wallace and Jim Erickson's *Hard Drive: Bill Gates and the making of the Microsoft Empire* (John Wiley & Sons, 1992).

In Microsoft, incredibly long hours were the norm. Weekends were for wimps. The Chairman Bill Gates' own terrifying focus on work above all else was communicated forcefully to the workforce.

If this is all true, yet Microsoft was the greatest business success of its time, how can we argue against measuring inputs like time spent at work? A number of reasons underlie Microsoft apparently bucking the trend. The key is the way that sheer enthusiasm and dedication to the possibilities of technology carried through the work. To the best Microsoft workers, what they were doing was fun with a capital F, because it was the most important, sexiest thing they could spend their time doing. Later on we'll cover energy – Microsoft is oozing with energy. Oh, and they've never fought shy of employing mavericks either.

In the end, Microsoft is the exception that proves the rule. It is only the combination of an exceptional man at the helm and the remarkable staff he recruited that makes it possible to maintain this company's attitude to work, and particularly time at work. For many at Microsoft who aren't near the top of the heap, work isn't such fun, and that's sad. The rest of us, short of finding another Bill Gates, need to employ other means. And, in the end, however exciting the experience of working under remarkable pressure, the result is burnout. What would you prefer?

'If you aren't part of the solution, you're part of the problem'

As a manager, this phrase is worth taking to heart. How much of what you do each day adds to the ability of your people to deliver? If you were to scrap all of the work that did not directly help them, how much of a job would you have? Frighteningly little. Using football as an analogy, how much of your time do you spend in the role of coach? How much of your time do you spend in the role of cheerleader? How much of your time is running interference – getting others out of the way of your players so that they can score a touchdown?

All of us tend to think highly of ourselves; why not ask your people what they think about you? If you really are as good as you think, they will give you a ringing endorsement and will rate you accordingly. If you are worried about the idea of asking them, you might learn something from that worry.

On the subject of asking people what they think, do you have ways of collecting anonymous feedback from staff? If you do, how much effort do you put into fixing the things that are not right? There are two prevalent attitudes to staff feedback. The first is that if you give people an opportunity to whine, everybody will take it and you will get a stream of useless, petty complaints. The second is that the feedback process itself is all that is required, as it gives people a chance to let off steam.

To the first of these attitudes, if you have such a low opinion of your people that you do not think them capable of giving useful feedback, then you can be pretty sure that the opinion is reciprocated and they think that you are a jerk. To the second, there is nothing more frustrating than being asked your opinion and having it ignored. This is probably worse than not asking in the first place.

Does this mean we advocate centre-driven 360-degree feedback with standard forms and timing? Not a chance. They are a cop-out. The aura of bureaucracy gives them the kiss of death. Staff think it's a chore and managers know they're only doing it because they have to. By all means provide guidance on how to elicit feedback, but let individuals do it their way. It's only then that it is liable to be effective.

Creativity

We make no secret of the fact that creativity in business is an obsession of ours. Our previous books and the consultancy work we do attest to this. This stems from the fact that we think creativity provides the single largest opportunity for any company to improve business performance. Increase the creativity of your individual staff, the teams they work in and, ultimately, your whole organization and you will have a recipe for business success. You are unlikely to predict the form that success will take. You may even end up in a different business to the one you started in. You will certainly feel that you are not controlling everything, but you will be successful.

An incidental spin-off of establishing a creative organization is that the people who work in it enjoy themselves, and the FQ rises inexorably. We cover weapons of creativity and innovation elsewhere in this book, and in more detail in other books, but the point of mentioning it here is that you see it not only as a weapon for new ideas

WATCHING

'All we can do is watch the herd and observe, with some relief, that in general it is headed in a Westerly direction.'

***Director of the highly fragmented engineering firm ABB, quoted by Charles Handy in* The Empty Raincoat.**

and solutions to problems but as one that will increase the fun levels of your company.

Energy

Have you ever stepped into a workplace that buzzes with energy? The energy of the human spirit is one of our greatest natural resources and most companies succeed in suppressing it, crushing it or, more commonly, allowing it to become diverted into working against, rather than for, the company. Getting energy from your people is like getting water from a well: the pump must be primed. You will get no energy out unless you put some in. If you want people to work with energy and enthusiasm on a project, then you must inject energy and enthusiasm at the start. This is not a question of playing the part well because if you do not really feel enthusiastic about a project, forget it. Nobody can sustain an act over a long period of time. Mind you, if you are not enthusiastic about it, ask yourself how much fun you are going to get from working on it. Why should you expect others to have fun, be motivated, give of their best when you will not be able to?

The learning organization

A very specific form of empowerment is sometimes described as 'the learning organization'. This is a concept designed specifically for a time of rapid change. In a learning organization, the employees are in a constant state of development. Just as an individual who is learning will change their approach, a learning organization will modify processes and decision-making procedures, evolving new ways of working as circumstances change.

Although the learning organization is a popular concept, it can never be a sufficient goal in its own right. In fact, the best way to achieve a learning organization is to put in place the changes needed for DisOrganization as the learning organization will follow.

So what?

So, look at your firm. What is its FQ? You can rate most businesses subjectively, just by getting a feel for a few other places of work. There is not a lot to choose between most companies. They are, as we said earlier, distributed without much spread around a soggy average that is neither terminally dull nor scintillatingly vibrant. If fun was once a possibility, it is quite likely to have been squeezed out by fear, and the pressure to succeed that fear brings. If the level of enjoyment will become a key determinant of who gets the scarce resource, what can you do about it? It is fairly clear that you will not be able to make your workplace fun overnight. Using the themes of power, creativity and energy, what practices can you change that will make a difference in the future? A lot depends on it.

FEAR AND FUN

'Fun does matter and the fun is there. But perhaps in the John Birt days there has been a squashing down. The collective fun of the BBC has been markedly reduced by the brutality of the change. I use that word advisedly. It's a brutality because of the very compressed timescale.'

Rod Lynch, Chief Executive of BBC Resources

8

Weapons of creativity and innovation

Creativity as an everyday management essential

The Imagination Engineering process:
Surveying – understanding the problem and its background;
Building – idea generation;
Waymarking – selecting and refining ideas;
Navigating – implementing ideas.

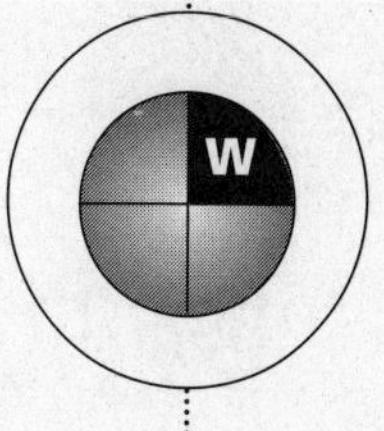

Creativity is marketing's job

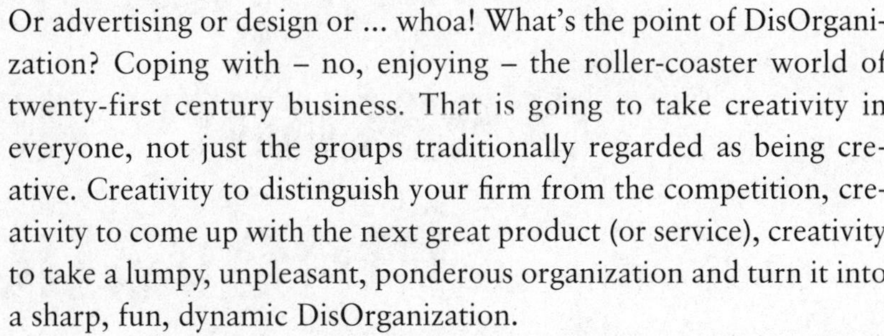

Or advertising or design or ... whoa! What's the point of DisOrganization? Coping with – no, enjoying – the roller-coaster world of twenty-first century business. That is going to take creativity in everyone, not just the groups traditionally regarded as being creative. Creativity to distinguish your firm from the competition, creativity to come up with the next great product (or service), creativity to take a lumpy, unpleasant, ponderous organization and turn it into a sharp, fun, dynamic DisOrganization.

CREATIVITY AND INNOVATION

'Imagination is the main source of value in the new economy.'

***Tom Peters, The Tom Peters Seminar: Crazy Times Call for Crazy Organizations* (Random House, 1994)**

It's a common fallacy that creativity is something you've either got or you haven't. In fact, whatever level of creativity you have, it can be stimulated and enhanced by a set of simple creativity techniques that have been refined over the last 40 years. Most people are familiar with brainstorming as an approach to idea generation or problem solving. The sad thing is, brainstorming is about the weakest tool in the creativity armoury, but it's about all that is normally used.

IMAGINATION ENGINEERING

For a complete framework and toolkit for business creativity, see our book *Imagination Engineering* (Pitman Publishing, 1996).

Systematic creativity is a big subject. We could write a whole book about it. In fact we did. All we can do in this chapter, however, is give a feel for what creativity techniques are about and how they are applied. Don't think that this is an optional extra. To become DisOrganized you are going to need all the creativity you can get. We particularly recommend trying out the exercises; creativity benefits hugely from practice, and it is hard to believe the benefits of creativity techniques until you see them in action.

What and how?

You need to be innovative. Great. What do you do? Go and sit under a tree and wait for an apple? It could be a long wait, especially if you've only got oak trees. Creativity is all about breaking out of the pattern of the past. It's looking at a problem from a new direction or seeing a market opportunity with fresh eyes. The trouble is, you often don't get inspired by sitting and thinking, even with a pencil to chew. What you need is something to break the pattern, to hack out of the tunnel of habit, something that creativity guru Roger von Oech refers to as 'a whack on the side of the head'. Enter the creativity technique.

There's nothing magic about creativity techniques. They are simple methods, tricks to force you to adopt a different viewpoint. Tricks that work again and again. At the most basic, a creativity technique might be simply to drop the problem and do something different for a few minutes. Everyone has experienced this phenomenon; the situation where an idea escapes you as long as you are searching hard, then pops up as soon as you start doing something else. It's easily done. Spend 10 minutes reading some fiction or listening to talk radio – or surfing the Internet. Come back to the problem both refreshed and with a possible new angle.

Heavyweight creativity techniques deliver more of a punch, but the effect is the same. There are many techniques available – in Imagination Engineering, we assemble them into a simple four-part framework to help you apply them. The framework is not obligatory, nor does it impose a great overhead, but most creativity practitioners, especially newcomers, find a structure helpful.

Surveying

Imagination Engineering uses the process of building a road or other travel artery as an analogy. The first step is surveying – checking out the lie of the land. Make sure you've some background information on the problem area first (for the purposes of this exercise, we'll refer to anything from idea generation down as a problem – OK, it's an opportunity, too, but don't you find that jargon dated?)

Now, let's use a simple technique. State what you are trying to do, then answer the question 'Why?' Take that answer and ask 'Why?' again. Do this a few times. It's surprising how often you get to a better understanding of what you really want to do by asking 'Why?' a few times.

WHY NOT

Consider your highest-priority task this week. Ask yourself why you are doing it. Then ask why of the answer. Repeat to taste. You may get some surprising insights.

Another purpose of surveying is to find a new direction. We recommend the level chain technique. It works like this. Suppose a paint manufacturer wanted to find a new way to sell paint. The level chain works by starting from a particular object or idea and moving up and down levels to more or less detail. For instance, I could move up from paint to the less detailed 'wall covering' or down to the more detailed 'powder paint'. Let's follow a chain. Say we're an office cleaning firm, looking to expand our range of services.

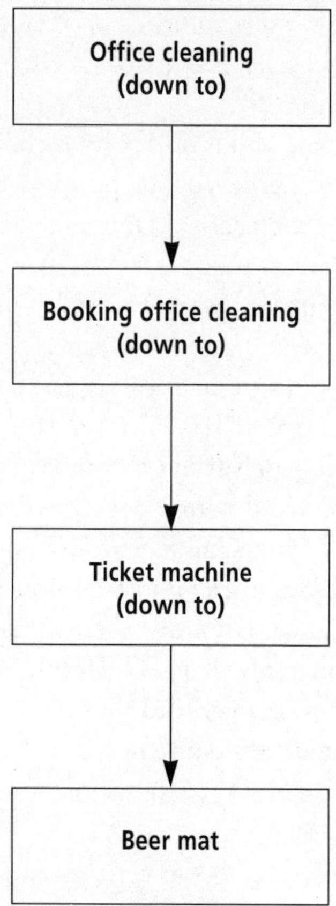

Oops! What happened there? We cheated. First we jumped to an object within the booking office, then made a sideways leap to a beer mat. Actually, we were about to put ticket, but thinking of rectangular slips of card made us think of the cardboard mats used in pubs to prevent marks on table tops from the bottom of glasses. Now here is a new market for us. We'd only ever looked into offices – not into cleaning bars and pubs and restaurants. After all, the working hours are often quite different, opening a new time window.

LEVEL CHAINS

If you are looking for something new, try the level chain on it. If not, start from Tax Returns and devise a new service for an accountant.

This is quite a good example (it genuinely worked and we didn't have any preconceived idea of what was going to come out), partly because of the randomness and also the cheating. Remember, creativity techniques are there to inspire innovation, not to keep you trapped by rules. In this case, each link was down a level, but you can go in any direction. Normally you would run a level chain several times, stopping wherever and whenever a good idea appears.

Whether you've asked 'Why?' or used the level chain, it's worth coming out of the surveying stage with a couple of statements of your destination. In the example we've just used, these might be 'how to get into cleaning bars' or 'how to diversify into cleaning for businesses open at different times'. Next, we can throw some heavyweight techniques at the problem.

Building

It may be enough to state your destination. Perhaps the idea of cleaning bars will send you off to test the field, but, often, using our civil engineering metaphor, you need to build the roadway. There is a whole raft of methods for breaking down barriers and jumping over problems. We're going to give you three quick tools:

- challenging an assumption
- someone else's problem
- random picture.

Challenging an assumption

Bearing in mind that creativity is all about getting away from habit and instead treading the familiar path, there are few more natural approaches than challenging an assumption. Whatever your problem or need, work out the most basic assumption you have about it and think of the implications of making it untrue. Let's say you wanted to break into publishing. What's the most solid assumption about it? Perhaps that publishers produce books. So, think about starting a publishers that *doesn't* produce books – how would you make it a going concern?

There are lots of possibilities. Perhaps you would simply buy other publishers and get them to produce books for you. Perhaps you would use non-traditional media. Perhaps you would consider that the main reason authors want publishers is to get their books marketed and distributed – these days, the business of typesetting and printing a book is relatively trivial. Instead of producing books, you could offer a marketing and distributing service to authors. There are plenty of other possibilities.

Once you've established the result of negating the assumption, you can replace it. But just because you will, in fact, produce books, there's no need to ignore all those other possibilities (unless you aren't in business to make money). By temporarily denying an assumption – make it as wild as you like, for instance, how would

ASSUMPTION EXERCISE

You may also need to challenge assumptions when DisOrganizing. Say you were trying to split up a very large programming team into smaller units. How would you write great software if no one in the team knew how to program? Now apply some of these thoughts to the original problem.

you make a skating ring work without gravity? – the ideas come flooding in.

Someone else's problem

With challenging assumptions under your belt, we can take on a very traditional method, but with a particularly creative slant. Most people recognize the advantage of bringing in someone else to look at their problem. Unfortunately, most of the people we bring in will already have a set view on what's needed, which may well be too close to your own. One solution is to look for someone with a totally fresh view – try asking a pre-teen child what he or she thinks about it. This may make you feel stupid, but can often result in remarkable insight.

VIEWPOINT

Take your company's best product or service. Imagine explaining it to Laurel and Hardy and asking for their views. If you can get any inspiration on your best, what could you do with your worst?

Alternatively, you can think yourself into the mind of someone very different. Pick someone well away from the problem. Perhaps a character from history or fiction or someone totally detached from your business. It might help to put together a list of such people and choose one at random. Think through what they would do in your circumstances; how they would look at your problem and its solution. What would the Pope do about your overmanning problem? How would a Star Trek character deal with the need to devise a totally new catering product? What would Shakespeare think of your standards manual? Or Plato (or Pluto) or a plumber or any one of a whole host of characters who are just waiting to help you out.

Random picture

Both these techniques appear to have a degree of logic. Equally powerful, sometimes more so, is the use of randomness. Remember, the essence of creativity is breaking away from the norm, so a totally random stimulation can often bring very positive results. A well-known form of this is random word – picking a word at random and using it to generate ideas. We are going to suggest a related, but often more powerful technique.

Put your problem to one side. Get hold of a randomly selected picture. If this technique appeals, pick up a photography book from a remainders bookshop. You know the sort of thing, a big glossy book with loads of photographs in it. For the moment, get hold of a Sunday supplement or other colour magazine. Choose a page at random – if it hasn't got a picture on it, choose another. Then, look at the first picture on the page, in detail and as a whole. What does it make you think of? What associations does it generate? Now bring those thoughts and associations together with your problem to generate new ideas.

Confused? An example might help. A chain of garden centres wants to improve profitability. What to do? They pick a picture randomly from a photography book. The picture (selected without cheating) shows an Indian temple. It is set on a lake. People are walking along a footbridge to it. Birds perch on the gilded dome. The Indian aspect makes us think of food. Perhaps the garden centres could hold a barbecue demonstration evening, giving out exciting ethnic food or a free recipe book.

PICTURE THIS

You are a motion picture company, wanting to expand into Australasia. Get hold of a newspaper and look at the lead story photograph. What does it make you think of? How might it help with what you want to do?

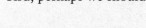

The lake reflects the temple; how does the appearance of the garden centres reflect on their quality? Do the centres look inviting from the street? Could they provide a virtual footbridge, something that would lead customers in? Perhaps by providing facilities on site (playground and animals to attract the children, toilet facilities, bar ... now there's a thought. Wouldn't having a drink make buying those garden essentials more palatable, plus there'd be profit from the bar's sales). And so on. The association could be direct – I see a bird, perhaps we should sell birds – or indirect, like the reflection.

Waymarking

The building techniques generate ideas, sometimes an awful lot of ideas. The third step of Imagination Engineering, waymarking, imagines that the road is complete, but we need to sort out the detail of signposts and rest stops. This is the fine-tuning stage. A useful first step is to try out a gut feel. Forget the logic and the numbers; what does the idea generated by the building stage do for you? Try to work out why you have this reaction – you may need to take some action, one way or another.

SIGNPOSTS

Take a current business proposal. Now spend three minutes each on identifying what's great and useless about it. Each time, stick ruthlessly to the subject: nothing negative first time, nothing positive the next.

Waymarking involves signposts. A useful exercise at this stage is to flag up what's good and bad about the idea. Take these as two entirely separate, short exercises. When you are thinking of what's good, can you make it even better? When you are coming up with negative points, how can you fix them?

It may be that waymarking destroys an idea and you have to go back to the building stage. A more likely outcome, though, is that it will help you round out and firm up the idea.

Navigating

The final stage is implementation. In our metaphor, we call this navigation, in the sense of travelling along the road (or whatever) you've constructed. If no one uses it, a road, however great it is, is worthless. If your idea is not put into practice, it isn't truly creative.

A few simple steps can ensure navigation has a chance of happening. First, draw up a plan. It doesn't have to be a grandiose affair, often something scribbled on a napkin will have more impact (if not weight) than a 500-page document. Consider using a rapid, prototyping iterative approach rather than the traditional, planned to the last detail methodologies.

Second, in packing your bag for the journey, remember the mobile phone. If you need to call for help, have you the means to do it, and do you know who to call?

Finally, make sure you've got some milestones along the way and you keep an eye on them. Make sure that arriving is one – celebrate completion for everyone's benefit.

Going further

USING THE WEB

The Internet is a great source of information on creativity. Try http://www.cul.co.uk/creative as a starting point.

Use the techniques we've outlined here. You don't need great expertise or detail to get something from creativity. This is enough to achieve DisOrganization. When you find the approach useful (and if you don't, blame us for not putting it across clearly enough), get some more detail. Read up on it. Consider getting a consultant in for a day or two to facilitate and train. Most of all, make sure that creativity is a constant business companion. DisOrganized companies don't have 20-page forms to fill in every time anyone wants to achieve something. They won't have a creativity police to check up on you and make sure you've been creative. But the benefits are immense, and it's fun, too.

9

DisOrganization: weapons

Each major section of *DisOrganization* is summarized in one of these mini chapters.

This is what I said

Communication begins with listening. The leaders of the organization can then decide what it is that makes the organization unique and set the direction based on this. This direction must set challenges that stretch the organization. Without this stretch you will be an average company, and today average companies do not survive long.

The communication process consists of setting the message, communicating it all of the time in everything you do and selecting the right range of media. Listening comes in again after communication as a way of checking understanding. Fundamental to this whole range of weapons is the point that people will always pay more attention to what you do than what you say. If you don't live the message, you will fool no one.

Do what's right – and enjoy it

There is a trend towards shortages of certain skills. In order to recruit and retain the right people to provide those skills, your organization's main weapon is likely to be fun rather than money.

The first step in making your workplace fun is to value your people. This is not about saying you value them, it is about doing it. In this area more than any other you cannot fake sincerity.

The second step is to provide them with real power. Nothing is more likely to make a workplace sparkle than the people who work there having genuine choice in the things that matter. This is not talking about the colour of the curtains or the supplier of the coffee. It is about the how and the what and the when and the why and the who of getting the job done. Again, the key is living the message. If you aren't actively making this stuff happen, you are preventing it.

Finally, injecting mechanisms of creativity and energy will ensure that the fun and empowerment become part of the fabric of work life.

Making creativity work

Creativity is part of everybody's role in an organization; it is not something that specialists do. There are techniques available that help to make individuals, groups and companies more creative. We have provided a four-stage framework based on a civil engineering metaphor. The stages are:

- *surveying* understanding the problem area and making sure that you are tackling the right issue;
- *building* generating ideas and building solutions;
- *waymarking* selecting from those ideas and refining the solutions;
- *navigating* travelling the route and making things happen.

Looking inwards

Having covered your organization's dimensions and the weapons of DisOrganization, we are about to move on to the inward channels by means of which these weapons can be applied. We are using the term 'channel' with a broader meaning than a sales channel: these are resources, the people, the mechanisms and systems that make your company function. The inner channels come together to form your hypercompany, providing different aspects of the organization.

PART THREE

Inward channels

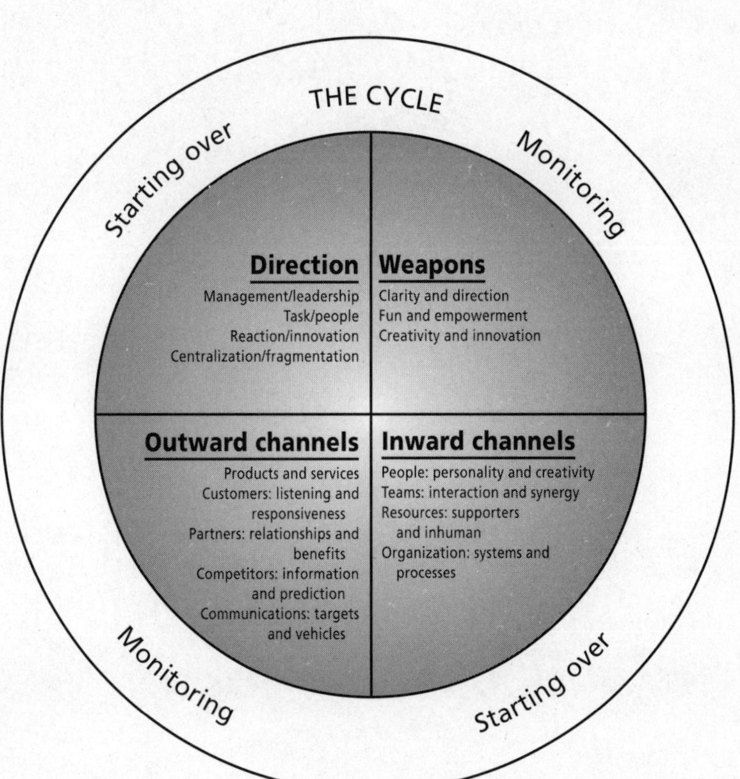

10

People: personality and creativity

- Knowing yourself and your staff
- The eight basic personality types
- Building on strengths and overcoming blockages
- Dealing with people in a DisOrganized company
- Career management, accommodation, unions and more

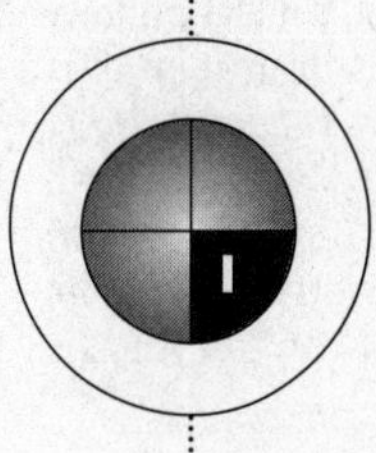

Know thyself

We're going to start looking at people by considering the effect of personality on an individual's work life, particularly creativity and willingness to change. Everything we say about personality applies just as much to you as it does to your staff. You need to be creative and flexible in order to be successful. Generally we are approaching this from a perspective of leadership or the organization, but the people aspect is more personal. If you don't understand what gets in the way of your personal creativity and flexibility, you will find it hard to remove the blockages.

An introduction to personality types

A large part of the material for the next two chapters is based on the work of Insights International in Dundee, Scotland. Insights has built on Carl Jung's studies of personality to develop a framework for understanding yourself and others.

INSIGHTS INTERNATIONAL

Insights' material is copyright and is used with the company's kind permission. For further information about its work, for an insight into your personality or the workings of your team, contact Andrew Lothian at Insights International, 29/31 South Tay Street, Dundee DD1 1NP, Scotland, or phone +44 (0)1382 229292.

Jung suggested that people have different preferences that determine their perspectives and cause people to react differently when presented with the same situation. These preferences affect all aspects of our lives.

When looking at a person's orientation to the inner or the outer worlds, Jung coined the terms *extraversion* and *introversion*. These terms are relatively well understood, but the following lists are provided for reference.

Introversion	Extraversion
Quiet	Talkative
Observant	Involved
Inwardly focused	Outwardly focused
Deep	Breadth
Intimate	Gregarious
Reserved	Flamboyant
Reflective	Action-oriented
Thoughtful	Outspoken
Cautious	Bold

In addition to extraversion and introversion, Jung also identified four other characteristics that he combined with the first two to create eight basic personality combinations. The second dimension of personality covers the 'irrational' functions and is derived from the way that people pay attention to and absorb information. Those who give more weight to their senses he called *sensing* and those who were influenced more by patterns and impressions he called *intuitive*. Sensing and intuitive people have the following characteristics.

Sensing	Intuitive
Specific	Take a global view
Present-oriented	Future-oriented
Realistic	Imaginative
Persistent	Inspirational
Down-to-earth	Are ideas people rather than practical
Practical	Conceptual
Precise	Generalize
Factual	Abstract
Like to do things step by step	Indirect

The final dimension covers the so-called rational functions and is derived from the way people prefer to make decisions. Those who prefer logic, analysis and an impersonal decision-making process he called *thinking*. Those who prefer decision making to be more subjective he called *feeling*.

Thinking	Feeling
Formal	Informal
Impersonal	Personal
Analytical	Considerate
Detached	Involved
Objective	Subjective
Strong-minded	Caring
Competitive	Accommodating
Correct	Harmonious
Task-oriented	Relationships-oriented
Systems-oriented	Morale-oriented

The possible combinations of the attitudes – extraversion and introversion – the irrational functions – sensing and intuitive – and the rational functions – thinking and feeling – give us the eight basic personality types.

Insights' Colours

Insights has used the Jung typology to produce two levels of personal understanding. The first is Insights' Colours (see Figure 10.1). These are related to the attitudes (extraversion and introversion) and the rational functions (thinking and feeling).

Figure 10.1 The Insights' Colours

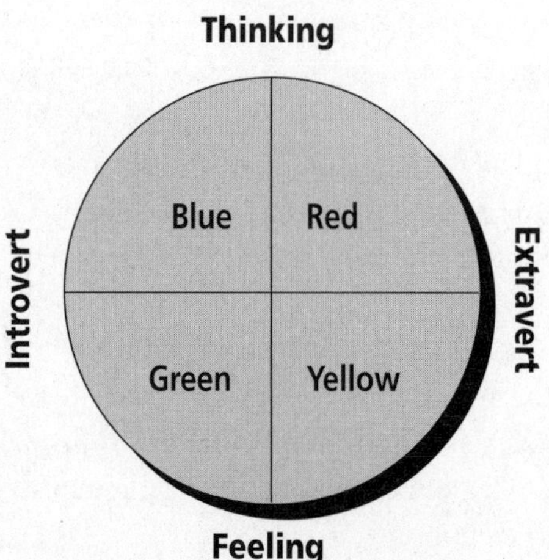

Fiery red

People in this group are extraverted and have high levels of energy. They are action-oriented and always in motion. They are positive, reality-oriented and assertive. They are single-minded as they focus on results and objectives. They will approach others in a direct, authoritative manner, radiating a desire for power and control.

Sunshine yellow

People in this group are extraverted, radiant and friendly. They are usually positive and concerned with good human relations. They enjoy the company of others and believe that life should be fun. They approach others in a persuasive, democratic manner, radiating a desire for sociability.

Earth green

People in this group focus on values and depth in relationships. They want others to be able to rely on them. They will defend what they value with quiet determination and persistence. They prefer democratic relations that value the individual and are personal in style, radiating a desire for understanding.

Cool blue

People in this group are introverted and need to know and understand the world around them. They like to think before they act and maintain a detached, objective standpoint. They value independence and intellect. They prefer written communication in order to maintain clarity and precision, radiating a desire for analysis.

What about the irrational?

As well as the four colours, Insights add the irrational functions, generating a subdivision of each colour to create eight basic types they call Reformer, Director, Motivator, Inspirer, Helper, Supporter, Coordinator and Observer. We will look a little deeper at these in the next chapter, but can't go into them in enough detail here to do them justice. To take this further, contact Insights.

What is your natural self most like?

To understand where you sit in Insights' Colours, work through this short exercise.

Look at Figure 10.2. This describes the main characteristics of each colour. Combine this information with that given in the descriptions of each of the colours above and you should have a pretty clear idea how you perceive yourself on a day-to-day basis.

Figure 10.2
Is your natural self most like this?

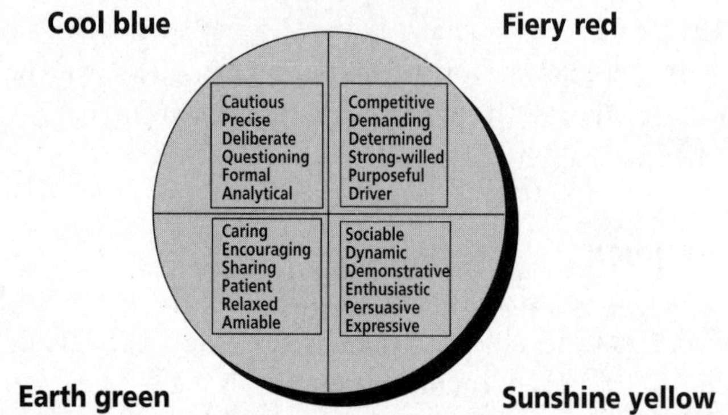

You may find that you are torn between two types. This may be because there are a mix of preferences within your perception of yourself. If you can, identify the one quadrant that is most like you. If you cannot, read through what follows with both quadrants in mind.

Remember also that the characteristics described so far have been ones that people in each quadrant are likely to identify with. On a bad day, they may not be so keen (see Figure 10.3).

At their worst these are also the characteristics that dissimilar types are likely to see in each colour.

Figure 10.3
On a bad day

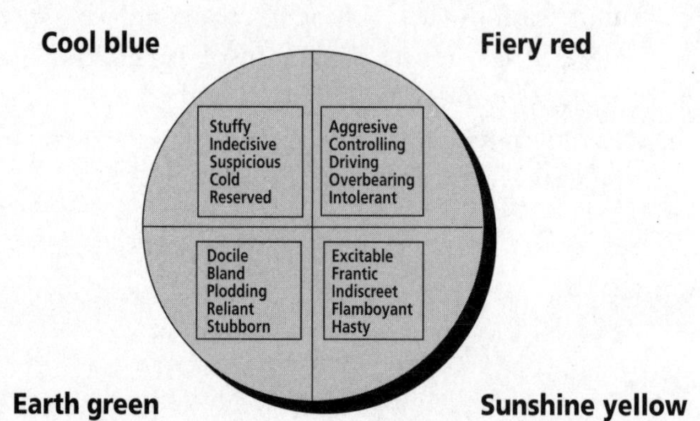

The colours and creativity

The colours can help with your creativity by providing a better understanding of what you will do well and where you will fall down.

Fiery red

Creative strengths

Once they've accepted a good idea, they'll push to make it happen. They are unlikely to be hung up on the way it has always been done and able to see new ideas as a path forward.

Creative blockages

Tend to be judgmental at too early a stage. They will kill half-formed ideas unless they can readily see an application. They are too impatient to wait for ideas to be developed. They want the results of creativity but don't want the sidetracks.

Sunshine yellow

Creative strengths

Buzzing with new ideas, they will be the source of many of the early, off-the-wall suggestions at any idea generation session. Their enthusiasm will encourage ideas from other participants.

Creative blockages

They will become impatient if ideas don't turn into reality quickly enough. They don't have the perseverance to follow through to make things happen. They will often be generating new ideas to solve new problems before anything has been done about the last set.

Earth green

Creative strengths

In a group idea generation session, they will be most aware of the other members of the group and will make sure that everyone has a chance to air their ideas. They are flexible and willing to listen to new approaches.

Creative blockages

Will often try to think through the effect that this idea may have on others. This may cause them to evaluate an idea too early. In trying to avoid disruption to others, they may appear to be inherently conservative.

Cool blue

Creative strengths

Once they are committed to a new idea, they will be able to plan and follow through its implementation. They are the most likely individuals to see a creative idea through to completion.

Creative blockages

The focus on logic and facts will mean that they are the most likely to evaluate early an idea that is not yet fully formed. They will tend to remain silent in group creativity sessions or, if they say anything it will probably be, 'but that's silly', or 'it would never work'.

Building on your strengths and overcoming the blockages

Fiery red

Reds will tend to generate ideas, provide thrust and act with decisiveness. They will take control and communicate openly.

To avoid conflict, ensure that they take responsibility for their actions. To overcome blockages and build on their strengths, give them plans, schedules, handouts and charts. Let them lead the process. Don't take offence at their seeming aggression.

Sunshine yellow

Yellows will express support for others and maintain networks. They will take action and enthuse others to join in. They are willing to participate and to be involved.

To avoid conflict, give praise for both individual and team successes. To overcome blockages and build on their strengths, give them the chance to talk and express themselves. Let them share their feelings. Be patient with them and don't shout them down (even if you are a red).

Earth green

Greens accept new ideas and will provide insight and flexibility. They know the environment and are keen to reach consensus.

To avoid conflict, be genuinely interested in team members as individuals. To overcome blockages and build on their strengths, give them space and praise for their work, even if it is incomplete. Allow them to work at their own pace and under their own steam.

Cool blue

Blues pay attention to the infrastructure and conceptualize problems. They look deeply into issues. They have a strong sense of responsibility.

To avoid conflict, give each team member undivided attention when listening to them. To overcome blockages and build on their strengths, give them time to study, reflect and contemplate. Ask them to produce a written analysis on a significant opportunity.

Moving forward with the colours

Awareness is a key part of progressing. Once you are aware of the pitfalls, you are much less likely to fall into them. Once you are aware of your preferences, you are less likely to exhibit bias. Once you are aware of your effect on others, you are more likely to affect them positively. Once you are aware of yourself, you may have started to become effective.

Look again through the things that are likely to go wrong because of the type of person you are and develop strategies for overcoming them. Look at the quadrant opposite you on the wheel and think of the positive benefits of some of the characteristics you most dislike. To be able to display these characteristics is unlikely, but it is quite possible, and highly beneficial, to value them.

Who's he, then?

If you aren't convinced of the benefits of DisOrganization yet, consider the alternatives. One of us was recently invited to a conference on competency. For a fee, we could enjoy two days of experts telling us how to cope with understanding what our people can do.

These experts are very clever folk, and are patching up a real problem – knowing your people in a huge company. Yet, all they can ever do is patch, because the underlying problem is not having inappropriate competency frameworks, it's having a monolithic organization. If you don't know your people well enough in a DisOrganized company, you don't need competency tools, you need firing.

How to ...

- get the right people for the job;
- manage careers;
- accommodate staff;
- deal with people's *real* motivations;
- bring outsiders in;
- deal with the unions;
- deal with power freaks;
- deal with staff;
- provide a point of contact;
- get and use ideas;
- deal with staff moves.

Getting the right people for the job

By now you are probably convinced that we are committed adherents to personality tests and that we are about to lay out a battery of personality profiling methods to use in selection. In fact, our experience of selection is that test results pale into insignificance when set against the weight given to a face-to-face interview. Tests may be a more accurate predictor (frankly we doubt it), but, even if they are, if the results are ignored when they do not agree with the results of an interview, why bother?

Selecting the right people has a lot to do with the skill set needed to complement the team, but it has at least as much to do with the way the individual will fit into the team. We will go into teamwork in the next chapter and there is certainly a place for personality profiling there, but primarily as a minimum requirement. One approach that may successfully combine personality profiling and interviews is a report produced by Insights that suggests interview questions based on the profile of the interviewee. Beyond that, profiling is much more useful as a way of understanding team dynamics and reacting appropriately than as a tool for selection.

Career management

The traditional human relations view of career management is helping an individual in their progression through the company with an invisible (actually, sometimes very visible) guiding hand. The alternative view sees it as something that an individual does for themselves.

In a DisOrganized world, there will be far fewer large organizations to move through. Progression may be within a mini company, but will, for most people, be across companies and even between industries. There cannot be the same paternalistic philosophy in such a world. For many this will not be a problem. Indeed, it will often be seen as an advantage. For some, though, the loss of a formal career management process is a significant drawback. For these individuals and many who wouldn't mind some pointers, the DisOrganized substitute is mentoring.

A mentor is someone who helps to guide career choices, but has no direct gain from the outcome. Mentors will often do this for people because they had similar assistance at some stage in their career. There is a strong feeling of, 'what goes around, comes around' in such a system. For the mentor, there is another, very intangible advantage and that is staying in touch. For the most part, mentors will be more senior than those they are mentoring and, as we all know, seniority is a sure recipe for losing touch. This may well be true even in a DisOrganized world. Mentoring discussions can provide an antidote.

How to be accommodating

As the watchword of the mini company is flexibility, there is likely to be a relatively unstable need for people within it. This implies an unstable accommodation requirement. How can a mini company, operating on tight margins, cope with this fluctuation? The workings of market economics means that short-term space, which is likely to be in high demand in such an unstable environment, will command a high price. If and when that happens, should the mini company buy into it?

In general, mini companies will be aware of their own volatility and will carry a small amount of additional space to cover short-term fluctuations. Beyond that, flexibility can be converted from a problem into a solution. In this instance, flexibility of using space. Teleworking, hot-desking and other flexible working methods will need to be the norm in mini companies and ought to be designed into the working processes from the start. The degree to which they are used will depend on the demand for space at the time and the needs of the staff.

There will be times when flexibility is overstretched and the mini company ends up paying over the odds for short-term space. This will decrease margins briefly, but will, hopefully, increase its profit. If it doesn't, why would it bother with the short-term expansion?

Dealing with people's *real* motivations

There has been a huge amount written about motivation, but it often seems to miss the point. Whenever we are dealing with people, there is a subtle dance between their true motivations and the ones they will admit to. Take a concrete example. One of us sometimes writes games software reviews. Although nominally this is done for the fee (and certainly wouldn't be done for free), the prime motivation is a childish enthusiasm for being given new toys and playing with them. At risk of being sexist, men seem particularly prone to the 'new toy' syndrome. You only have to look at the effort put into choosing a company car.

Real motivations can't be assessed by using forms. Sorry to say this, but people lie. The mini company structure gives you a better chance of knowing your staff and, hence, understanding why they are doing things. Leadership abilities put a manager in a position where they are more likely to be able to discuss real motivational issues, but the main thing is to remember that unknown motivations exist. We all have hidden agendas that we are likely to consider too silly to put on the table. If you can be aware of those in the people of your organization, you've a better chance of getting them on your side.

Bringing outsiders in

One of the effects of flexibility and changes in size is that there will be a growing need for temporary and part-time staff. If they are not in line with the culture of the DisOrganized company, they will do more damage than good. To achieve this alignment, effort in selection, orientation and ongoing reward is required. At the heart of this is the notion that temporary and part-time staff are fundamental to the success of a mini company and that their input is as important as that of the people who are directly employed.

Very few companies put outsiders through the same degree of introductory and ongoing training as permanent staff, nor are they usually fully exposed to the culture of the host company. Even if the company uses Insights, it is unlikely to apply the technique to temporary staff, but they are still part of the team. Unless contractors or temporary staff have the same view and provide the customers with the same feel, they will entirely undermine your business. Don't think of it as an unnecessary cost, think of it as part of the price of flexibility.

YOUNG AND ALIVE?

Retail outlets often use school-age staff to fill in during school holidays and weekends. They may lack experience, but they have a huge resource of energy. You wouldn't think so when you are served by them: often their performance is, at best, lacklustre. There's a huge opportunity here, if only these people were treated properly. They have vitality – use it, don't squash it.

Dealing with the unions

Many mini companies will be elements of previous conglomerates that have been broken up. They will have brought with them some of the baggage of the larger company and this may well include union representation.

Transferring staff to another company will, in most countries, require a transfer of undertakings that will keep pay and conditions the same in the new as it was in the old. In many cases this will include union recognition. It is possible that this will result in a period of difficulty and confusion. It is, for instance, likely that staff in a large organization are represented by more than one union. It is unlikely that this will make sense in a mini company. There is almost certainly going to be a period of rationalization. In the US, this needs to be negotiated at the end of each of the contract periods or, if the contract allows, at an interim negotiation. In the UK, the change will be simpler if the staff agree, but will also need to be negotiated.

One of the effects of DisOrganizing is likely to be a shrinking of union involvement. There are two extreme explanations for this. On the one hand, the employers will tell you that there is no need for staff representation in a small outfit where communication is easier. On the other hand, the unions will tell you that small companies tend to be more exploitative and can get away with more if unions aren't involved.

There is some degree of truth in both statements. Some employers would prefer not to have the unions involved in their firm because it makes their job less complicated and may even allow for exploitation. Some unions would like to be involved in firms even where there is no need for representation because they want the increased membership and the associated dues. Not all employers are nice guys and not all union officials are saints.

There are no hard and fast rules as to how the mini company should develop over time. In general, union involvement is likely to diminish as a result of lack of need. There will be a transition period with a duration that depends on the degree of trust between the staff and the employers in the mini company. Generally, the most successful mini companies will be those that look after their staff extremely well, but there will be significant exceptions and, for these exceptions, there will still be a need for union involvement.

Dealing with power freaks

The traditional measure of a manager's success has been the size of their organization. In the DisOrganized world it isn't the size that's important, it's the way that you use it. Big is no longer beautiful. There will be a lot of people who do not get this message and will strive to control more than a single DisOrganized company. Our contention is that they will be less successful than those who are focused, directed and who keep it small.

Those in the net company need to pay particular attention to this. If there is an amalgamation of mini companies over time, there are two risks in this. The first is that the service provided by these companies will diminish as a result of a lack of focus and direction. The second is that the mini companies will start to wield too much power in relation to the net company and that the ultimate weapon of withdrawing a contract will no longer be a viable option.

Dealing with staff

Throughout the transition from the traditional dinosaur to the mini company, it is essential to pay attention to the staff. They will feel sold out. They will feel that they are losing their employer. They will have learned their organizational skills in a different world and some will not be able to cope with the change. How can we handle this?

The first and most important aspect of the preparation for the transition is communication. The benefits of working for the mini company must be made to be at least as good as the previous company offered and this must be communicated. The concerns and fears of staff must be heard and responded to honestly. This means a huge amount of work, but this work is essential.

Next, there must be a strong point of identification with and pride in the mini company. One of the key points of DisOrganization is that the staff of a mini company identify personally with its successes and failures. If the facts of what is happening to the company are not communicated, there is no chance of identification and the mini company will fail.

Some staff will find it impossible to cope with life in a DisOrganized world. Ideally there should be a way of helping them move into a dinosaur company somewhere else. We believe that, for the foreseeable future, there will be large companies out there, even when the DisOrganized companies of the world are demonstrably more successful.

NEW SKILLS

The range of new skills needed for survival in modern business is well-covered in Brian Clegg's *The Chameleon Manager* (Butterworth Heinemann, 1998).

Providing points of contact

Communication between companies in a DisOrganized world is fundamental. If it falls down, then the whole system collapses. This communication depends on individuals, and they need other individuals to talk to. This means that every mini company must have a single point of contact with the net company. Every mini company must have a single point of contact with every other mini company. Where mini companies do not deal regularly with one another, there must be a simple way of putting one in touch with another. Remember, this whole notion depends on individuals talking to individuals.

Getting and using ideas

We have said that creativity is at the heart of DisOrganization before, but we must stress it again. Great ideas can come from anywhere, so there need to be efficient mechanisms for collecting and using ideas from people throughout the structure. Generally, the mini company will be small enough to make this relatively straightforward. Talking to people and e-mails should be enough.

If ideas aren't forthcoming, the traditional approach is to bring in suggestion boxes and suggestion schemes with financial incentives. Neither is appropriate for a DisOrganized company. Suggestion boxes generally don't work because little is done with the ideas submitted. Administrating such a scheme is a chore, and the ideas provided are rarely viewed positively by management. The culture of a DisOrganized company should allow anyone with a suggestion to walk up to the boss and explain it or e-mail it to him or her – and have something happen. Further, with the extra insight workers in a mini company have, they may well be able to make the suggestion direct to the person who can do something about it.

Schemes with financial incentives are disasters for morale. Certain parts of the company, because of the nature of their work, often come up with the vast percentage of money-saving ideas. Either you irritate these people by not rewarding them or you irritate the rest because it's always 'them' who get the big payouts. A decent, performance-based pay scheme should take into account an individual's overall contribution without such an abomination. However, if you do want a structured approach, how about having facilitated problem-solving sessions with the entire mini company once in a while? Otherwise, use Nick Spooner of Internet commerce specialists Entranet's approach of walking a problem around your staff. There is no business in the world that doesn't have problems. Using the brains of everyone to solve them must give a business an edge.

Dealing with staff moves

People will move. They will sometimes move within the mini company. They will often move between companies. If and when they do, it will cost money to recruit and train others to replace them. It will cost more for people to move between mini companies than it would have cost for them to move within a dinosaur company. There is little that can be done to alleviate this. The cost is necessary. You cannot afford to bring people in without giving them a proper grounding. This cost, we believe, pales into insignificance when set against the advantages of doing this.

11

Teams: interaction and synergy

- The nature of teams
- Interaction of personality types in teams
- Cross-company teams
- Performance-related pay
- Production lines and airline checking in services

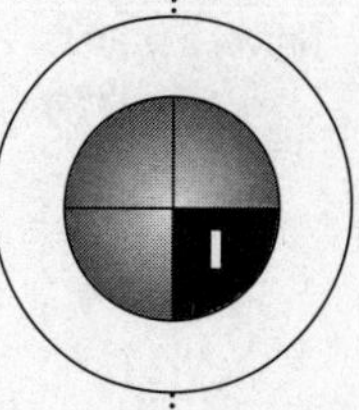

All together now

Teams and the ways in which they work, develop and fail are areas that have fascinated management practitioners and social scientists for many years. There is something interesting about the chemistry that makes some groups work significantly better than the sum of the individual members' efforts, while others fail abysmally even to get off the ground.

In this chapter, we will look at the reasons behind this and develop an understanding of the blocks and hindrances to the creation and success of teams in your organization.

What is a team?

TEAM

1 a set of players forming one side in a game (a cricket team). 2 two or more persons working together. 3 (a) a set of draught animals. (b) one or more animals in harness with a vehicle.

Concise Oxford Dictionary **(9th Edition, Oxford University Press, 1996).**

A team is a group of people who work together in some way. The use of the word 'work' in that sentence should not be taken to imply that teams are only employment-based – that is obviously not true. Teams crop up in all sorts of human interaction. The lessons in this chapter are primarily aimed at organizations – particularly DisOrganized organizations – but can be applied to any form of endeavour.

Why teams?

When discussing teamwork, a question that is often taken for granted and rarely answered is, why would you bother with teams? Indeed, they can often seem more trouble than they are worth.

A well-structured team working on a particular issue can achieve far more than the sum of the individuals in the team could ever do working separately. This is really an area where the overused word 'synergy' comes to mean something real and substantial. Teamwork is driven by a combination of the ability to spark ideas off each other, the interplay of different skills and the ability to multitask in a way that is impossible for an individual. Having said that, a team performing poorly will suck any effort that the team members put into it and will still fail to deliver as much as those individuals could have done on their own.

Nick Lopardo is Chairman of State Street Global Advisors (SSgA), the institutional investment management arm of State Street Corporation. SSgA was established in 1978 and is now the third largest money manager in America, and in the top ten worldwide.

Do small working units of around 50 people make sense to you?
I am not sure that the 50 people level is the right number, but the direction is appropriate in my opinion, in that I feel smaller groups tied to a common goal, target or even enemy, for that matter, will enable an organization to feel empowered and react appropriately to the goals. Smaller groups allow for closer ties and more recognized common accomplishments.

Let's not lose sight that large businesses can *feel* small when communication is excellent, missions are clear and the small groups' targets are in sight and focused.

What's the difference between management and leadership?
I don't view leadership and management similarly. Good managers tend to be well-organized while leaders are more charismatic but rely on managers to deliver the goods. A good find is a leader who can also manage. I would tend to not want to burden the leader with implementation – let the leader dream and share the vision, and if the person can also lead by example, what a bonus! SSgA, I would like to think, is well-managed and well-led. We all share a passion for the mission to be the best global money management firm in the business, as demonstrated by assets under management, breadth of customers around the world and repeat business from those customers.

Business leaders are all doers in SSgA – we all do our own computer analysis, but we also can inspire team members to follow us into the fray!

How should companies be organized to be effective?
I believe the effective company of the future is the holding company that allows its businesses to run their show, but be mindful of their impact and influence on other family members in the conglomerate. I also think it is appropriate to tie this holding company into one reward system so that nobody cares who gets the credit as long as the family thrives and grows.

How do you balance reaction and innovation?

Both reaction and innovation have a role to play: it is healthy to create differentiation for your company – something that sets you apart and makes you different or unique; this creativity enlivens the atmosphere and charges the troops up with enthusiasm. However, let's not forget to react when appropriate, when time is of the essence and you don't have the opportunity to create the newest idea – execution is the requirement and one must be able to respond effectively and quickly to stay in the game at certain times. Take well thought through and calculated risks.

Should work be fun?

Fun is not necessarily popping Champagne bottles – fun can be the thrill of victory or the satisfaction of a job well done. Fun to me is knowing that when the alarm rings in the morning, the first response isn't 'Oh no, it's a work day.'

What about teams?

Team is the essential ingredient in SSgA today – a more appropriate characterization is family. We care about each other, but, more important, we respect each other – if we also like each other, that is a bonus.

Back to Insights

Personality types, and their implications for how people interact, have an obvious application to teams. The Insights wheel (see Figure 10.1, page 96) can help in understanding the way that teams function or fall down. In order to explore this, we will need to extend the original Insights wheel from the four we have considered so far to our eight basic personality types.

Eight basic personality types

The eight basic types are shown on the extended Insights wheel in Figure 11.1.

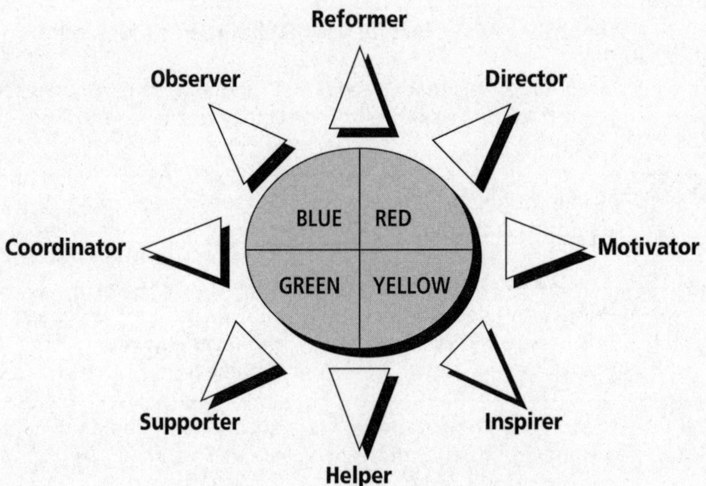

Figure 11.1
Eight basic personality types

In the team roles these types can be expressed as:

- *Motivator* creating new ideas;
- *Inspirer* promoting ideas to others;
- *Helper* consulting with others;
- *Supporter* providing structure and support;
- *Coordinator* keeping to established procedures;
- *Observer* checking systems;
- *Reformer* establishing methods;
- *Director* testing and implementing.

The shadow side

In general, those at any position on the wheel will have the greatest difficulty with team members at the opposite pole to themselves. So, a Reformer will find it difficult to work with a Helper, a Director will find it difficult to work with a Supporter, a Motivator will find it difficult to work with a Coordinator, an Inspirer will find it difficult to work with an Observer, and vice versa in all cases.

Perceptions of types by their opposites

An important step in working more effectively with your team is to understand your reaction to your opposite type. An important step in getting a whole team working together is to imbue all team members with a similar understanding. Table 11.1 shows what each type is seeing in themselves and what their shadow sees in them.

Table 11.1
Perceptions

Type	What they see in themselves	What their shadow sees
Reformer	'Sometimes this team needs a jolt to get it back to work.	'Stop being so blunt, you seem totally unaware of others' feelings.'
Director	'Some tough work needs to be done right now.'	'Stop driving us so hard – time to understand one another is essential to a good result.'
Motivator	'Innovation keeps the business coming in.'	'Stop launching new ideas. If we never deliver anything we'll never be successful.'
Inspirer	'Getting to know people and having fun is important for the success of the team.'	'Stop talking and do something.'
Helper	'Attention to each person's needs is good for the team.'	'Stop worrying about everyone and focus on your job for a change.'
Supporter	'Exploring our deeply held beliefs and values keeps this team on the right path.'	'Stop taking offence and develop a thicker skin.'
Coordinator	'Precision and accuracy of information allows our team to produce good work.'	'Stop nitpicking. Let's go for being roughly right rather than precisely wrong.'
Observer	'Teams need to analyze concepts carefully before they can work effectively.'	'Stop being so theoretical. Let's allow the ivory tower people to worry about the concepts and we'll go for actually doing things.'

Combining types to maximize effectiveness

The fact that a particular type finds it difficult to work with their shadow does not mean that teams should be formed only with similar types. Teams that are made up of similar types will get on well together and will reach consensus swiftly. They will, however, have blind spots, overlooking opportunities (and threats) in their mutually weak areas. Teams consisting of different types take longer to reach consensus, but are likely to achieve better results because of the balance in the team. Less will be overlooked.

The very nature of teamwork is that the differences in the team fuel the synergy. Indeed, a truly effective team will have individuals who are able, to a greater or lesser extent, to display the characteristics of all of the Insights types. This does not mean that you always need at least eight people, each with a different personality type. Look at the desired outcome and balance the team accordingly.

Different aims, different teams

To read some of the literature, you would think that one formula can be applied to creating a team and that this formula will be effective in any and all circumstances. It is almost axiomatic that, for different tasks, different types of team will be required. The suggestion that Insights makes is that the balance referred to above is achieved by mixing opposites according to the needs of the team.

So, if you have a need to hit a production deadline, you are likely to want to have an Observer, a Reformer and a Director in the team. This would provide strong results orientation. It would also make for an unbalanced team. Into this mix you could drop an opposite type, perhaps a Helper, in order to provide balance.

Similarly, if you want a people-focused human resources team, you could select a Supporter, a Helper and an Inspirer. To provide balance in this team, you would put in a Reformer.

Life would be hard in such teams for the opposite type, unless all team members understood the importance of their role. Even then, there would need to be frequent opportunities to express opinions and misunderstandings.

Self-managed teams

In recent years, there has been a great deal of talk about self-managed teams. They are seen by some as the panacea to replace all previous panaceas. Realistically, there are no panaceas.

There is a place for self-managed teams, and when they work they seem to work very well indeed. Those who work in them often find that the freedom to make choices about the inputs to work that determine the outputs is enough to make a real difference to their enjoyment and commitment.

How long should a team 'live'?

A classic 'How long is a piece of string?' question. A team should last as long as is necessary for an objective to be achieved. However, there are some guidelines that might be useful. Some teams will be formed and disbanded in a very short period of time. This could be as little as a few hours for a very specific, tactical objective. Some teams will last for years. In general, those projects that will last longer than a few months should be regarded as a series of projects. You will often find, if you view them this way, that the skills required for the different stages of the completion of the project are different. These different skills could call for different teams, or different team members, to complete them.

The length of life of a team should be considered when setting it up. If it looks as though it will extend beyond a few months, think again about the project and work out ways of subdividing this life. Having done this, it might well be that the project really does last for a very long time and it is, genuinely, one long piece of work that cannot be sensibly subdivided. If this is the case, at least you will know and can warn the team accordingly.

How should it 'die'?

Once the task that a team has been created to achieve has been completed, the team must not only die but it must die publicly. Its achievements should be celebrated, its members should be thanked and its passing should be mourned. Allowing a team to quietly fade away is not a good idea. Even a team that is regarded as a failure should have a funeral of some sort. Without some sort of rite of passage it is unclear where the members of teams stand. Without a clear watershed there is little to differentiate one day from the next. Without a public thank you there is little incentive to put in so much effort next time.

How big is your team?

A team can be as large or as small as you want. In reality, most working groups will be between two and ten people. Fewer than two is obviously not a team; more than ten will tend to result in some subdivision for all or some of the workings of the team. Having said that, the person running a department, either the relatively small ones of DisOrganized companies or the larger ones of dinosaur companies – may well regard their department as a team.

How to ...

- create cross-company project teams;
- deal with rogue mini companies;
- organize within a mini company;
- handle performance-related pay;
- work a large production line;
- check in at an airport.

Creating cross-company project teams

This is always going to be difficult. Unfortunately it is not possible to say glibly, 'It will be easier because DisOrganization makes it easier'. In fact, it will be harder. Cross-company teams become more likely in a DisOrganized world because companies are smaller and interactions are greater. The directions of companies may be closely aligned, but individual loyalties will still be to the company rather than the team.

THE IMATION EXPERIENCE

See the Imation interview, page 187.

We have had significant experience of cross-company teams in the past and there are a few lessons that can usefully be applied. First, the objectives of the companies in forming the team need to be similar. They need not be the same, but they should require similar outputs from the team.

Second, the members of the team must have a strong point of contact and support in their company in order to talk over conflicts and difficulties.

Third, and most important, the team must be colocated, ideally in territory that is neutral to both companies.

Dealing with rogue mini companies

Given that the mini company can be viewed as a team, we need to consider how to deal with one team that is working at odds to others around it. In the case of a rogue mini company, the ultimate sanction is that the net company will no longer choose to deal with it. Ideally, the situation would not reach this state.

The initial direction that other mini companies need to take is communication. Explaining the problem is often halfway to solving it. This assumes a degree of goodwill on both sides. If this is not there, the next stage must be to apply some sort of sanction.

If this is done from mini company to mini company, then it is likely a feud will develop that will get out of hand. The ideal situation is that the net company is involved in order to examine how the long-term aims will not be met if the rogue mini company does not toe the line. Obviously there is an implied threat in this conversation of ultimately withdrawing a contract. If there is no risk to the aims of the net company, then there really is no issue, other than a degree of competition between mini companies. This they will have to live with.

Organizing within a mini company

In a traditional, dinosaur company, the organization often happens without much thought. Even where it is planned, it is often to a model. In other words, should it be functional or geographic? If functional, then it should look like this or like this. Within a mini company, however, such models do not apply. A large organization is structured on the assumption of overhead. There will be staff performing a range of overhead functions and there will be yet more overhead providing support to those staff. Yes, we know that almost every company has gone through significant downsizing in the last 10 to 20 years, but, beyond 50 or 100 employees, there will still be diseconomies of scale built into the structure.

A mini company cannot afford such luxuries: there must be a purpose for everything and, in almost all cases, this purpose is defined by the end-product or end-customer of the company. This degree of focus is the primary key to the organization of teams. They will be focused, aimed at specific, measurable results. They will often be short term. The longer-term thinking will tend to be in the hands (or the head) of the leader of the mini company.

Handling performance-related pay

It may seem strange that we've put performance-related pay in the chapter about teams rather than the one about people. It would fit there perfectly well, but it's here to make a point. Personal performance tends to be the only input considered in performance-related pay schemes. There is likely to be a large company performance element at a directorial level, but not below. It's no use saying you've got profitsharing. Profitsharing doesn't give buy-in. Profitsharing is what shareholders get. If staff are really to support the company, they should have performance-related elements to their pay at the company, team and individual level. To miss out the team is a real mixed message. You tell them that teamwork is crucial, but then don't reward them for doing it well.

There is a concern that the mini company structure will get in the way of a fair pay scheme. After all, surely a performance-related pay scheme can only be fair if it is uniformly applied across the hyper-company?

There's no perfect solution, but we believe that the best way to apply performance-related pay is to give individual managers the freedom to decide. From the pot available, they should allocate pay appropriately. In some circumstances, this will fail. The manager may be vindictive or simply not trained well enough to make the allocation correctly, but look at the alternative.

Take it out of the manager's hands and put it under the control of a 'fair', company-wide system. First of all, what does that say to your managers? We don't trust you. Simple as that. You can't cut it. And what does the system do? It applies distributions or relies on some mechanical linkage that ends up with half the staff getting entirely the wrong message. Giving managers freedom will fail sometimes, but an imposed system will fail every time.

A final essential with performance-related pay is to consider the impact of your award. You've either got to do it so it makes an impact or not do it at all. If you pay someone a performance bonus and they aren't impressed by it, you might as well save the money. We have seen performance schemes that allow for a one-off bonus to reward a special effort made in that year, but then restrict the amount payable to a paltry sum. It's simply not inspiring. If money is really that tight, don't give them cash, give them a gift. Get their manager to choose something appropriate. Somehow a reasonable, personal gift feels much more rewarding than an almost-invisible extra little bit of money on their payslips. If the gift has clearly been chosen by their manager and some thought has gone into it, it is invested with even more value.

THE BONUS GAME

Jot down the cash amount you would need to make a financial bonus really significant. Then consider what luxury household goods you'd really appreciate, but don't have. What would they cost? Check out the different values – there's a lesson there.

Working a large production line

So, within the DisOrganized structure, how do you cope with the demands of a traditional factory production line where there may well be more employees than our ideal mini company size? We see two solutions to this.

First, you could break our rules and structure a mini company that is larger than 50 to 100 employees. We do not like this solution because it will be the first, rather than last, resort of the traditional manager. Everybody believes that their industry is unique and that its uniqueness explains the need to do things in their own way. In most cases this is sloppy thinking. We would only ever advocate large mini companies as an absolute last resort, when all other avenues have been fully explored and rejected.

The second approach would be to identify the factory itself as one mini company, to be run as a sort of logistics exercise, but with no staff and no production output. This factory space would then be leased to a series of mini companies that would perform elements of the production process within this factory space.

In a car assembly works, for instance, there are already splits between those producing the chassis, those painting it, those producing the engine and so on. These splits could be the boundaries between mini companies. Alternatively, mini companies could see whole cars through production based on model or market.

Is this just being done for the sake of it? We would argue no. Are such splits advantageous? We would argue yes. The series of mini companies that result from such splitting would not have the massive human resource, finance or IT support that you would see in the old company. Nor would the sum of the tiny levels of support they would have be anything like the size of support in the parent. Somehow small companies manage with a fraction of the kind of infrastructure large companies have. If you were to add enough small companies together to equal the number of employees in any large company, you would still have far less of this kind of support.

Not only are small companies less bloated, they are also more focused, more effective and more results-oriented. Many of the historic problems that have plagued large factories in the past would be inconceivable if the staff in those factories genuinely identified with the success of the business. Somehow, in a large organization it is possible to develop aims that are not in support of the customer. Indeed, they are often diametrically opposed to the needs of the customer.

Checking in at an airport

Another area that has been pointed out to us as a possible difficulty is the checking in process of a large airline. Generally, this is handled by vast numbers of staff who work a variety of shifts to provide adequate cover. How would you organize this army into mini companies when there are no clear functional divisions?

Our first thought was to make a split by time of day. Set up mini companies that provided a checking in service over only one shift. However, this is less than ideal for a couple of reasons. First, there may well be a requirement for more staff than you would want in a mini company.

Second, you would be employing staff on the basis that they would work only one shift – always nights or always afternoons. As these staff would have taken their original job on the basis of a range of shifts, this would be a significant change in their terms of employment.

Our next thought was to organize the mini companies by checking in area. That is, to allocate groups of routes to different mini companies and have them supply the staff to check in customers for those routes. The checking in desks and infrastructure would be owned by another mini company. This approach has some obvious advantages, in the forms of improved product knowledge and greater focus. It has disadvantages, too, in that there might be a fluctuation in the demand for staff by area.

Finally, we thought of a totally arbitrary division of staff and then having work allocated to their mini companies on the day. This has the advantage of smaller mini companies, each focused on providing service, but has no real product knowledge advantage. It also adds a level of organization in the form of work allocation.

It's probable, in fact, that the best approach would be a hybrid of the last two ideas. Mini companies could have specialist product knowledge – one, for example, might specialize in first-class travel, another in leisure flights – but such divisions would be on a broader basis than destination, and it would be quite possible, if there were shortages, to provide cover for other mini companies (at a price).

12

Resources: supporters and non-human

- The need to add value
- Mini company support departments *are* front-line ones
- Handling purchasing, accounting and IT
- Dealing with property
- Disposing of head office
- Brands as resources

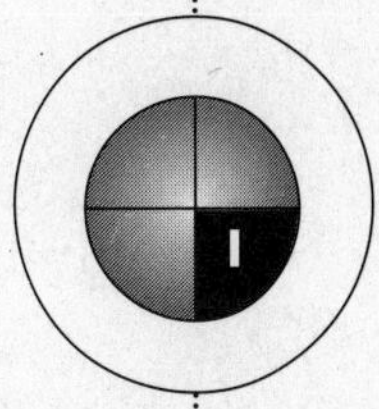

Does it add value?

We've already looked at people and teams in general. Here we're considering the support staff and the non-human resources – such as the buildings, technology, assorted hardware and software that underpin the front line. When dealing with resources, there should be a constant refrain – does it add value? Whether you are talking about a headquarters building or a finance department, don't *assume* it has a positive benefit – make sure it really is doing something worth while.

Without the mini company structure, support workers have a hard time. They will be regarded, and often regard themselves, as second-class citizens. Always in danger of being closed down or sold off. Always being reminded that they aren't at the core of the business. That's rubbish. And a lot of the blame for this poor state of affairs should be taken by management thinking. For too long it has been trendy to emphasize the core nature of the company above local functionality.

Say we're dealing with the IT department of a construction company. IT managers who want to get on have been brainwashed into thinking they should be construction people, not IT people. Result, their staff get into the ghetto mind-set. With mini companies, the business is turned around. The IT department becomes one or more IT companies, with particular expertise in construction. They are no longer trying to be something they aren't. The staff become front-line IT workers.

As far as the rest of the hypercompany is concerned, the IT mini companies are one possible source of IT. The big extra they can provide is expertise at working in the particular industry. It doesn't mean, though, that they should be the sole resource or even be used at all if they're ineffective. Note that the mini company approach differs markedly from two other reactions to dissatisfaction with support departments – kill them and sell them off.

Those who are of the 'kill them' school are so fed up with bureaucratic delays and irrelevancies that they want to sack the whole support department and get on with things themselves. This throws out the baby with the bath water and isn't fair on a jolly nice bunch of people.

Of course, mini companies must be able to make their own decisions. Say we're dealing with purchasing. If mini companies want to buy their own pencils (or PCs or real estate), they must be able to. But if a purchasing department really delivers, mini companies ought to be queuing up to get goods at bargain prices. Particularly with less routine items, negotiating expertise could come in real handy.

You may or may not agree that purchasing people are nice. Even so, the company employed them in good faith, so give them a chance to make their mini company a success.

The 'sell them off' school of thought is, at first sight, closely related to DisOrganization. We've nothing against mini companies being floated in their own right – it is often a great way forward. What is totally unacceptable, though, is to sell off, say, the IT department to another big company. There are small potential savings from the new contracts that would result, plus a wider base of people to call on, but selling off a resource to a dinosaur is no answer. You get none of the support mini company's advantages and the entire bureaucratic overhead.

If we're being hard on the support departments, we ought to be even harder on non-human resources. This isn't the same as being tight-fisted. If your staff need a better tool to get the job done, it's a necessity. If you've engineers struggling to design cars or develop software on three-year-old equipment, you deserve everything you get. Good physical conditions for your staff – down to free coffee and soft drinks – are no problem as they are contributing directly to a prime driver. However, all non-human resources should pass the added value test or be sold off without delay.

Resources as blockers

Like every channel, resources can act to block the effectiveness of your business and your ability to make organizational change. Support departments traditionally contribute unnecessary work, delays and fudging. Extra work? Ever seen a 17-page form to buy a PC? We have. Delays? You need the software today; the support department can get it for you in three weeks, but, hey, they've got you a small (very small) discount over the local computer superstore, so why are you complaining? Fudging? A particular tool will help you get the

I NEED IT NOW

Jot down half a dozen business essentials you may need at very short notice. A phone, a hire car, a toner cartridge for a printer, a laptop PC, a security pass, a bunch of flowers. What's the fastest you could get it in an emergency? What's the routine time? Why the difference? Why are any of them more than an hour?

job done quicker – sorry, you can't have it: the company standard is different. You want specific figures – sorry, accounts (yes, accounts is a support department) only provides information in this format.

It's easy to see how people can get in the way, but what about the non-human stuff? Property is a prime blocker. Want to bring your mini company together? Can't do that, we've got accommodation problems. Want to dispose of the headquarters building? Don't be silly; we've spent millions on a half-constructed site with all the requisite fountains and landscaping. Oh, and you can't have Apple computers, because we have a PC network. OK?

How to ...

- manage a complicated project;
- manage non-human resources effectively;
- handle purchasing;
- handle property;
- blow up head office;
- manage brands;
- handle IT;
- handle accounts;
- develop large IT systems.

Managing a complicated project

A large project will span many mini companies and require a whole host of resources. Of itself, DisOrganization does not bring any new problems to the table. Large projects usually involve coordinating a range of companies – it's just that more of them may now sit within your hypercompany federation. More interesting is who manages the project. Don't fall back into pre-DisOrganization thought patterns. It isn't the net company because the net company isn't 'the boss'. It sets overall direction and decides on the constitution of the hypercompany, but beyond that it's a support group. Project management will be the responsibility of the owning mini company.

Take a large construction project – a hospital, for example. Either the project management comes directly from the mini company that is going to run the building or from one specializing in construction of this sort of facility. The project manager will have to know the hypercompany well to make sure that all the contributing mini companies are involved – as always, information is an essential to making it work. That apart, it's business as usual.

Has DisOrganization got more to offer project management? The imperative for clarity and direction makes us wary of some aspects of the traditional approach. Yes it is useful to adopt detailed project management tools and techniques to be able to engage the right resources, but there is considerable doubt that putting a huge effort into monitoring all aspects of the plan has enough value to make it worth while. It is important that all those involved know what has to be achieved, have clear milestones and share a common aim; it is less important that we know that three more rolls of masking tape were used than was originally planned for.

It is hard to imagine fun entering project management spheres – there are few stuffier aspects of management. Yet, large projects inevitably have small setbacks, which can be celebrated with humour to bring the participants together. Empowerment is the real breakthrough, though. Traditional project management sits like an unwanted monkey on everyone's back, always keeping tabs. By giving the project teams clear principles and goals, and ensuring that they have accepted an appropriate culture, it should not be necessary to have the system constantly chase them. They will chase themselves – and spot plenty that wasn't in the original plan, getting it fixed rather than worrying about integrating it into the Gantt chart.

CREATIVE PROJECTS

It's Friday. Your new outlet opens on Monday. All that remains is the interior décor. Your contractors pull out. Use a creativity technique from Chapter 8 to come up with five different ways to solve the problem. Are any better than using the contractor in the first place? Would you have thought of them if there hadn't been a problem? There's a lesson somewhere.

Large projects are oozing with opportunities to involve creativity. Each large project is littered with problems crying out for a creative solution. Whether it is 'How do we manage a building housing 5000 people when we've only car parking for 2000?' or 'How can we design a staff restaurant that's cheap and attractive?', creativity has its part. Why not constructively use some of the time you've freed up by disposing of all that detailed planwatching – have a weekly creative ideas session. Just half an hour, spending five to ten minutes on the hottest problems and requirements, employing a creativity technique. Who knows, projects could become fun after all.

Managing non-human resources effectively

A large company will have a whole range of non-human resources, from paper-clips to costly plant. It is entirely reasonable for a mini company to deal with its own paper-clips. There is something ludicrous about having a central bureaucracy to deal with paper-clips. Whether the mini company decides that one member of staff can pick them up from the local stationers in their lunchbreak or get them from the in-house supplies mini company, which has them on special, it's their business.

Other resources cannot sensibly be the sole responsibility of a single mini company. Take a car plant. There are several ways in which the automobile company can DisOrganize. Say each model was owned by a separate mini company. Each would require use of the bodyshop, but none of them would individually want to own the bodyshop. So the bodyshop is run by the net company? No, no! The net company coordinates and sets overall direction; it isn't a place to amalgamate everything that doesn't fit elsewhere. Instead, the bodyshop will be the responsibility of another mini company, selling its services to the model teams. You get the picture.

Handling purchasing

Take a moment to think about the purchasing (procurement) department. What comes to mind? Write down the first three things you think of. We've got a real conflict. On the one hand, we see real professionals – sharp individuals who can spot a discount a mile off and can come up with some genuine opportunities for partnership. On the other hand, it's hard not to think of all the times necessary purchases have been held up or of crazy schemes where the best product has not been chosen because it's all part of a larger deal. For instance, XYZ makes great mainframe computers, but terrible PCs. We need a new mainframe. XYZ will offer us a huge discount if we commit to buying all our PCs from them. The fact that they cost 10 per cent more than ABC's models and are half as fast is irrelevant; the company is getting a good deal.

This approach to purchasing simply won't hold up in a DisOrganized firm. If a mini company has the choice of good PCs for price X or rubbish for X plus 10 per cent, which is it going to buy? What about the greater good? Sorry, we don't do that sort of deal. If we need PCs (and if not, why are we buying them?), we need the appropriate tool for the job, not one that will get us a discount elsewhere. It's a bit like eating food you don't like to get a discount on a holiday.

Can the purchasing department survive? Tom Peters has always advocated disposal, but we're not sure. Certainly a purchasing mini company will be leaner than any current department (remember that the limit of around 50 is a maximum – there's nothing to say that a mini company can't be just 2 people, or 1 for that matter). After all, it will have to pay all its wages out of the percentage of the saving it is allowed to hold back. Perhaps 10 per cent, as this seems to suit most agents. On the other hand, there's plenty of incentive there in some businesses. However, remember the cardinal rule: use of the purchasing mini company will always be optional. All of a sudden, there'll be a way to get things faster, not to introduce delays. Wow.

Handling property

We've seen how big plant and other expensive resources could be shared between a number of mini companies. Presumably this holds true of property, too? Maybe, but only maybe. There's a big difference between a bodyshop (or a plane or a film stage) and office space. Most big resources are ideal for timesharing. Office space is more personal. Some of the best work comes from teams that have their own small building (or at least offices that feel isolated) rather than occupying mainstream, faceless office space. You only have to look at the way the Apple Macintosh was developed with a skull and crossbones flag flying over the development site.

INSANELY GREAT

The life and times of the Macintosh are eloquently described in Stephen Levy's book *Insanely Great* (Viking, 1994).

On a smaller scale, both of us were involved in a British Airways project that named itself 'The A Team'.

Back in 1984, personal computers were beginning to emerge as a real force in business. Until then, the IT Department had effectively ignored them. Now an outside consultancy had been engaged and was in danger of showing up the IT Department.

The IT Director had the brilliant idea of throwing together a small team to provide a response. The team was housed in an inaccessible room, lurking in the depths of the airport terminals, and this had huge advantages. It had independent space where it could do its own thing, and it was right on top (well, underneath actually) the customer. When, later, an expanding team was brought back to the off-site, open-plan office, alongside other IT teams, it lost its edge and, ultimately, its reason for existence.

Giving a mini company control of its own space is an important part of the freedom that is necessary to make DisOrganization work. Before you assume that the only practical approach is to stay with the huge, open-plan offices you've already got, have a creativity session. Does the current approach maximize mini company interaction with the right partners (internal and external)? Would teleworking enhance your mini companies? Would a small building on a new science park be a more stimulating workplace than your current 1960s' concrete monstrosity?

DisOrganization doesn't always mean disposing of your property, but it ought to be considered. Some existing buildings may have merits, with the probable exception of head office.

Blowing up head office

Attractive thought. Why not (or at least sell it off)? Fragmentation has done away with the need for a large headquarters building. It has a mild attraction because it looks and feels impressive, but what does it actually contribute? Do you buy Mars bars because Mars has a sexy HQ? Do you know (or care) what the headquarters of most of your suppliers (business or domestic) look like?

Clarity tells us that the large, expensive building on prime land has no real business benefit. Let's sell it quick, while everyone else still thinks that such a location has kudos. Fun and empowerment certainly isn't impressed. Try word association: could anyone seriously associate 'headquarters' and 'fun'? Instead, the HQ is the antithesis of empowerment, emphasizing how separate and irrelevant the centre is from the front line. Try saying to someone 'I'm from head office, and I'm here to help', and watch them crease up. At least you'll have brought a little laughter to their day.

So, bring on the creativity. What does the headquarters do? Houses management, but managers should be with their mini companies. Then, the remaining net company is much too small to need a palace like this. Houses the Board, but its members often have a little hideaway closer to their appropriate financial partners anyway; if not, set one up. Acts as a PR front for the organization. Get a shop in a high-class shopping district instead.

Try all the possibilities. List the functions of the headquarters then use a creativity technique to generate alternatives.

There is one possible exception: where the headquarters houses the entire company. Even then, think twice. If it is most important for your mini companies to be housed together, then a single building isn't a bad idea (though make sure you spend your money on great facilities, not an expensive, trendy location), but make sure colocation is a real business driver. Check out what Michael Skok has to say about AlphaBlox. Colocation with potential alliance partners was of prime importance. Maybe it's more important for a mini company to be located alongside external partners than another part of the metacompany.

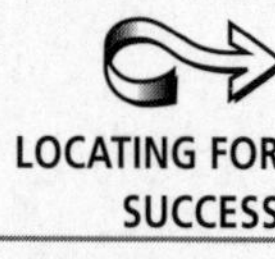

LOCATING FOR SUCCESS

See page 193 in chapter 17.

Managing brands

Where a DisOrganized hypercompany presents a coherent brand to the consumer that is independent of the mini companies, that brand needs to be owned and managed centrally. The brand is often a key resource that sets a company apart from its competitors. Allowing it to dissipate and disappear as a result of DisOrganization is a real danger and must be prevented.

This implies that there is a need for centralized management of the brand. It need not be the well-stuffed brands departments that you see in many large companies, but it does need to know the brand, know what makes it work and have real power in setting the contract terms that lay out the delivery of the brand by the mini companies. This could be seen as a franchise operation, where the brand is owned and controlled by one company but delivered by another DisOrganized set of companies. It is tempting to put brand control into the net company as one of its coordinating roles. This might work, but there is a grave danger of overloading the net company by broadening its focus and increasing its size. Preferably a brand management entity should be a separate mini company.

Where a single mini company delivers the brand, there is no need for central ownership. As the success of the mini company will be directly linked to the success of the brand, central ownership would remove power from the mini company and that would be severely detrimental.

Handling IT

IT is an unusual support function in that it can represent a key business differentiator. To paraphrase American Airlines' CEO Bob Crandall, a big airline can be seen as an airline booking company that flies planes rather than an aircraft provider that has a computer. Large companies will need to divide the IT function into a range of mini companies. Some are pure support and off-the-shelf supply. Others produce code. Others run complicated systems. Each needs to be treated separately.

A particular concern in the move of the IT department into the independent mini company structure is standards. Few issues cause more irritation and concern than standards. DisOrganization can only work if mini companies are allowed to buy whatever IT equipment and software they like. Of course, the IT mini companies can stick to standards, and can use the benefits of standards as part of their sales pitch, but there can be no compulsion. What is going to happen?

Some mini companies will break away, the mix of hardware will become more complicated, yet most third party maintenance firms are quite happy with such a mix. Different versions of software or even different products will be in use from mini company to mini company. When dealing with simple documents, this isn't much of a problem. One of us regularly writes for a magazine that uses a different version of the same word processor editorially, and typesets on a totally different hardware platform. The other works with a group of consultants who use Lotus word processing and presentation software while we use Microsoft, yet electronically transferred documents are the order of the day and rarely cause a problem.

At a more complicated level, the net company may require certain minimum abilities to be part of the operating network. Yet, such abilities can always be defined in terms of interfaces. It's not uncommon for a company to require a supplier to be able to communicate or use joint systems, yet it would cause real raised eyebrows if a customer expected to tell you who to buy your PCs from and which web browser to use.

Handling accounts

Like all support departments, accounts began with the best intentions, but all too often the finance guys have started to think they run the company. This delusion isn't helped by a common trend to appoint chief executives who have a financial background. Does this mean that you can simply dump all accountants and accountancy? Sadly, no. Yet, just as mini companies draw on the benefits of interaction that small companies enjoy, so they can look to small companies for a model of how accounts should work.

In a large company, the accounting systems take on a life of their own. In a small company, only the minimum required to get through is undertaken. An accountant will deal with the reporting required by law and will point out potential savings. Simple, almost back-of-an-envelope calculations will do for budgeting and management accounting. After all, a budget is never more than an educated guess – what is the point in guessing to two decimal places?

This isn't to say that a DisOrganized company doesn't worry about accurate information. When it comes to customer reaction or competitor awareness, accuracy and timeliness are everything. However, when all sensible management activity is suspended for two weeks because it's time for the annual plan to be worked out in endless detail, we've got problems. When budgets are cut because they're not spent up, we've got lunacy.

Should accountants be banned then (or, even better, drowned at birth)? Not at all. We can't, in all frankness, say that some of our best friends are accountants, but one of us used to sing barbershop with an accountant, the other has to admit to spending a while as a financial controller, and our own accountant is a very nice person.

An accounts department, though, is a different beast. Most mini companies will probably want their own accountant. It won't be a full-time job; the person who does it can therefore do some real work as well. As part of the mini company, based in their offices, this person ceases to be one of 'them' and becomes one of 'us'. Similarly, the net company may well need an accountant or two to pull things together, but let's not get carried away.

Developing large IT systems

See under 'Managing a complicated project' – the first How to – it all applies. It has been known for a long time that you don't develop a complicated IT system by throwing several hundred people at it. Known, but often unrecognized. After all, the author of the classic treatise on the stupidity of throwing huge teams at a problem – Frederick P. Brooks – was an alumnus of IBM, the ultimate champion of megateams. It is only by splitting the system into manageable chunks and putting small teams onto them that a successful system can be built. DisOrganization naturally supports this approach.

MYTHICAL MAN MONTH

This classic book was updated for its twentieth anniversary: Frederick P. Brooks, *The Mythical Man Month: Essays on software engineering* (Anniversary Edition, Addison Wesley Longman, 1995).

Many of the problems that have arisen in the development of large systems have been due to lack of user involvement. Of course, they signed off the specification at the start, but this process depends on the entirely unjustifiable assumption that anyone can decide in advance exactly what they're going to need, and that the world will stay conveniently still while it is developed. Dream on. Empowerment requires user involvement in the development – all the way. In such a project, clarity is reached by taking an iterative approach, prototyping rapidly to give the user something to use, then responding to feedback.

Many large in-house systems are generated because an off-the-shelf product would only cover 80 per cent of the need. If the user of the system had to pay the 200–300 per cent increase in cost directly, closing the 20 per cent gap would probably seem terribly unimportant.

Creativity, too, has its place. Often it is relatively clear what is needed, but not how to go about – a creativity session can help clear the way. Equally, the development of a large system is a time to sit back from the way it has always been done and ensure that:

- it ought to be done at all;
- there isn't a much better (and simpler) way of doing it.

Don't just computerize an existing process or develop a system to support an unjustified structure. First, have a creativity session to generate alternatives. You may still go ahead with your original intentions, but it's surprising (if you are flexible enough to change) how often a better, simpler approach will be produced.

13

Organization: systems and processes

- Organizational killers – hierarchies, departments, job titles and job descriptions
- The dangers of processess and systems
- Breaking up a big company into mini companies
- Financial issues
- Dealing with the Board
- Killing bureaucracy
- DisOrganizational structure

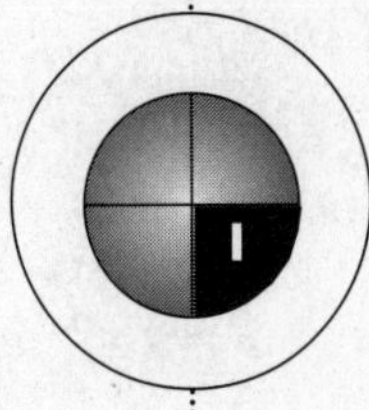

The golden trap

ORGANIZATION

'1 the act or an instance of organizing; the state of being organized. 2 an organized body, esp. a business, government department, charity, etc. 3 systematic arrangement; tidiness.' Concise Oxford Dictionary *(9th Edition, Oxford University Press, 1996)*

THE PARADOX OF ORGANIZATIONS

'So they go on in strange paradox, decided only to be undecided, resolved to be irresolute, adamant for drift, solid for fluidity, all-powerful to be impotent.' *Sir Winston Churchill, speaking in Parliament about the government, but his remarks could apply to any organization.*

Depending on your point of view, an organization is a life support system that binds together the activities of your people or a strangling sea of red tape, always attempting to stifle change and originality.

Realistically, it's both. Without organization there is anarchy, yet the systems and processes that an organization builds to protect itself and make things happen will inevitably, over time, become barriers to activity. If left unchecked, they become activities in their own right.

It would be tempting to think that having DisOrganized your people, your teams and your resources, the organization would also be brought into line. Certainly the changes that are required to make your people more effective will help battle against organizational difficulties. If necessary, your DisOrganized staff and teams will step around the organization to make things happen. If you've got your resources right, the organization will find it harder to resist. However, in themselves, such changes are not enough. The organization can exhibit a destructive form of synergy; it becomes more than a sum of the negative aspects of its parts. It is therefore necessary to work on the organization itself as well as its constituents.

'I wouldn't start from here'

One of us recently turned up for a meeting at a large corporation. The offices of the company are spread across a large site, with entry controlled by electronic gates. As a regular consultant to the company, I had a security pass. When it was swiped through the reader, I was informed that the pass had expired. With the meeting time fast approaching, I hurried to the security building.

'Oh, yes, your pass has expired,' I was informed. 'You will have to get a form signed by a manager to have it renewed.'

I explained that I needed to get in right now, and could I have a visitor's pass.

'I can't do that,' the receptionist informed me, 'we can't issue visitor's passes to holders of consultant's passes.'

'But what about my meeting? There are senior managers of this company waiting to meet with me. How can I get in?'

'You'll have to get a signature from a manager and bring it along here. I'm sorry, I'm a contractor myself. I just have to follow procedure.'

There's a horrible echo of the old joke of the motorist asking for directions, only to be told 'if you want to get there, I wouldn't start from here.' If the receptionist had been DisOrganized, she could have found me a way around my problem. Failing that, I was blocked by a system that was designed with a perfectly sensible goal – the security of the establishment – but that achieved something quite different. To emphasize just how far apart goal and reality were, while I was waiting, several couriers came in, waved a delivery slip and were sent straight through. No checking at all. The system was not delivering security, it was delivering activity and rules to give the impression of security.

Brian Thomas is Financial Director of Allied Dunbar, a UK financial services organization that is part of the BAT Group.

For 20 years, Allied Dunbar was a young company enjoying all the benefits that brings – a group of people with enormous energy, clear focus, on first-name terms and relaxed. Having a good vision and clear objectives led to a successful 20 years. The company became highly centralized, a classic, centralized, medium-sized organization. Decisions were made very much at the centre. It was a single business with a single focus. Then you could see new strands coming in. We started with direct sales only but indirect channels grew. You could no longer have a simple product structure.

That was Allied Dunbar as a quoted company. Latterly, as part of BAT, Allied Dunbar was positioned alongside Eagle Star. We have been bringing the two together in a single structure of four business units, underpinned by four service units: finance, business services (IT), marketing/brand development and legal. There are very different dynamics. Now there is more delegated authority. People feel more empowered, with a stronger sense of purpose. The business units are more focused and precise – the business was getting too diffuse, making it harder to identify with the whole. The business units don't contain all the resources they require. For example, not all of the finance function is in the finance business unit. The whole thing depends on cross-connections. If you put everything into the unit it may have the best shape in isolation, but run into large diseconomies of scale and feel less inclined to consider corporate needs. In part, we use the service groups to link the business units.

The centralized approach in a small- or medium-sized business is very powerful; it pulls everything together as a centralized team. The business units let you do things more quickly, but come with their own tensions. Individually, with delegated authority they can make a change of direction that's well understood in the business unit, but in another unit they're screaming because they're losing market share. Medium-sized companies tend to reach out for the business unit concept too early. Even in a very large company you can achieve a lot by being very clear about objectives.

In the end, your success is about the quality of people you've got, the way that they feel empowered. The organizational structure should be organized around the talent, the people you've got and the stage of their development. The structure could be completely different in a year's time; you've got to be fluid.

Structures

A handful of structures is used to great effect in blocking organizational change and effectiveness. Never underestimate the contribution that organizational hierarchy, departments, departmental and group boundaries, job titles and job descriptions make to the ineffectiveness of a company.

Organizational hierarchies

Like almost all blockers, organizational hierarchies began perfectly innocently. The aim was to make clear the chain of command, identify sensible groupings and establish who does what. While most activities bringing together numbers of people require structure, it is very easy to let the hierarchy run away with itself. As companies get bigger and feel the need to centralize services to bring efficiencies of scale, the tree grows. As new individuals are brought into the organization, status requires that they are given a certain level of authority

– the tree grows some more. New technologies, new requirements, new business, all deepen the structure of the tree. In the 1950s, Peter Drucker suggested that seven levels of management were a recommended maximum. By the 1980s, Tom Peters was demanding no more than five. As he points out, the Catholic Church has managed pretty well on five layers for a good while now.

EFFICIENCIES OF SCALE

And why they are a fiction – see page 232.

What's the problem with a deep organizational tree? Who cares how many layers there are? After all, a structure with many layers allows each manager to concentrate on a tight, focused span of work. It limits duplication of effort and makes vertical communications easier. And there is an attractive career path, with many steps to take, each an obvious advancement. The trouble is that every advantage brings greater problems. The easier communications are beset by distortion as a result of the many layers they travel through, so that the message originated by top management is not the same one received by the staff – and any feedback is equally garbled or sanitized.

The many steps on the career path make promotion a much more significant goal than broadening experience, breeding managers who are less effective for the company. Tight management focus is another term for parochialism. With a flatter organization, managers have a better chance of relating to the company's goals. Crucially, management of a flat organization is closer to the coalface where revenue is generated. And although there may be some duplication of effort in a flatter structure, it is more than compensated for by the new approaches it enables and the unnecessary centralization that is avoided. In the end, the taller the hierarchy, the less responsibility the individual is given, and the less benefit they can bring to the company.

Occasionally, a matrix organization is brought forward as the solution to the problem of the burgeoning tree. If implemented correctly, a matrix organization ought to be superb. Matrix organizations recognize that quick response often requires fluid project teams to be assembled to meet a particular need, then re-formed to attack the next challenge. Such cross-boundary teams still have to be managed, so the outcome is a matrix. In our example shown in Figure 13.1, managers are listed across the top. Projects run down the side. Responsibility for the project or activity is indicated within the matrix by an open (information) or filled (control) circle.

In practice, matrix organizations are rarely successful. The theoretical advantages are crippled by the resultant tying up of authority into a tangled web. It is rarely clear just who is responsible for mak-

Figure 13.1
Matrix organization

Project/Activity	Manager 1	Manager 2	Manager 3 ...
A	○	●	
B	●	○	
C		○	●
D	○	●	●
E			
F	○		●
...			

Key

○ = receives information about project

● = controls project

ing a decision about a project, so the outcome is, typically, that everyone gets involved, causing the decision-making process to grind to a halt. The problems of matrix management are not an excuse for avoiding cross-disciplinary teams, but suggest that such teams should have a different reporting structure.

ORGANIZATION CHART

In *Further Up the Organisation* (Michael Joseph, 1984), ex-Avis Chairman Robert Townsend points out that a dotted line on an organization chart indicates a troublemaker or a troubled relationship.

Even the organization chart – the representation of the hierarchy on paper – is a problem. Simple, high-level charts can be an effective introduction to a company, but detailed charts are a disaster. In the first place, a detailed chart is make-work – any sizeable organization is constantly changing. Even if the pressures of change haven't resulted in a departmental shake-up in the last few weeks, individuals will have left and joined. As soon as an organization chart is committed to paper, it is obsolete.

Detailed charts are also morale killers. Their hierarchical nature emphasizes status, while the typographical approaches taken to make them look more interesting irritate many of the people in the company. Take a typical, top-level chart of a large company. For the directors there may be photographs. Next level down has fancy type in a box. Next level down is in microscopic lettering on scrawny little lines. The level below isn't on the chart at all (you have to see the page detailing their department). If you aren't a director, you are immediately made to feel inferior. If you aren't on the chart at all, or even worse, if you were on the previous version, but a reorganization slips you off it, you might as well give up now.

Departments and boundaries

Departments are supposed to exist to bring clear control to an aspect of a company. They can be organized by function, by product or by market, but the underlying intention is the same. Yet the existence of departments resists organizational reform. Departments rapidly become tribal, fighting for resources and power. Tinkering with departmental boundaries can cause nearly as much ill feeling as if they were national boundaries, and the resultant wars can bring nothing but disaster to the company.

TEAM STYLES

See Chapter 11, Teams: interaction and synergy, page 110.

Departments can drain a company by transferring effort from the company's goals to the department's own. Companies generally strive to minimize the size of the workforce. A department's hidden agenda is often to increase in size, to increase management power. The perfect service department aims to bring about its own demise, yet few have this as a departmental aim. In the ideal world, there would be no departments. In practice, however, a company of more than six or seven people becomes difficult to manage without some structure. Even mini companies will generally have some structure, but will avoid the dangers of departments. Paradoxically, the move to mini companies, which sounds as if it ought to magnify the departmental problem, actually removes it. Although each mini company has its own goals, it still buys into the underlying principles of the net company, and it doesn't have the departmental urge to profligacy – any inflationary action hits the mini company's bottom line. The huge differences between a department and a mini company are a mini company's meaningful profit and loss control and accountability.

Job titles and job descriptions

Job titles can cause surprising difficulties. As the organization changes, there is a temptation to rationalize, bringing together different jobs under the same title from a sense of structural simplicity. At best this causes irritation; at worst staff can feel demoted and undervalued, when doing the same job for the same reward.

More insidious are job descriptions and associated evaluations. The job description is the justification of the jobsworth ('I'd love to help you, I really would, but it's more than my job's worth'). Job descriptions are the product of the production line, a rigid division of labour organization. This is what your job is and you must focus on this to the exclusion of all else. Even when the environment is static, this is a dangerous approach. Staff (and managers) will come across eventualities that are not covered by their job description. When everything is changing furiously, the outcome is confusion. The conventional job description, always questionable, has become worthless.

By now, there may be shrieks from human resources and the unions. Without a job description, how can you have job evaluations? And without job evaluations, how can you rate jobs mechanically? Simple answer – you can't. Such points-based systems are built on a flawed foundation. Standard jobs, filled by standard people are OK for the mechanical business models of the past, but they have no place in DisOrganization. There may still be lots of people doing similar jobs, but the individual cannot be rated on their performance against a frozen job description. The contribution that individual makes to the company may far outweigh anything that can be deduced from the description. Equally, the description could oversell their contribution. Evaluation needs to be a continuous process, not an unthinking procedure. Sounds like we're making a lot of work for the manager? Maybe, but there will be plenty of compensations.

Processes and systems

There is no end to the problems that processes and systems can cause. A system is put in place to make something happen – whether it's to deliver a product or solve a problem. From day one, the system may have negative effects. Many systems – especially large systems that haven't evolved from a smaller one – have minimal relevance to the task they are meant to support. Whether or not there is a match, it is a practically universal law that systems will grow in size and complexity with time – and that they are horribly difficult to kill off.

SYSTEMANTICS

John Gall, *Systemantics* (New York Times Book Company, 1977).

Systems can mislead management, by appearing to do what is required, but actually delivering something different. In *Systemantics*, John Gall has an excellent example that we shall paraphrase here.

Let's say our aim is to deliver a fresh apple to a customer. The impractical, non-systems approach might be to plant an apple tree at his house and let him pick an apple when he wants one. Outcome – a perfect, ripe apple. With a small system in place, a grocer might buy apples by the vanload from a commercial orchard 20 miles away. Outcome – not quite so good, but still acceptable. The large system is the supermarket approach. Pick the apples green, ripen them in a controlled environment, ship them chilled halfway around the world and produce a 'fresh apple' that bears almost no resemblance to the original product. The supermarket's management may genuinely believe that their system produces what the customer wants, but who is being fooled here?

Most dangerous is the process that becomes an end in itself, where following the procedure is more important than the intended goal. Rigid processes and systems are ripe targets for a changing world. Just think of a very simple case. We are providing a scout with a procedure to follow to navigate by the sun. We observe the sun first thing in the morning. Checking with a compass, we instruct the scout to head in the direction of the sun to travel in an easterly direction. By the end of the day, our scout, still following the sun, has gone horribly wrong. It was easy to predict that a process linked to a well-known change would falter. The trouble is, few of the changes in the business world are as predictable. Inflexible and unchanging processes and systems are a recipe for disaster.

How to ...

- get a big company from here to there:
  - can it ever happen?
  - how to divide it;
  - how to make the transition to a mini company;
  - set up the net company;
  - set up the systems;
- pay the piper;
- deal with the Board;
- decide whether or not to spin off mini companies;
- get rid of unnecessary bureaucracy;
- trim processes and systems;
- control a hypercompany;
- give freedom without anarchy;
- reorganize mini companies;
- shut down mini companies;
- restructure the hypercompany;
- cope with an expanding mini company.

Getting a big company from here to there

There's no doubt that the easiest way to put together a DisOrganized company is from scratch. Companies such as ABB, the Scandinavian engineering firm headed up by the charismatic Percy Barnovic, and to some extent Richard Branson's Virgin (though it's arguable that this was always DisOrganized) show that it is possible to DisOrganize a dinosaur corporation, but it's an uphill battle. There are many people and systems that will be fighting the move. At a high level, the Board and executives may feel they are losing control. Middle management will be concerned for their jobs and powerbase, while staff may feel that they are losing the (largely illusory) security of a job with a corporation.

We can't offer a universal panacea. Each company needs to develop its own path to DisOrganization, using the weaponry that we have suggested, bearing in mind all the channels. Yet, there are some considerations that will transcend most vertical market boundaries.

Can it ever happen?

We've got some bad news. Awful news. Many large companies will find it impossible to DisOrganize. Not just difficult, impossible. The reason is the chief executive. If your chief executive won't buy into the idea 100 per cent, you can forget it. You have two options: move to a different company or wait for the current incumbent to be fired. If you are the chief executive, start thinking hard. With the CEO behind DisOrganization, there is one other obstacle: the immediate team around the top can make or break such a radical change. Either they too have to have total buy-in or at least be malleable enough to trust the person at the top and go with their judgement. Given that top-level support, we assert, any company – *absolutely any company* – can DisOrganize. Without it, there is no hope.

How to divide it

SERVICE DEPARTMENTS

See Chapter 12, Resources: supporters and non-human, page 124.

An early task is the division of the operation into appropriate chunks. It would be a mistake to assume that this has to be on existing departmental lines. For example, as we established in the Resources chapter, service departments may well be split among mini companies. The guiding principles are these:

- a mini company should be small enough for everyone to know everyone else and work effectively together (our guideline is no more than 50–100 people; the minimum size, clearly, is 1 person);

- a mini company should have a clearly identifiable role, one that the staff can understand and buy into, one that would work (and may well work in the future) for an independent small company;
- there may be several mini companies undertaking the same activity in parallel.

How to make the transition to mini companies

Along the way to forming mini companies there will be some problems. Managers will be taking on new responsibilities. Individuals will be less cushioned by bureaucracy and structure. Some will not like the flexibility that is expected of them. Yet the opportunities, when explained properly, will prove attractive for many. After all, a mini company is not tied to a corporate reward scheme – it can give its employees pay that is appropriate for their contribution. Achieving a successful transition will need support from everyone. A huge boost can be given to the transition by sending the whole mini company on a seminar. This should concentrate on the new roles, giving the staff a genuine input into how the mini company will work, encouraging early buy-in. This is a heavy set-up cost, but remarkably easy to justify.

Setting up the net company

The net company's two roles – setting direction and providing excellent information flows between mini companies – come from different parts of the old company. The net company will require both the executive input of senior management and expertise in information technology and interpersonal communications. The change of executive role from dictator to mediator is not a trivial one; there is a real argument for either a significant influx of new executives (with the equivalent outflow of old) or setting up a major training exercise.

Just as individual mini companies may contract for each others' services, it is also essential that there is a clear contract between the net company and the mini companies, making it clear what each will deliver.

Setting up the systems

The systems aspect of DisOrganization should not be underestimated. First, there has to be change in mind-set. The net company's systems are there to serve the mini companies. The mini companies are not minions, responding to the demands of the centre, but partners who expect to be given the support they need. This will be part of the contract. Systems should involve minimum effort for the mini companies and maximum gain.

To achieve this, the net company needs to poach the brightest and the best of the IT staff. These need to be people who are not concerned about protocol or doing it by the book, only with results. They should be zealots, obsessed with making their systems easy to use and provide all the necessary information. This is because information is the lifeblood of the hypercompany: without adequate two-way flows, mini companies can't interact properly with the net company and the net company can't manage the overall direction. Be wary of thinking, though, that the net company sets up the IT systems. It owns the systems and information flows, but will get mini companies to execute them.

Paying the piper

It is not obvious to start with how the finances of a hypercompany will work. The net company is financed by the mini companies, much as a writer or actor pays an agent. In pre-DisOrganization days it would be considered an overhead, but now it is an explicit levy for the functions the net companies provide. From the mini companies' viewpoint, the net company is a source of work.

Individual mini companies, whether spun off or still technically part of the metacompany, which is comprised of the net company and the owned mini companies, will have their own profit and loss figures. If individual, the net company will be paying them for their services, just like any other external supplier. If part of the metacompany, the finances will be amalgamated for reporting, but will still operate individually at the local level. Without this, we are not dealing with mini companies or DisOrganization at all. The hypercompany has no legal existence – and, as such, no financial concerns; it is merely a word to describe the combination of the net company and all the mini companies, internal and external, that fall within its influence.

Dealing with the Board

Boards of directors can be a problem. Not only do they tend to be conservative – and there's just no such thing as conservative DisOrganization – but also they have a vested interest in keeping power centralized. The major obstacle that will be faced when dealing with the Board is their legal obligation to protect the value of the shareholders' investment in the company. To break up a large organization into a loose network of mini companies, it will be necessary for each new mini company to reimburse the shareholders of the existing company for the full value of the assets (and possibly even good will) that are taken out into the mini company. Alternatively, if this break-up is done via outsourcing, then the assets may be available for sale, either to the new mini company or a third party. Where the new mini company remains a part of the hypercompany, there is no need for the transfer of funds. Being easier does not make it the right decision, though.

It is possible that the move to mini companies will mean less public ownership, as mini company-sized organizations tend to be private limited companies. This may not be a bad thing. Shareholders are mostly institutions with no interest in the way the business is run. The German model, where few companies are public, may represent the future (by a strange coincidence, many dinosaur German companies move in the other direction).

Deciding whether or not to spin off mini companies

So, is it best to launch mini companies as independent companies or keep them as part of the hypercompany federation? There is no simple answer. Generally, the decision should be a joint one, between the net company and the mini company; it should not be imposed. The net company may also feel that some mini companies are too crucial to the existence of the hypercompany to spin them off. However, this is a dangerous line to follow. It is the first step of rebound. If the mini company really wants to go it alone, it will be operating suboptimally if it is forced to remain a part of the hypercompany. In such circumstances, the net company must ensure that appropriate contracts (and payments) keep the mini company part of the whole without actual ownership. With time, it is likely that many mini companies will want to become independent. This is healthy for all concerned.

DRESS CODES

There are few rules more contentious than dress codes. But don't fall into the trap of thinking that throwing aside a formal dress code means everyone should wear jeans and a T-shirt. That's a dress code, too.

Getting rid of unnecessary bureaucracy

The move to mini companies will inherently kill much of the bureaucracy, as what seems reasonable in a company of 50,000 becomes a joke in a company of 50. Other aspects have the ability to survive the change, however, and need to be weeded out ruthlessly.

Whether it's dress codes or allocated car parking, bring in your task orientation and your creativity. Use the 'Why?' creativity technique on all bureaucracy. Why do we need a dress code? Why should anyone have allocated parking spaces? Why do you need to fill in a form to ask for leave? (I don't, of course, as a senior manager, but I'm trusted.)

Bureaucracy is a persistent weed. However effectively you root it out, it will return, often in a new form. Make a five-minute bureaucracy hunt a regular feature.

Trimming processes and systems

A related need is the pruning of your processes and systems. You might not consider your invoicing system to be bureaucracy; it is, after all, a necessary part of the business. Still it will proliferate with time. Harsh pruning is beneficial to both the users and the system. Have you a complicated rewards system? A lengthy project justification process? An unwieldy process for claiming expenses or monitoring sales? If it is not all needed (check everything and consider moving any process or system that doesn't influence the bottom line into the bureaucracy class), get out those secateurs.

Controlling a hypercompany

The net company has the responsibility of pulling together the hypercompany. Control is a delicate balance here. Directives can no longer be dispatched from on high; instead there is more need for communication. We have emphasized the importance of systems, but, equally, the net company's managers should expect to spend a sizeable part of their time on their feet, going out to the mini companies and engaging in face-to-face communication. It might seem painful at first, but eventually you'll even come to like it.

Giving freedom without anarchy

A real fear at the prospect of the move to mini companies is anarchy. Where is the stick to keep them in line? There isn't one. The mini company structure depends on something much more important to keep the mini companies on track: real support for what the mini company is out to achieve; understanding of, and commitment to, the principles that drive it. There won't be anarchy, because it won't benefit the mini company, but, equally, there won't be any toeing the party line for the sake of it.

Will the mini company's goals always line up entirely with the hypercompany's? No. Sometimes a mini company's actions will not deliver maximum benefit to the company as a whole. However, this is much better than the other extreme, demonstrated amply in IBM in the 1980s when consideration of effects on every other part of the enterprise, especially the one-time flagship mainframe business, bogged down practically every attempt to deliver an exciting new product.

ANTI-SYNERGY

Bob Carroll's *Big Blues* (Crown Publishers, 1993) gives an excellent insight into IBM's troubled passage through the 1980s.

Reorganizing mini companies

The initial structure will not be right. Even if it is right, needs will change over time. A hypercompany is much more fluid than a traditional corporation. If it's simply a case of changing to use a different mini company, there isn't much of a problem; it's just like changing a supplier. However, where there is a need to reassess the balance between mini companies, the negotiation is much more delicate.

As always, the essential tool for making mini companies work is to treat them as independent entities, even if they are still owned by the net company. Traditional companies have often changed shape in the past. Perhaps a hotel chain might drop a leisure club to focus on its core business, selling the club off to a leisure specialist. Similarly, if part of a mini company simply isn't working, the options are to split it off as its own mini company or sell it to one of the other minis.

What, though, if the problem is more fundamental? Let's say the original company was split up on product lines. This proves impossible to work. Instead, a market split seems more appropriate. Avoiding such problems should be a major input to the initial splitting process. If the mini companies have been set up effectively, morale would be shattered by throwing all the mini companies up in the air and coming up with a totally new arrangement of people. It may not even be practical if mini companies have been spun off. Instead, the existing mini companies have to form the core of the new structure. What was a product-oriented mini company must become market-oriented.

There will need to be some transfers of staff, but perhaps fewer than you may originally think. After all, the whole point of mini companies is to harness the incredible amount of ability that is normally wasted in a corporate structure. You are no longer dealing with a huge oil tanker that has to travel some way to be able to turn round; this is a motorbike that can turn on the spot.

Shutting down mini companies

Not all mini companies will succeed. This should be a given, and not be regarded as a problem. In fact, if there are not some mini companies failing, it's time to be suspicious. Someone, somewhere is executing a cover-up. We have consistently emphasized that the net company does not control, it simply binds and supports. So, how do we get rid of failing mini companies?

They have to get rid of themselves. To enable this, it is first necessary to have an ethos where recognizing failure and doing something about it is viewed as a positive asset. Tom Peters advocates celebrating failure – not considering it a desirable end, but a necessary and useful step on the road to success. So, what happens to the failed mini company? If it was working effectively, it may become the seed of a new mini company (see below). Individuals may take up opportunities in other mini companies or they may leave. Sometimes this can be to everyone's benefit. If they have really bought into DisOrganization, they may then set up their own mini companies to serve the hypercompany.

What, though, if the mini company failed at an essential service? Give someone else a shot. Start a new mini company to approach the aspect of business in a different way. It may wish to recruit from the old mini company or not. Does this all sound risky? Which part of your MBA course said business wasn't risky? If you've not got an MBA, excellent – you've much less to unlearn!

Restructuring the hypercompany

The net company must always be looking at the components that make up the hypercompany. Are these the right mix? Is something new needed? Part of the communication exercise with the mini companies must be details of such considerations.

Mini companies should be given the opportunities to expand roles if required. It may even be that a mini company expands so much (see next section) it splits into a new hypercompany. However, the current span of the hypercompany will not cover all eventualities, and there will be a need to add other, external mini companies to the portfolio. If those mini companies are already part of another hypercompany, the temptation might be to assume that it's the net company that has to be approached, but that's old thinking. Even if the mini company is still technically owned by the net company, it is the mini company that will negotiate and establish a contract.

Coping with an expanding mini company

Some mini companies will have a roaring success with their particular fragment of activity. This will lead to growth. There will come a point where the mini company will be too big to function effectively. The time will have come to spawn a new hypercompany. The mini company will split itself into a net company and mini companies. There is nothing surprising about this; it is perfectly natural. The original net company will now have several mini companies to deal with rather than a single one, but all the structures will be in place. The new hypercompany is not a competitor. Its business is not the same as the original one. For instance, the original hypercompany might be a supermarket chain. The mini company might be a bakers. The new hypercompany is also a bakers, not a supermarket.

14

DisOrganization: inward channels

Each major section of *DisOrganization* is summarized in one of these mini chapters.

The easy bit?

In theory, the inward channels are the easy part of making DisOrganization happen. After all, external forces are much less in our control, aren't they? Yet, it is often the case that internal resistance proves the hardest aspect of making something happen. There's a paradox that is rather similar to fixed and variable costs. When costing an enterprise, it is usual to consider fixed costs (those that will not change however much product or service is consumed) and variable costs (which are linked to the number of sales). In fact, despite the titles, it is often the fixed costs that are optional and the variable costs that are set in concrete.

Never a number

The Insights Colours technique gives some useful guidance in the contribution people will make and how they will work together. Without the backing of your staff, DisOrganization can never succeed. This includes your whole staff, full-time or part-time, on the payroll or contracted. In a DisOrganized company, staff can never be considered as an interchangeable resource. One of the huge advantages of the mini company structure is that it is much harder (we were going to say 'impossible', but it can be achieved with hard work) not to know your staff. And knowing them as individuals is the first step to getting the most out of them for the company and helping them achieve their goals.

Team spirit

It is impossible to think of the workplace today without thinking of teams. DisOrganization does not have a huge influence on how teams work. It may mean that teams crossing mini companies are a little harder to establish, but the cross-fertilization is just as effective. And, of course, mini companies themselves reflect the team structure. A key point to remember is that team results should be reflected in performance-related pay, just as individual and mini company results are.

The B Ark

In Douglas Adams' masterly comedy *The Hitchhiker's Guide to the Galaxy*, a planet disposes of all its support workers, from telephone sanitizers to management consultants, by telling them a disaster is about to strike the planet and sending them off in the B Ark (the A Ark is for the useful people). There is, in fact, no A Ark, and everyone else lives very happily without the unnecessary people until the whole population is wiped out by an infection caught from a dirty telephone. This dramatic scenario reflects the reality that most support workers are considered second-class citizens in a company.

DisOrganization has two key effects. It gives those in support departments back their self-esteem, as their mini company is genuinely about their job. If you look after the airconditioning in a film studio, you are no longer irrelevant to the core business of your company, because its business is airconditioning. The second effect is that support departments no longer have a stranglehold. With their newly found self-esteem comes a need to sell their services and justify themselves. Win–win.

Unravelling the organization

This book wasn't called *DisOrganization* by accident. One of the biggest barriers to improvement is the organization itself. Whether it's the processes that are in place to maintain the status quo or the systems that act as a constraint, organizations are not comfortable with change. The move to a hypercompany/mini company structure will involve tearing apart much of what makes the organization its current unwieldy self, but it won't inherently dispose of confining bureaucracy. Keeping things simple will remain a battle.

They're out to get you

We now look outwards, through the halfway house of products and services to the external channels. Traditionally, in the 'us and them' culture, practically every external channel has been regarded with suspicion. While DisOrganization doesn't mean complacency – some of them genuinely *are* out to get you – there is a need for a more constructive way of working with others.

PART FOUR

Outward channels

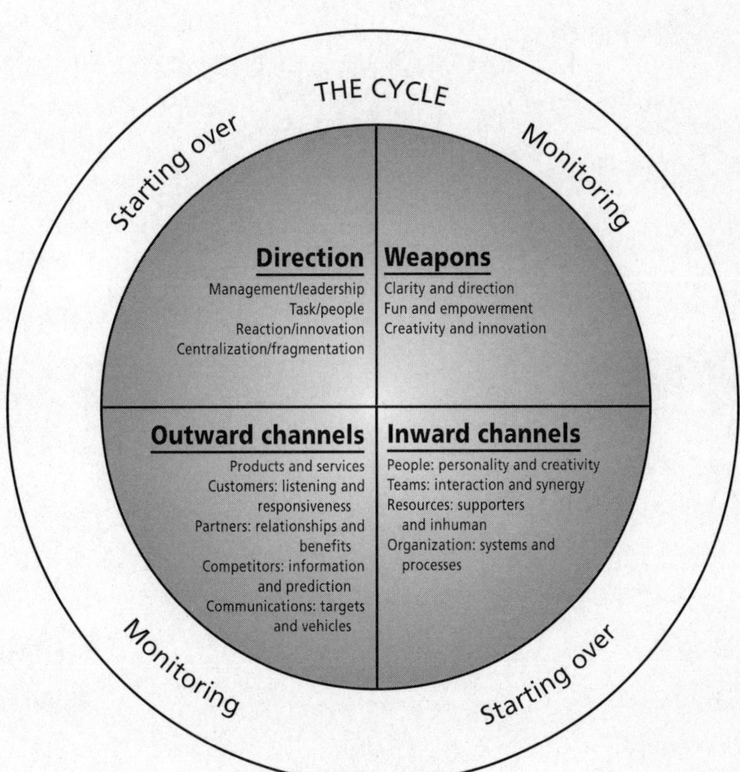

15

Products and services

- Loving your products and services
- Keeping it simple
- Systematic innovation
- Building on the competition
- Killing unwanted products
- DisOrganizing a supermarket, IBM or an airline

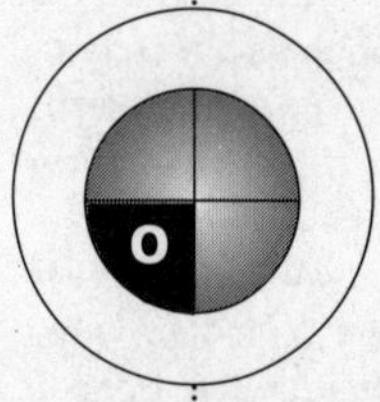

What are we here for?

Thoughtful, philosophical questions rarely sit well in business books. Somehow, you've only got to combine a deeply held belief and a business imperative to get a pompous or spaced-out trip into the impractical. Despite this, we're going to take a quick voyage into our navels. We'll limit ourselves a bit – the question is not 'Why are human beings here?', but 'What's the point of my company?' This is uncomfortably close to the sort of exercise that generates woolly mission statements, but don't be put off. Let's get some tight, specific reasons – just two or three, we want real focus. If you've a minute to spare now, have a go for your own company. If you don't have a minute to spare, stick in a bookmark and come back to this point when you do have time.

There may well be something in your list about profits and/or shareholders. There may well be something about your staff (there had better be; if you are in business and your staff aren't a prime driver, it's time to get into something more relaxing – say, Tournament Russian Roulette). Often, though, there won't be anything about your products and services. It's the same kind of problem as thinking that once you're good at *a* business you can run *any* business without learning more. There's no doubt that business and people skills are essential, but so is some specific knowledge that only resides with the people who really know the job, and any decent manager is going to go in there and make it damned obvious they are eager to learn.

WET BEHIND THE EARS

UK banks went through radical reform at the end of the 1990s. Number one complaint from staff was that the young new managers introduced in the process had never worked in a branch. It would never have been a problem if the managers had gone in with an 'I need to learn' attitude.

The thesis that causes the confusion is that all businesses are, in essence, the same. It doesn't matter if you're selling bagels or nuclear reactors. Rubbish. (Yes, they would argue, it even doesn't matter if you are selling rubbish. And they probably are.) Unless you love your product, unless you live your service, you aren't going to excel. That goes for your salespeople and for your management. One of us bought a new lawnmower recently. The typical sales pitch from a DIY store was not impressive: 'There they are'. At a (more expensive) lawnmower dealer, we were served by a lawnmower fanatic. He spent half an hour explaining why a recycler would be a good idea. Why it was better than a mulcher. Why we shouldn't buy the (more expensive) ride-on machine that we had gone in intending to buy. To be frank, he could have bored for his country on lawnmowers, but he made the sale.

Sadly, as we'll see in Chapter 16, Customers: listening and responsiveness, product knowledge and attention to your customers won't always make the sale, however much we'd like them to. However, lack of product knowledge, and product enthusiasm, will certainly do wonders for demolishing your company's edge. Surely it's enough for the salesperson to know all about it, though? Think again. The mini company is small enough for the whole company to be legitimately regarded as part of the sales team. One of the ultimate joys of the mini company is that lots of painfully inaccurate slogans become truths. When a large company says 'you're all salespeople', you know it's in trouble; when a mini company says it, it's true.

If you don't love your product and know it inside out, how are you going to do deals and establish new product lines? How are you going to understand your competitors if you don't understand what they're competing against? How can you run an IT company without having a good understanding of how to use a computer? How can you run a pet shop without any pets? How can you make good television if you never watch it ('No time – I'm always at the theatre or the opera')?

This is an easy enough proposition if you have a sexy product, but what about something deeply boring? Hopefully you aren't bored by what you do. After all, if you weren't excited by smoked haddock or sewage pipes or accountancy, why did you get into the business in the first place? If you are doing something that doesn't interest you, there's no doubt about the solution – get a new job. If you find yourself thinking there must be some products, some services that no one would find interesting, worse still if you find yourself running a business dealing with them, look again. We can't imagine anything that, looked at the right way, with the right approach (because we don't want an ordinary, everyday approach – remember your weapons of creativity and innovation), can't be made interesting to someone. Maybe not you, but someone. Just look at Rubbermaid, business books' favourite star. It couldn't be dealing with a more generic, commoditized set of products, yet it's obvious that someone (everyone?) in that company loves them.

For that matter, what about a product or service you couldn't pos-

GOLDEN OPPORTUNITY

You sit next to the chief executive of a potential client on a conference shuttle bus. How can you sell your key product to them in under five minutes?

sibly use yourself? Say you made surgeons' masks or left-hand angle bend pipes for oil rigs. You can go some way with the masks. Have you tried the masks on? Have you tried to open the packaging and put them on someone else while wearing gloves? Have you kept them on for five hours while doing stressful work? With either product, with any product or service, have you been to see them in use? To see how people react to them? There are plenty of ways in which you can get close to your product, even if you can't be an everyday user. (There is no excuse to avoid using computers or having pets or watching TV, though, or, for that matter, eating in your restaurants or using your telephone enquiry service. If you *can* be an everyday customer, you *must* be one.)

Done all that? Wonderful. Now you can try your competitors' products and see why they're better.

Troubleshooter

The UK edition of *PC Week* magazine regularly carries a troubleshooter column, relating the experiences of a fictional consultant. The following example is particularly apt when considering the importance of product knowledge.

PC WEEK

This 'Troubleshooter' article first appeared in the 24 June 1997 UK edition of *PC Week* and is reproduced with the permission of VNU Business Publications.

To the Travel Sector Account Manager, Slaughter McTone Regis Consultants

BritBreak's new IT Director, Mike Rapton, has put the cat amongst the pigeons by showing real enthusiasm for IT. The department heads are horrified; they're determined to maintain the status quo. The wonderful thing is, both Rapton and the heads think I'm on their side. Each confides in me, and I tell them they're absolutely right. Of course, if you weren't a consultant, you might think this two-faced, but that misses the point. After all, the only side I'm really on is mine.

My first priority was to arrange management training. Rapton wants every IT manager to be PC-literate, handling his or her own typing and e-mail. He will be attending the first course next week along with his team. Shortly after hearing this I attended a battle-planning session with the department heads.

Network Manager Brian Finlay opened the batting. 'This training is an excellent idea,' he said. I was surprised – Finlay knows less about using computers than the average cat (at least cats understand mice). 'Enhanced communications will benefit everyone. And middle managers frankly don't need secretaries. Of course, we would love to be able to get rid of our secretaries too …' (much nodding around the table) 'but unfortunately the complexity of an executive's calls and diary makes it quite impractical.'

'I agree,' said Arnold Potter, the DP Manager. 'In principle it would be excellent for me to make use of the e-mail thingy. Realistically, though, we have to remember that executive secretaries are PAs. It's essential that Christine sees all my mail and letters, so she might as well type them. I could look at them on the screen, though – that would save time, I'm sure.'

'Absolutely,' said IT Security Manager, Rufus Tanner. 'I'd do that too, only I'm out of the office so much that it's easier to have my e-mails printed out on paper. I just scribble a reply for my secretary to type in. But I'm all behind the concept.'

Fiona Rhees, the Desktop Manager seemed puzzled. 'Surely we can't expect our managers to give up their secretaries, then keep ours? We should be leading from the front – that's what modern management is all about. I could get rid of Susan tomorrow; I'd be quite happy dealing with my own typing.'

'I'm sure you would,' said Arnold Potter with deep condescension. 'We'd all love to get our hands dirty, but it wastes company money. We're paid too much to do the typing. If you've a problem keeping Susan busy, I can give you some suggestions on making extra work. The important thing is that we show solidarity. Losing our secretaries is the thin end of the wedge. It'll be the company cars next, believe me.'

Fiona reluctantly agreed to go along with the rest. It will be fascinating to see how the branch heads manage the course itself. I'll be along to facilitate – I wouldn't miss it for the world.

Keeping it simple

It might have been more appropriate if the serpent in the Garden of Eden had offered Eve a huge choice of apples. Not so much, 'try this apple' as 'which of this baffling range of apples, with no real information to help you choose between them, would you care to nibble?' The mini company approach of DisOrganization will help to keep your activities focused, but you need to ensure that the focus extends to your product and service range. Of course, you must offer everything your customers might want, but check that it is simplicity itself for the customer to make an informed decision.

We recently bought a few hundred pens for a seminar series. We approached three companies. The first said 'Here's a catalogue – tell us which you like and we'll tell you what it costs.' It took a long time to find out which pens were in our price bracket. Once we had, and asked for a quote with printing, they said 'We'll get back to you'. They didn't. When we called them up, they said 'Oh, yes, sorry about that. We've got some details, but we need to check with our supplier. We'll get back to you.' They didn't. Neither did we.

The second firm said 'We'll send you a catalogue. Choose a pen and we'll talk about costing.' They did send the catalogue (though it took three days to arrive). There was page after page of pens, from which we selected a few. We then had to get back to them and get a full costing.

The third firm asked about our requirements. Within an hour they faxed through two pages featuring five pens in our cost bracket. Accompanying it was a simple calculation to work out the final pricing including printing. They also dropped off samples of the pens we liked and offered to pick up our artwork for the printing when we were ready.

Guess which firm we went with? Number three, Allsons of Swindon. They no doubt had the same product range as the rest, they didn't particularly have better prices than the rest, but kept it simple. They did more than that of course. They were timely and polite – but most of all they kept a focus on what was needed. AlphaBlox's Michael Skok says, 'Almost every company going through hypergrowth does *one* thing really well. They've established every bit of the infrastructure.' Such focus keeps the approach to products and services simple.

How to ...

- innovate systematically;
- build on your competitors' successes;
- kill off existing products and services;
- run a supermarket chain;
- run IBM;
- run an airline;
- sell our stuff.

Innovating systematically

Creativity runs throughout DisOrganization – in how you work and how you organize – but there is nowhere more in need of innovation than products and services. Think of your customers. Do they turn to the new product pages of your catalogue (or however you let them know what you're doing) and say 'Wow, that's great' or is it a case of 'More of the same; throw it out'?

Creativity needs to come in at every stage of your product/service development cycle. Use creativity techniques when exploring new directions and product lines. Use creativity techniques when looking at how to beef up a flagging line. Use creativity techniques to use and improve on what your competitors are doing.

Creativity isn't an option to slot in when you've nothing better to do – systematic innovation is the order of the day. When dealing with new products, creativity is as necessary a tool as your computer or your white board. It means a little more planning – you can't just walk into a product development session with a blank page, you need to have your creativity toolkit ready to deliver the goods.

Building on your competitors' success

As you'll find when we go into this subject in depth in Chapter 18, your competitors should be very important to you. It's important to know *their* products as well as your own – and have a good guess at where they are going with them. Remember the reaction/innovation spectrum. Yes, you've got to be innovative with your products, and slavish copying is a road to second-rate performance, but there's nothing wrong (and everything right) about noticing what's working for your competitors and bettering it. They will discover new opportunities you never thought of – don't waste them.

COMPETITORS

See page 197.

COPYING

'To refrain from imitation is the best revenge'
Marcus Aurelius, Emperor of Rome AD 161–180

All of the weapons in the DisOrganization armoury are necessary to make this part work. You need clarity and direction to find out the right information about your competitors and use it. You need fun and empowerment – your employees are often best placed to get an idea of what the competitors are up to. We aren't advocating industrial espionage, but they will gather legitimate information from all kinds of sources that you might not think of. Make it fun for them; make knowing about the competition and doing something with that knowledge an attractive exercise. Creativity is equally essential. It's not enough simply to copy; you have to transform what the competition has done into something better.

The mini company structure is ideally suited to knowing your competitors. The focus it provides makes it easier to know what to watch. It also allows you to regard other mini companies in your hypercompany as pseudo-competitors for the purposes of improving products and services. It doesn't mean that you have to compete, necessarily, but you can build on the ideas of the other mini companies.

Killing off existing products and services

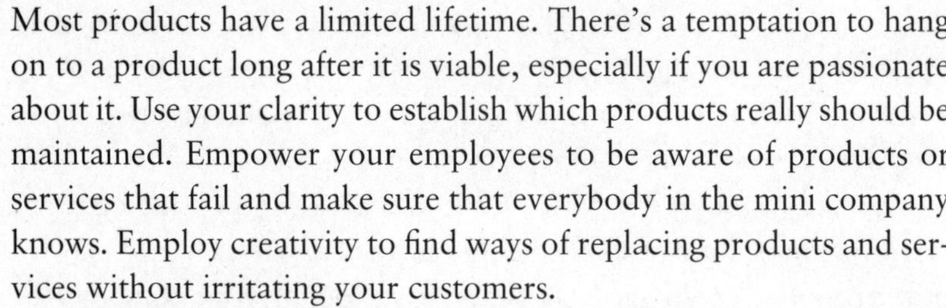

Most products have a limited lifetime. There's a temptation to hang on to a product long after it is viable, especially if you are passionate about it. Use your clarity to establish which products really should be maintained. Empower your employees to be aware of products or services that fail and make sure that everybody in the mini company knows. Employ creativity to find ways of replacing products and services without irritating your customers.

BACKING UP

We were recently talking to a company that uses computer tape back-up drives to exchange large amounts of information with a partner company. When they had come to equip a new batch of PCs, they found that the manufacturer had stopped manufacturing the old tape drive. The new one was a bargain. It had three times the capacity for the same price. However, you couldn't interchange tapes, so the companies would have to replace all their existing drives to expand. Oh, and any back-ups would be lost if one of the old drives failed.

This is a classic mix of reaction and innovation. You need to be aware of how a product is going down to deal with it with innovation, not simply by knee-jerk reaction. Again, the mini-company structure is perfectly suited to keeping the product line lean, mean and targeted on what the customers want and what the customers will want in the future.

Running a supermarket chain

We're going to look at a number of specific businesses, to see how DisOrganization might apply.

First, let's take as an example a chain of supermarkets.

It seems likely that each shop would be at least one mini company. It might be the case that in a large shop departments such as the bakery could operate separately; there may also be some specific roles that could be supplied by a mini company. However, we would not recommend a mini company of shelf-stackers or checkout staff, because these may well be too specialist to attract employees. It would be better to have one or more parallel mini companies covering a section of the shop, giving the employees more of a range of opportunities.

There is, then, the interesting consideration of how the shop itself is operated. Should there be a secondary hypercompany, consisting of an individual shop, or simply another mini company with store management responsibilities?

The answer to this depends on how unique the stores are. If each is very similar to the next, with similar information requirements, it would be sensible to run the shop with a management mini company, relying on the net company to supply information to and collect it from each mini company. If, however, this was a specialist supermarket with shops in London, New York and Paris, it is quite possible that the information needs (and perhaps the legal requirements of the company) would be such that each would have its own net company, forming a secondary hypercompany within the larger one.

Superquinn Supermarkets

Feargal Quinn is Chief Executive of the Superquinn chain in Ireland. His ideas for the retail sector, described at a Management Centre Europe conference, make so much sense we fully expected them to be picked up across the industry. They haven't been. To give a few examples, he changed the title of his Head Office to Support Office. A small matter, but indicative of something bigger. He put every member of staff in charge of an area of the shop they work in. Even if it is only making sure the trolleys work, they are in charge (we say 'even', but don't you hate those trolleys that constantly try to drag you into the shelves?). The staff member has their photograph by their point of responsibility – they are clearly identified to the customers.

Every Thursday morning, the previous week's results are shared with the staff. Most important of all, Quinn made the entire organization into a listening system. All executives have to spend at least an hour a week working in the shops. Every two weeks, the chain holds a customer panel, in a different shop each time. All executives have to do their own monthly shop. The manager's office in each shop is on the shop floor, not walled. Quinn was asked, 'But doesn't that mean that they get bothered by customers and are unable to do their real job?' 'No, because customers *are* their real job.' Sounds trite? Try it sometime.

Clarity, direction, fun and empowerment all figure strongly in a distributed retail environment like this. There are all manner of requirements that have to be followed very precisely by the employees – from hygiene regulations to display formats – yet there is also much scope for flexibility. How often have you been in a supermarket and stood in line behind others while tills remained idle and employees stood around, doing very little. What if they could start up a till at a moment's notice without supervision?

Supermarkets are doing a lot to make the shopping experience more enjoyable and to hang onto their customers. Cafés and post-boxes are certainly great amenities, but it sometimes seems that there's not been much thought put into making the experience fun for the customer. Dig out that creativity toolkit.

Running IBM

Much of what we've said about supermarkets would apply equally well to a bank or a hotel, but what about a corporate monster like IBM? Would it be possible to DisOrganize there? Absolutely. It would mean destroying a lot of the tradition that has required every part of IBM to be happy with a project before it goes ahead, but this tradition seems to be falling by the wayside.

For many years, IBM was incapable of producing competitive PC software. Almost everything was wrong with the approach they took. They threw huge numbers of programmers at a product, when computer programming can only be made to work with mini company flexibility and shared knowledge. They insisted that products fitted with their other lines and didn't threaten other products. They wanted staff around the world to get involved. They wouldn't price to the market. Yet, by the end of the 1990s, IBM was producing speech recognition software that was tight, cheap and designed to work with the best-selling word processor, even though it came from a competitor.

You can see the effect of partial DisOrganization elsewhere, too. The Lexington printer plant went from a no-hoper to a real player in the printer market when it was sold off. IBM has many characteristics that suit it to DisOrganization. It has a long tradition of having subsidiaries in other countries that feel truly local. IBM UK, for example is more British than almost any other UK subsidiary of a US company in the IT business. However, this apparent independence is coupled with rigid central control.

To achieve DisOrganization in IBM would require the Armonk Head Quarters to release its grip. While there is no doubt that this is possible, it is not certain that the senior management of such a dinosaur would be prepared to go through with the change. The jury is out.

Products such as the speech recognition software signal a real future for IBM, but the original IBM PC development was started as a mini company, then subsumed back into the line of command, wrecking its chances against the competition. If these old tendencies dominate, IBM's future (and the future of many, many similar corporations) in the chaotic new world of business is highly uncertain.

Running an airline

An airline is a complicated business that is, perhaps, one of the hardest to imagine DisOrganized. Yet, an aircraft crew operates very much as a small company in its own right. There are specialist areas such as IT that could easily form mini companies (indeed some airlines' IT or operations research departments have already done so). And the hundreds of staff required to operate checking in desks at large airports fall into the same pot as assembly line workers or any other task where hundreds or thousands doing the same essential job are required.

In all these cases, the workforce is much less homogenous than a superficial glance would suggest. Employees are divided between different factories and shifts. They have different skills. They often operate as teams already. Thus, whatever the current set-up, there is nothing to stop the division of these types of workforce into mini companies providing the same services, but which are then still small enough to feel that staff have real communication with management. After all, it is in such workforces that disputes most frequently occur because there is lack of communication, lack of shared goals. The chances of this happening in mini companies would be significantly reduced.

Selling our stuff

There is a concern that the fragmentation of DisOrganization will make it difficult to have a company-wide sales approach. In fact, in some cases this will be true. Where a mini company has total responsibility for a product, it will handle its own sales – and who could do it better? It doesn't mean, though, that there can't also be a central sales arm, acting as an agent for the mini companies, just as a wholesaler sells on goods from a range of manufacturers.

Where mini companies are only responsible for parts of a product, then the central sales arm becomes more important, but it is only another mini company. To work properly, a DisOrganized firm may need to stop a mini company forming links with other hypercompanies and selling through them as well. As we mention elsewhere, if the net company or the sales mini company wants to own a mini company's output in its entirety, they must be prepared to pay appropriately for a restrictive contract.

16

Customers: listening and responsiveness

- Customer service horror stories
- The 'global village' myth
- Customers across the hypercompany
- Listening to customers
- Knowing your product line

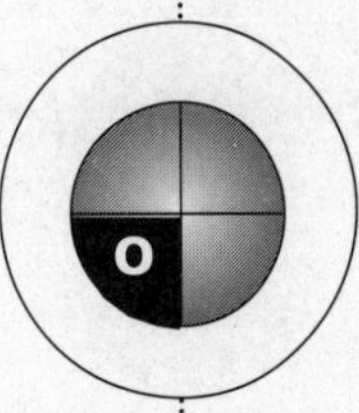

'We've heard it all before'

If you took all the management books off the shelf in your local bookshop and read every one of them, you would find a lot of disagreement. (You would also have a serious headache and an irritated bookshop manager.) No doubt you could find a book with a totally opposite message to DisOrganization, advocating a happy medium between all those extremes we're demanding. Worrying isn't it? But there's one message that is almost uniformly pushed by everyone: customers are important, so treat them nicely. Without them, life might be a lot easier (if more boring), but cash flow certainly won't.

Yes, you've heard it all before. So why aren't you doing it? Why do the horror stories you'll find in the next section still happen? We need to work it out – and make sure that DisOrganization enables you to do more than simply recognize that customers are important and that is to be able to do something about it. Before we tread where most customers fear to step, however, one word of caution. Great customer service is hugely important. You can't do without it. Yet, it isn't the universal panacea that some of those tomes that are lying on the bookshop floor would have you believe.

There are distinct market segments where customer service *isn't* high up the list. Awful customer service may put you off, but great customer service isn't going to differentiate you much from the average business in your area. The classic example is the supermarket. For all Feargal Quinn's genius, great customer service won't influence most supermarket shoppers.

SUPERQUINN SUPERMARKETS

See page 167.

If we analyze why we go to a particular supermarket, there are probably three prime influences:

- *location* we don't want to drive too far;
- *cost* when you're buying a can of baked beans off a shelf, pennies are a big influence;
- *loyalty schemes* a new differentiator.

Of course, there are extremes that will push you away – if there are never any checkouts open, if the goods you want aren't in stock

– but, generally, an average supermarket is not heavily influenced by customer service.

It might be wonderfully impressive if the person at the fish counter of a supermarket not only knows what fish is good, but how to cook it and what to serve it with. It is impressive, but it isn't going to influence most of us to change our regular supermarket shopping habits. This doesn't mean that Feargal Quinn is wrong to take the approach he does. Apart from anything else, what we have said so far applies almost entirely to out-of-town supermarkets. If you're up against a decent fishmongers next door in the high street, you've got a different sort of competition. And there will always be a proportion of people who will go further for great service in commodity shopping, but they will not be the majority.

Tales of terror

Bad customer service doesn't have to be earth-shattering to be off-putting. Rather than relate third party horror stories, these are real, everyday customer service problems we've experienced. Just two of us. And these are only the handful we remembered immediately. Now, multiply that by the population of the country. Frightening, isn't it?

- You approach the checking in counter of an airline. The person behind the desk is not wearing a uniform. She is shouting at the passenger in front of you. He wants to go to London. Can't he see that she is checking people in for Manchester? She points at the sign over her head that he can see, but she can't. It says London. He points this out. At first she doesn't believe him, she tells him he is wrong. Finally, she climbs onto the desk and looks up. Does she apologize? No. 'I don't believe this,' she says, 'this is ridiculous. They've put the wrong sign up. Do you realize I've just checked in half a dozen London passengers on the Manchester flight? It's going to take me ages to sort this out.' The customer feels like he should apologize. Later he feels like he should never fly with that airline again.
- You buy a computer modem by mail order. It doesn't work properly. You ring the manufacturer's helpline and the person you speak to confirms that there is a fault with the modem. So, you ring the mail order company to find out how to get it replaced. 'Sorry,' the person there says, 'if there's a fault, you have to send it back to

the manufacturer. It's policy.' You point out that they have a legal obligation to sell merchantable goods. OK, you'll have a refund. 'But the policy is that faulty goods have to be sent back to the manufacturer. It's not our problem. We can't do you a refund.' You point out their legal obligation again. It is only by talking to a manager that you get a sensible response. And choose a new mail order firm in future.

MYSTERY SHOPPER

Do you employ mystery shoppers? Nice idea, wrong implementation. Your senior executives should be mystery shoppers. Try it, this week. It's more important than anything in your diary. Worried you'll be recognized? Unless you've a small business, you probably won't. If you are, the staff will get a positive buzz out of seeing you at the coalface.

- You go to buy a new cordless telephone. The branch of the national chain you go to has the telephones in a locked glass cabinet. After a while of standing around, none of the half dozen sales assistants on the floor take any notice, so you walk over and speak to one. 'Can someone help me with cordless telephones?' Rather grudgingly, he comes over. You ask what the difference is between digital and analogue telephones, given that they're more than double the price. 'They're clearer, and they work further away from the base.' How much clearer? He doesn't know, he's never used one. Can we try one out? No, sorry, there isn't any way to do that. After a while, despite the service, we try to buy a telephone. No, we can't have it, it's the one in the display, they haven't got any more and they can't sell the one in the display (or else presumably they couldn't then irritate other customers).
- You ring three builders to give you a quote for doing some work. Two have answering machines. You leave a message; they never ring back. The third answers. He arranges to come and look at your house. He never turns up, and doesn't call to explain.
- When you have arranged for builders to do the job, you start dealing with builders' merchants. This is truly an area where customer service has never reared its head. You spend an entire morning calling a variety of merchants for quotes on materials for building a significant part of a house (a large amount of money). Only one of them bothers to call back. When you call the remainder, they are annoyed at the fact that you aren't prepared to wait for them to call you.
- You call three PC mail order companies to purchase a PC projector, a rather expensive item. You explain the requirement and ask for a catalogue. Two out of the three fail to dispatch the catalogues.
- You buy 23 windows for a house and half of the ones delivered are the wrong size. The building work is significantly delayed as a result, so, in a superb piece of service recovery, the company offers

a free front door as compensation. A less than superb example of service is that the door fails to arrive and it is only by chasing that anything happens.

- You stay in an airport hotel with your family and, in need of a boost, you all go for a swim. You are told that the children cannot go in the pool in the evening. After much arguing they are allowed in, but then you are told that there is an exorbitant charge for the use of the pool. This is naturally not something that is mentioned in any of the literature or anywhere else until you are changed and ready to enter the water.
- You change credit card company, but only on the condition that the credit limit you had on your previous card is matched. This is agreed, but within two weeks your card is returned in a restaurant because it is over the limit. You call the card company and they explain that the person who sold you the account had no right to offer you that limit and, not to worry, after a year or so they would be willing to raise it. You cut up the card while on the phone to them.
- You are travelling on a trans-Atlantic flight. The meal is delivered and the table collapses, depositing the meal in your lap. The stewardess watches it happen and then moves on to the next customer as though nothing is amiss.
- You are called by a double-glazing firm. Apparently, to celebrate its anniversary the company is offering a 30 per cent discount, plus an extra sum off each window, and you can reserve as many windows as you like without payment, then decide over the next few years when you would like them installed. When the salesperson calls to arrange the visit, it seems that only the money off part of the deal exists. Not many sales opportunities there.
- This one isn't personal, but we couldn't resist including it. A representative of a major dry cleaning chain appears on a TV consumer show to defend the company from customer complaints. 'Customer service is very important to us,' the representative says, 'We have millions of garments brought in and very few complaints. If anyone has a problem they only need get the damage assessed by an independent assessor and, if we're proved to be at fault, we'll compensate them in full.' If there are only a few complaints, why not assume the customer is in the right? Why make them prove (at their own expense) that your company made a mistake? Customer service? We don't think so.

- Then there are the shops that mysteriously lose their stock rooms on a Saturday. 'If it isn't on the shelf we haven't got it.'
- What about the defence mechanisms that surround the important people in a company? One of us recently had to talk with a very senior executive whose PA said that he was busy (every time we called) and that she would pass on the message. After five or six tries, we left it with her. The executive then called a few days later, furious at the fact that we hadn't bothered to call.

Mark Ralf is Group Purchasing and Property Director of health insurance group BUPA

I like the discussion you have of leadership and management. The distinction between the two is how broad a piece of the business you are looking after. Managing can be a myopic subset of the whole. Managers will tend to find metrics that cause them to act in certain ways. When the business moves, they are at most risk of losing it because the metrics they have are no longer appropriate. It is not only the managers who lose direction, but all of the people working for them will have the same problem. They will tend to move in all sorts of directions and from then on it's like herding wild mustangs. Those who extol leadership may allow freedom to act, but they also have a huge degree of control of their organizations. When you work for these people they will not allow you to wander away from the values. People who do not like the direction will leave the company.

People working for a company feel that they have a direct connection to the business, so they need to know what the business is about. If there's no one communicating the business direction, then they will make it up for themselves.

Often you will see a small entrepreneurial company turning from a leadership model to a management one when it grows. To avoid this, the business needs to stay small. Look at Richard Branson – his approach is to break up a business when it gets too big for everyone in the company to know everyone else.

Large companies become overwhelmed by support departments. The danger in support departments is that you will often find people who identify more with alliances outside the company than within. Information technology departments or human resource departments are usually full of people who identify more with their specialism than with their customers. This leads to them supporting their own objectives rather than the customers'. If you aren't directly serving the customers of your business, then you'd better be serving someone who is. Forgetting this is what leads to things like HR specialists setting up career management schemes that serve neither the end-customers of the business nor the people serving those customers.

Business strategy is an area that can make a real difference. Strategy is not what most businesses see as strategic planning. When you have a bunch of companies in an industry who all see their problems in the same area, who are all advised by the same consultants, then it is not surprising that they all end up heading in the same direction. This leads to massive overfishing. The leaders of a business need to find ways of seeing different things in their market.

Another reason for overfishing is that businesses believe that they must be customer-led. If everyone is being led by the customer, then they will all head in the same way. A business needs a front end that is customer-led and a back end that is ahead of the game. You need to be able to change the field of competition. Don't compete on equal terms. If everyone in your sector is improving their track shoes, you must get a pair of spikes and move the competition to grass rather than track. Sustainable competitive advantage does not come from reading the gurus. Everyone else is reading the same gurus. Consultants will not help either. They do not define a new point of view; they systematize success and sell it to those who are trying to catch up with those who have successfully changed the orthodoxy. There are some consultants who are radically trying to change the way people think, but they are few and far between.

The degree to which you can effect change depends on your level of control. Unless you are the Chief Executive or have the Chief Executive on side you will not be able to change the whole business. The best you will do is protect your people from the madness in the rest of the organization. Remember also that in the right hands radically changing the business can lead to success based on a strategy of unpredictability. In the wrong hands it can lead to uncontrolled, continuous chaos.

The world is not a village

'Global village' – there's an evocative term. It emphasizes how much modern communications have made it possible to communicate with others anywhere in the world. How we can no longer ignore someone else's plight, just because they're on another continent. Evocative, yes, but of course, it's rubbish. There is no global village. In a village, you know how other people will behave. You know because you share a culture and an identity. You can work out, on the whole, how the villagers will react to your customer service. Forget that in the real world; it ain't like that.

CULTURE SHOCK

For an excellent assessment of the impact of cultural differences on business, see Fons Trompenaar's *Riding the Waves of Culture* (The Economist Books, 1993).

It's easy to assume that because certain brands, often American, have a worldwide appeal, that you can transport the whole customer service approach with it. Wrong. Take apparently similar cultures – certainly with a lot more in common than most – such as the USA and the UK. The fine distinctions are those that get the hackles rising. If a US company innocently encourages its staff to suggest that British customers 'have a nice day', they are liable to lose custom. In Britain, the expression seems entirely false and manufactured.

Similarly, what could be more natural than for a waitress to come up and say 'Hi, I'm Sally, I'll be your waitress today; how can I help you?' Yet this is guaranteed to irritate many British customers. They are not used to such familiarity from staff, and they don't want to be helped, they want their order taken. The discomfort extends beyond words. Try to park someone's car for them in Glasgow and see how they treat you.

EUROCULTURE

The quotation is from Bill Bryson's book *Neither Here Nor There*. Copyright © 1992. All rights reserved. Used by permission of Jed Mattes Inc., New York, and Random House, UK. For a wildly entertaining view of the differences between European and American culture, see Bill Bryson, *Notes from a Small Island* (Doubleday, 1995) and *Neither Here Nor There* (Secker & Warburg, 1991).

Of course, the comparison works the other way, too. The superb American travel writer, Bill Bryson, with many years living in Britain under his belt, sees the opposite side of the coin in his masterful *Notes from a Small Island*, and here discovers Parisian customer service for foreigners in *Neither Here Nor There*:

> You would go into a bakery and be greeted by some vast slug-like creature with a look that told you you would never be friends. In halting French you would ask for a small loaf of bread. The woman would give you a long, cold stare and then put a dead beaver on the counter.
>
> 'No, no,' you would say, hands aflutter, 'not a dead beaver. A loaf of bread.'
>
> The slug-like creature would stare at you in patent disbelief, then turn to the other customers and address them in French at

> much too high a speed to follow, but the drift of which clear was that this person here, this *American tourist*, had come in and asked for a dead beaver and she had given him a dead beaver and now he was saying that he didn't want a dead beaver at all, he wanted a loaf of bread.

Yes, customer service matters, but make sure that your measurement of good customer service is made with local knowledge. Stick the global village concept where it belongs: in the global toilet.

What caused the terror tales?

The problems with customer service we, and most customers, come across can be boiled down to a few, simple causes. Lack of interest – not caring about the customers. Not believing the customer, and showing it – yes, customers are often wrong, but you shouldn't flaunt the fact. Lack of information – not realizing, for instance, that they were obliged to give a refund for a faulty modem. Lack of product knowledge and experience – how can you sell a telephone on improved reception if you've never used one? Making it seem that your custom isn't important to them. In the end, a lot of it is about listening, appearing to value the customer and knowing your products.

How to ...

- know about customers for the whole hypercompany;
- listen to your customers;
- get staff to know the products;
- give customers an easy point of contact.

Knowing about customers for the whole hypercompany

Customer information is an excellent resource, if sometimes overrated. Overrated? Surely this is a heinous suggestion? The customer drive of the 1980s and 1990s was founded on the principle that to know your customer was to be able to squeeze every last drop of cash out of them. In practice, customers have proved a rather more sophisticated bunch than the marketers hoped. Just because you target them with products centred on their interests, just because you call them by name and refer to the fact they used your services seven months ago doesn't mean they're going to go all gaga and never use the competition again. Either they're too cunning or too fickle. Still, that customer data is valuable; it will get you extra revenue if it is used properly.

The DisOrganized company has both pros and cons when it comes to using customer data well. Because the company has to have an excellent communication network to function, it already has the infrastructure in place to share information with speed. However, the fragmented nature of the company can lead to a tendency to cling on to customers who approach a particular mini company. It's here that the leadership and management axis comes in. The DisOrganized company needs to have strong enough leadership to make everyone aware of the benefits of sharing – and good enough management to establish the procedures to get that information around. Creativity can come in, by making it a positive benefit (or even fun) to share customer data.

Listening to your customers

Of course you listen to your customers; doesn't everyone? Not if you believe our terror tales. DisOrganization gives a unique opportunity to listen, because no one knows their customers better than a small company. Of course, this opportunity only arises if the mini company split is on a customer basis; this sometimes won't be the case. Even so, the information networks, as we have just seen, are an ideal means to communicate customer feedback.

What comes across time after time in our terror tales is a lack of willingness to listen to the customer. The wrong attitude from customer contact staff. This in turn is driven by a focus on management instead of leadership. If you take the DisOrganized view and make strong leadership an essential accompaniment of task-focused management, a number of things will happen. Recruitment should make enthusiasm for the customer an important part of the job specification. Training is absolutely essential. Not the mechanical training of the fast food joint or the rudeness training that seems to be given to the staff of most retailers, but training in flexibility – in thinking on your feet to give the customer the right experience. How about creativity training? Not because you want your customer contact staff to start using a creativity technique every time they have a customer problem, but to get them into a more flexible mode of thought.

Only when you've got staff for whom the right response is second nature, staff who depend on acting flexibly based on a set of principles rather than responding to the rules like robots ('I don't make the rules, I just work here') will you have staff who will genuinely listen to customers and do something about what they hear. Whatever needs to be done will be done. A refund where it's required. The right level of service. Feeding back a suggestion for a product improvement to the designers. Whatever, however big or small. But what about customer surveys and focus groups and customer complaint centres? All valuable – and all useless without the right attitude. In fact, if your customer contact staff are reacting the right way and feeding back to the right places, you can probably do without surveys and focus groups; your whole customer base is being surveyed and focused on every time they use you.

Getting staff to know the products

It's not enough for staff to know about customers, as we've already seen in Chapter 15, Products and services, they need to know their products, too. Is this all sounding like it will be a bit much for the morons you've got working in your retail outlet? Oh dear. Why is that, exactly? Why do you think you can get away with employing dross in your most important jobs? We were speaking to a 17-year-old student recently. He has a Saturday job with W. H. Smith, the UK's largest newsagent and bookseller. His assertion was that he and the other casual Saturday staff ought to be paid more than the regular weekly staff. Why? Because like many town-centre retailers, Smiths does practically as much business on a Saturday as the whole of the rest of the week. So, Saturday staff are very valuable. He has a point. This isn't to say that you need graduates, with graduate salaries, but you certainly need to make sure you bring out the best in your staff. Think about it.

OUT OF THE MOUTHS

Do you employ part-time or casual staff? If so, get a few together and ask them what's good about what they do and what can be improved. It'll take a while because to start with they won't understand why you want to listen to them, but it's worth the effort.

Back to those products. Remember our experience in the electrical retailer? How could they expect their sales staff to have a chance when they had no experience of the product? Can't afford the time to keep them up to date when things are changing so fast? You can't afford *not* to. Remember the PC projector? We ended up buying it from a shop rather than by mail order. After an excellent job of customer service and the cheapest price by far, the staff asked if we minded them trying it out before delivering it because they had never sold this model before and were keen to get to know it for future customers. If you aren't in retailing, you are probably feeling quite smug by now. Sorry: the examples may be from the shopping centre, but the lessons are the same. You've got customers; you've got products and services; your people need to know both.

There are probably still a few of you with a touch of smugness left. Let's say you're an Internet bookshop. No customer contact staff – no problem. Wrong. First, there's your web site. That is a prime part of your customer contact. How well does it 'know' the product? Is it organized the way you work – or the way customers work? Can they find what they want easily? Has it the full product range? There's nothing more frustrating than an e-shop with a subset of the 'real' shop's products – that was probably the biggest reason, bigger even than early suspicion about security, for Internet shopping being so slow to take off. Oh, and there is real customer contact, too. How well do you handle e-mails? We recently tried out an Internet bookshop that boasted that its database covered the whole product range. We sent an e-mail pointing out an error in its catalogue. A week later, we had not received a reply and so sent another. Still no reply after a few more days. Bye-bye smugness.

Giving customers an easy point of contact

In the DisOrganized company, there may be mini companies that have a customer interface. This tends to cause panic in the top ranks. A classic example is the corporation's IT department. With plenty of development teams, different operational support groups based on technology, service agents and perhaps specialist teams such as PC support and operations research, the IT department seemed a nightmare to the pure management school of the 1970s and 1980s. The answer was the help desk. All calls had to be routed through the help desk, even if you were sitting next to an IT expert who could solve your problem in 30 seconds. It was a classic, totalitarian, for the greater good of the masses solution, and it still holds in many corporation's IT departments.

The DisOrganized company can't work this way. The net company has not got the power to enforce such an approach on the mini companies. Yet, there is a problem. It can be confusing for a customer if they have to deal with several elements of the hypercompany. Where the mini companies have their own, distinctive branding, there is no problem. No one has difficulties with the fact that there isn't a single point of contact for both Mars Bars and Pedigree Pet Foods (in fact, they'd probably be rather uncomfortable if there was). Where the branding is at the hypercompany level, there is the possibility of confusion.

The DisOrganized answer? Everyone who has customer contact is part of the help desk. If you usually deal with Sue Williams in mini company X, and you want a product from mini company Y, or you've got a problem with your supply from the hypercompany, then Sue is the person you'll deal with. She can handle it for you. End of story; end of help desk.

Troubleshooter

Another *PC Week* column, with a particular message for the help desk.

To the IT Sector Account Manager, Slaughter McTone Regis Consultants

Pete McShane, Customer Service Manager for Nanoware UK, asked me to spend some time with their helpline provider and report back on possible improvements. I produced the standard Slaughter McTone Regis briefing (never less than 40 pages: the client expects value for money).

At the presentation, I broke down the call process. The average caller waits 15 to 20 rings before getting through. This could be fixed by increasing switch capacity. McShane nodded without comment. When the customer does get through, it takes between 2 and 20 minutes before they speak to anyone. McShane looked worried now. 'We'll have to look into this,' he said. 'It should be between 10 and 20 minutes.'

It's apparently company policy that there should be ten rings before the phone is answered, then ten minutes before reaching an agent. This makes sure that everyone who gets through has a real problem, rather than wasting help desk time with trivia. Why ten rings and ten minutes? Apparently ten is Nanoware supremo Jim Toren's favourite number, and it's best not to argue.

I moved on to the touch tone menu, used to select an appropriate agent. It has too many levels, each entry is extremely long, and the whole structure is changed every four weeks. Again, McShane informed me, this is intentional. While delays put off home users, corporate callers just leave the phone open and get on with their work. By requiring several interactions, and regularly changing the structure so it can't be learned, Nanoware ensures that corporate support staff don't phone up with questions they could answer themselves.

PC WEEK

This Troubleshooter first appeared in the 24 June 1997 UK edition of *PC Week* and is reproduced with the permission of VNU Business Publications.

By now my next observation was redundant. Despite the complex menu, pinpointing the reason for the call, the help desk selects an agent at random – but I had misunderstood the menu's purpose, so I hurried on. The agent answers 'Nanoware Help Desk?' I felt it would be friendlier if they said: 'Nanoware Help Desk, Simon speaking – how can I help you?' McShane nodded. Progress.

The agent then follows a script. They have no technical expertise whatsoever. If the script fails, the call is passed on to a technician. I suggested either using an expert system to help the agents, or putting technicians on the front line. Apparently neither is acceptable. It's company policy to only use Nanoware products, and they don't make expert system software. As for techies on the front line, apparently they cut to a solution much too quickly, removing much of the necessary pain from the process.

My final suggestion was that anyone with a bug should have progress reports on a fix, then be sent a free copy of the updated software. Again McShane had two problems. Progress reports require communications with the software developers, a dangerous prospect, while updated software implies that UK-originated bugs are fixed, which is pretty unlikely.

Not a bad session. After all, my suggestion that agents should give their name was accepted without a quibble.

17

Partners: relationships and benefits

- Partnership is inherent to DisOrganization
- Moving away from 'not invented here'
- Partnering a dinosaur – necessary, but be wary
- The shareholders are partners
- The customers are partners
- The members of staff are partners

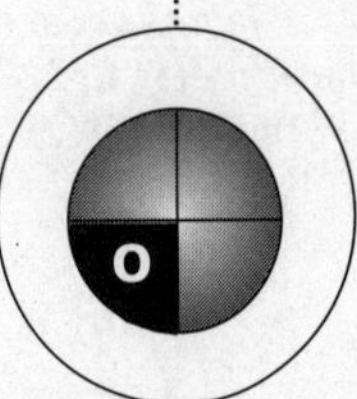

Howdy partner

Partnership is vital to business success. Read that sentence again. Partnership is vital to business success. Few would disagree with it. In the world of the DisOrganized company, this statement becomes even more true. If it is so true and so obvious, why do we all ignore it in the day-to-day running of business? Other companies in the same sector are usually treated as adversaries. Suppliers are at best regarded with suspicion and at worst looked on as a resource to screw down as part of any cost-saving initiative. Employees are seen as part of a win–lose relationship; anything you gain must, perforce, be something I lose. Even the most obvious partners – companies in business alliances – view one another with suspicion or even open hostility.

This state of affairs must change. Even if you reject all of the notions of DisOrganization and even if the business world turned its back on the idea of creating smaller, more manageable companies, there has to be sense in reducing the warfare and increasing the partnership. This plea is not made in the spirit of a hangover from the 1960s. It is not simply a feeling of having to love one another and put flowers in our hair.

COMPETITION

'Government and cooperation are in all things the laws of life; anarchy and competition the laws of death.'
John Ruskin, nineteenth-century English social commentator,* Unto this Last *(1862)

Cooperation is more effective than confrontation at achieving results. This isn't a plea to abandon the capitalist economy and move to some sort of socialist Utopia. Capitalism appears to work, but the fact that it works does not mean that it should be taken to the lowest extreme, that everyone should compete with everyone else. Nor should it necessarily be taken to the next level, where every company competes with every other.

Competition works in the marketplace. Where consumers have genuine choice among providers, then they seem to get the best deal. The companies involved work harder at producing more for less and economic growth is the spin-off. Yet the companies that offer this choice need not be stand-alone entities. More and more are seeing the benefits of working with others to produce what consumers want and need. The problem is that we are so embedded in our traditional models of business that we are, frankly, pretty damned poor at anything but competition. There are very few companies that manage successful cooperation with others. Almost all formal alliances fail. Even mergers cause huge indigestion until one party is completely subsumed in the other.

What is it good for?

One issue that is at the heart of this problem is language. The analogy used for most business interaction has, for a very long time, been that of warfare.

Warfare does not lend itself to cooperation. The enemy is the enemy and, without a total surrender, will always be hated. Similarly, partners are usually short-term political expedients who serve a need and are then ditched. Alliances move with the fortunes of war and so are not to be trusted. Even those on one side have inter-group conflict. The front-line troops do not trust the generals. One regiment will try to outshine another. Rivalry and conflict are at the heart of the model.

We are proposing a more cooperative model for business. The DisOrganized company will compete with other companies and the consumer will be offered choice, but at the heart of the model is the notion of cooperation. One mini company cannot survive without the others that help it to meet the needs of its customers. The net company does not make sense without the mini companies it organizes. The hypercompany is merely a notional construct and doesn't even exist in any real sense. Without cooperation they are none of them viable.

This interview is unusual in that it was with two people. Clifford T. Pinder is President of Growth Technologies and Vice-President of Imation Corporation. Michael E. Sheridan is Vice-President of Operations at Imation. Imation was the media production arm of 3M, but is now a separate company.

Why was Imation spun off from 3M?

The top-line objective was the significant difference in focus in the markets 3M participates in. Such a multimarket conglomerate spreads across many different areas with different capital requirements, different markets progressing at a variety of different paces, and also with different bottom-line results. Companies making 5 or 10 or 20 per cent can all be very effective business models, but if the focus in the corporation is more to one end or the other, the outlying businesses are in difficulty. The corporation will try and force them to an objective that has very different dynamics to the overall market in which they participate.

We had different financial results, time to market, capital requirements, all not fitting the model of 3M. I think the corporate executives understood, but it meant taking more of their time, time away from the other 90 per cent of the corporation where the top leadership should focus more time. Now we don't have to spend time internally selling to the main organization, we can spend more time on the external market. The issue is focus and speed. If you aren't focused you can't be fast. If you are fast and unfocused, you'll probably make lots of mistakes. In large corporates today, focus is a real problem. To go further, what we have to do is to develop internally the start-up company attitudes and processes that cause a company with zero sales and a brilliant idea to get to market quickly.

Has working with strategic partners anything to do with location?

Communications are important, and having no barriers caused by distance can make a big difference to getting things done. We won't have an ideal position internally. Our factories are in several US states, the rest of the company in Minnesota. I worked in Japan for a couple of years. We had a single site: honestly speaking I had no idea which engineers were in manufacturing and which in the laboratory because they just worked together and got things done better. Ideally we should colocate, but getting people to move is difficult. It's not practical.

We've had a lot of experience with external partners. Having a common language and understanding is important. Cultural differences can make you think you're understanding the same thing, but you aren't. Also a good fit for objectives. If they're the same, you're synergistic, you can get a good outcome. If there's a mismatch, plus perhaps some misunderstanding, you can run into problems.

Is partnership with 3M easier than it is with other companies?

We treat it as an external relationship, but it is different, as there's a thread that goes back to our internal relationship. It works both ways. On the plus side we've got history – an understanding of the people and a clear knowledge of what works. On the other hand, it's a different relationship for both of us. The method of working together needs to be different. Some of our old 3M colleagues would like to use the old systems, but we can't.

How do you find appropriate alliances?

We have relationships, good and bad, with everyone in the industry. We talk to our colleagues in the industry on a regular basis. We know where to go. The other thing that's happening, as we're smaller, we need to be faster. That sometimes can be achieved by going outside. There's more outreach to the periphery of the business.

Tear out my heart why don't you?

This notion of cooperation extends beyond the individual hypercompany. It is easily possible to envisage a mini company working for more than one hypercompany. Indeed, today suppliers will provide goods or services to competing customers and there is nothing strange in that. Suggest that this should happen with a department in a large organization and you would think that you were suggesting ripping the heart out of a living company.

CORE AND PIPS

Jot down on a piece of paper the main activities of your company or department. How many are performed by internal staff? How many would make a difference to the company's success if they weren't? Why? Make sure you can answer why in every case.

If, for instance, a company that made wangle plungers bought in the widgets that were a necessary subcomponent, there would be no difficulty in the company that supplied the widgets also supplying a competitor. If the wangle plunger manufacturer made its own widgets, it would not consider allowing its widget factory to become a supplier to a competitor. If the wangle plunger manufacturer DisOrganized and the widget factory became a separate mini company, then it would have to give the mini company the freedom to trade where, and with whom, it liked.

The instant reaction to this is that it is a dangerous loss of control. This is only true if the widget subcomponents being made by the factory were significantly different to those in the competitor's product. If making its own widgets gave our imaginary company a sustainable competitive advantage, it would have to DisOrganize in a way that forced the mini company to trade with it and it only. Unless this is done on a commercial basis – paying the mini company so much that it is willing to enter into an exclusive contract – such an action immediately loses a significant chunk of the advantages that accrue from DisOrganizing.

The temptation for most companies is to say that everything they do today provides a significant and sustainable competitive advantage. Even down to the provision of commodity services and products such as office cleaning and computer support. This is obvious nonsense. However, while it is obvious nonsense when you are looking objectively at another company, it is not so clear in the case of your own. The problem is that no one else understands the special circumstances that apply in your business. More nonsense! It is always possible to convince yourself that you cannot allow elements of your current business to trade with competitors. It is rarely a sustainable argument. If you really, really, really believe that you could not buy in most, if not all, of the things you currently do for yourself, then you need help. Someone who is not wedded to the shape, size and structure of business that you have today may provide a more objective view of those elements that genuinely provide sustainable advantage.

We have been making various contentions throughout this book. Companies of around 50 people are more effective and more easily managed than larger companies. It is possible to break monoliths into smaller units. It is necessary for these units to cooperate in order to succeed. Partnership is a good thing. To sustain these arguments, we must look at the benefits of partnership.

You've got a friend

At the softer ends of the partnership benefits is support. Having someone that you can turn to when times are rough is always useful, but when you are in charge of a business, it starts to be essential. The loneliness of command is a phrase that brings to mind an image of the destroyer captain standing alone on the bridge. It is a phrase that can equally apply to modern business. Just having a group of other people facing similar demands on a day-to-day basis can make a real difference. And, let's face it, when you pay high salaries to the top people because of their effect on the business, any difference you make to them has a leverage effect on the bottom line. If it doesn't, cut their salaries.

Anything you can do, I don't need to

Dividing expertise among companies results in specialization within each company. This results in the companies being more focused and more able to provide the very best of what they do. When a mini company becomes truly responsible for its own bottom line, it will work very hard at finding those elements of its business that are duplicated elsewhere in the hypercompany and cutting them out. The real focus DisOrganization brings is on the results.

How to ...

- make alliances work – synergy;
- cope with geography;
- DisOrganize research and development;
- network for business;
- locate for success;
- hold hands with a dinosaur;
- partner shareholders;
- partner customers;
- partner the staff.

Making alliances work – synergy

There is an old English nursery rhyme:

Jack Spratt could eat no fat,
His wife could eat no lean.
And so between them both,
They licked the platter clean.

SYNERGY

'The interaction or cooperation of two or more drugs, agents, organizations, etc., to produce a new or enhanced effect compared to their separate effects.'

Concise Oxford Dictionary
(9th Edition, Oxford University Press, 1996).

Obviously a synergistic marriage. Unfortunately, in business such meetings of opposites have been rare. Alliances have not worked in the past. In most cases, this was because neither partner was willing to give up something they regarded as fundamental to their success. Without any movement, finding true synergies relies on the potential partners having gaps in areas that happen to be covered by the other. In the traditional business model it is unlikely that successful businesses can have survived in this state.

The DisOrganization model is different. By DisOrganizing, you are setting up mini companies that require interaction with their partners for their success. True synergies are not only possible, they are inevitable.

There is a danger that mini companies will become nervous about their reliance on partners and try to create, within the mini company, those functions provided elsewhere in the hypercompany. Frankly, this is unlikely because the successful mini company will keep itself as lean and focused as it can. As the mini companies must be provided with a high degree of autonomy, there is only one real defence – selecting the right chief executive for the mini company. If the person running the company believes in the cooperative model of business, as opposed to the adversarial one, they will be more likely to rely on trade to buy in services rather than try to provide everything themselves.

Coping with geography

These days, everybody is using the term 'glocal' to describe a global business with a local feel. In most cases, in most large companies, it is actually shorthand for, 'I haven't got a clue what's going on in those markets, but I'll treat them just like the ones I understand'. In the DisOrganized company, there is a real possibility of presenting a global brand in truly local ways because the mini company that represents the brand really does understand the market.

So far, much of the discussion of the mini company split has been functional. That is, if you have a discreet area of production or provision of service, you can see a natural boundary. Another split is geographic. If you have a local representation in other markets, you can see a natural boundary there.

DisOrganizing research and development

Developing new directions, new products or new services could be a casualty in a DisOrganized world. Without huge corporations with their massive research and development spend, where will the novel approaches come from?

In our opinion they'll come from where they've always come from – the small companies or the individual entrepreneurs who risk their own future to make a vision into reality. What's more, as DisOrganized companies they will be fuelled by systematic creativity.

Large research projects of corporations do not deliver as much as those who populate the R&D departments would claim. If your industry happens to be one where there are massive amounts of money spent on research and where the small entrepreneur cannot be effective – the pharmaceutical industry springs to mind – you can set up mini companies that are pure research companies, funded by the mini companies that sell the products. Those that invest share the benefits, those that choose not to do not.

Networking for business

If you knew all of the people we know and we knew all of the people you know and they all knew all of the people ... Imagine the networks you could plug into if you truly cooperated with others to the extent that you shared contacts and leads. Naturally, where you are in competition with others, or even just naturally suspicious of them, you will not share such information. When you move into a world of true cooperation, then this becomes far more likely.

You could view this as a profit stream; you get paid a finder's fee for new business you generate elsewhere, but it is more likely to work on a mutuality of benefit – you scratch my back and I'll scratch yours. It sounds warm, cuddly and Utopian, but it already works well in the consultancy world. If there is an area in which you cannot provide a particular service or that you cannot handle alone, then you pass work on to others in the sure and certain knowledge that one day your generosity will be repaid. It works, don't knock it.

Locating for success

Despite the way that geographic spread becomes more practical when underpinned by partnership, Michael Skok, Chairman and CEO of AlphaBlox Corporation, is convinced that, in some markets, the right location is essential for effective partnership – and effective partnership is equally essential for success:

> In software, the US market is so dominant that if you don't claim an early market here, you don't get global success. Paradoxically, part of the reason that location is so important is the Internet explosion. It is all driven from Silicon Valley – even Boston is too far away. This ironic development in a business of instant communications is endemic to a technological industry where you are developing leading, or even bleeding edge products. You can't avoid the need for 'face time'. You can't do this sort of development with the asynchronous communications of e-mail or battling against time zones. The only efficient way to do it is face to face.
>
> When I think of a virtual organization I have to look not just within the company but the industry. To be a leader, dominating a particular space, we need to think of every single alliance that is part of our virtual space. At AlphaBlox, 2 out of 50 staff are full-time on alliances – plus it's on my own priority list. The really

great companies of the future will be those where many other companies profit from their success. This is where location is so important. I can walk down the road here to many of our strategic partners. Others are a 30-minute plane ride away, and in the same time zone. The really successful corporations will be those that form an ecosystem around them where their allies benefit from such partnerships.

If we stand back and look, this is a trend, not just a fad. The complexity of current systems and products leads to the need for specialist knowledge. The implication is more and more partnerships are needed for complete solutions.

Holding hands with a dinosaur

One very real problem with DisOrganization is that it will not happen everywhere overnight. There will be a long period where this business model coexists with the current adversarial model. Mini companies will have to do business with dinosaur organizations that still work to the 'big is beautiful' and the 'screw them before they screw you' models of business. How do you partner a dinosaur like this?

The first answer is similar to the answer to the question, 'How do porcupines make love?' – very carefully! Naturally the mini company has to draw up contracts and establish the standard statutory protections. Having done this, there is then a huge degree of trust. We recently considered doing business with a huge multinational and had some problems with the contract, which was internally contradictory and unenforceable. An expert in contract law told us not to worry ourselves about the detail. A précis of the conversation would be, 'If they choose to screw you, you will get screwed whatever the contract says'. We ended up not doing business with these people. In similar circumstances, with similarly sized companies we have felt more comfortable because we have trusted the individuals we were dealing with.

Trust is important, even when dealing with a dinosaur. Nevertheless, it is worth establishing the basic protections that a contract can offer. It's a bit like Ronald Reagan's maxim, 'Trust but verify'.

Partnering shareholders

The shareholders are partners, too. Yes they are, they own the company, remember? It is tough to think of them on a day-to-day basis, but at the point the company DisOrganizes, they come to the fore.

At this stage, the real issue is to be able to provide adequate reassurance to them that the value of their company is not being destroyed by the moves you are making. This is not as easy as it may seem. Remember that for the majority of businesses, most of the shareholders are likely to be conservative. They will have developed their understanding of business on the old model and will equate growth and size with success.

Convincing them is not a lost cause. The bottom line is still the bottom line. If you can provide shares that are at least as valuable as the initial investment and can demonstrate a future that is at least as bright, then the model of the business will be secondary. It's not unusual for monolithic companies to increase in value when they are split up. Often there are subsidiary businesses that are less risky than their parent. They will have been valued at the risk level of the monolith and so separating them will increase their value. Of course, the opposite could be true, but it is unlikely that a business that is perceived as a low-risk one contains a large number of risky sub-businesses.

Partnering customers

So far we have not mentioned one group with whom you must establish a rock solid partnership: your customers. Isn't it enough to give these irritating people their own chapter? No. It costs you a great deal of money to win new customers; it costs far less to keep those you have. Establishing a partnership with your current customers is not only possible, therefore, it is good business sense. There are a few things you can do that will help with this.

If you have a small customer base, then getting to know them all individually is essential. Setting up a simple customer tracking system, knowing what they have bought, when and why is the very minimum. Knowing what they are buying elsewhere is useful. Knowing what they do in their spare time, what family they have, what makes them tick, is all very useful. This information does not make many demands on your brain, your PC, your notepad or whatever you happen to use as a retrieval system. Just make sure it works.

If you have a larger customer base, then it gets much tougher. You could set up a massive database that stores vast amounts of data, but the chances are that this will have limited payback. You could, on the other hand, work at finding out what is important to your customers each and every time they interact.

The hotel business provides good examples of the best and the worst in this regard. There was a period when one of us was spending most of his time in hotels. For well over a year in Arlington, Virginia, and then, later, for almost a year in the UK. The stays tended to be in the same hotels, week after week after week. None of them picked up the fact. None of them commented on the repeat business or even recognized it. Contrast this with the hotel in Sydney that, on just the second visit, recognized this and sent a bottle of wine to the room as a thank you. The bottle of wine cost them a tiny fraction of the business generated as a result of the recommendations.

GREAT PARTNERSHIP

Note half a dozen instances of great service you've received recently. What made them great? How could you apply similar benefits to a business partnership?

Another example is the hotel in Singapore where the porter asks if you've stayed before while helping you in. If you have, then they signal this to the checking in desk where, instead of saying 'Welcome' the person there says 'Welcome back'. It's a tiny, almost trivial, point, but it does make a difference.

The first step on this road is to view your customers as partners rather than one of the resources of business.

Partnering the staff

If you need a rock solid partnership with your customers, just think of the reliance you are placing on your employees. Every day of the week, every hour of the day, for better or worse, one of your employees is representing your company. If you treat them like dirt, think about the kind of representation they will be offering. Even if you feel that you have a good relationship, it is unlikely that you view it as partnership.

We have mentioned before the win–lose philosophy that many businesses have with regard to employees. If you viewed the relationship as a partnership, you would always be on the hunt for win–win solutions where you both gain.

There was a piece on the radio about flexible working. The person was saying that employers see flexibility as a one-way street. Employees are at their beck and call while businesses do nothing to accommodate the needs of their people. Just think how powerful it would be to set up a flexibility deal with obvious and tangible benefits for both parties. To do this means moving away from the mind-set that anything they gain is something I lose. Indeed, that could be a summary of the whole notion of partnership.

18

Competitors: information and prediction

- Partnership doesn't mean an end to competition
- Identifying competitors
- Getting the information
- Estimating is often enough
- Where to look

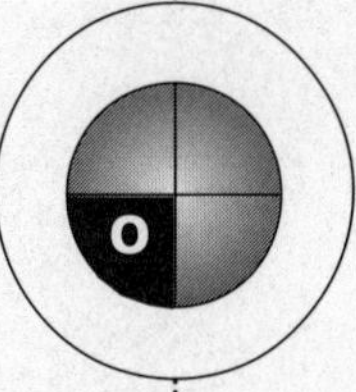

What a wonderful world

Lest the last chapter has led you to believe that we are envisioning a world of cosy cooperation where no one competes with anyone else and everybody holds hands and smiles, let us reassure you. We have not gone soft.

Partnership is essential in the DisOrganized world, but so too is competition. There is no conflict here. The market-driven world in which we live relies on competition to keep the wheel spinning. Until and unless we find a more effective model for doing business, competition is an essential prerequisite. Without it, atrophy sets in and business grinds to a halt.

The point of the last chapter was that you must be clear about who you are competing with and then be prepared to cooperate with those non-competitors. You may even set up temporary cooperative alliances with competitors, but there are some pretty obvious risks down that path.

KNOWLEDGE

'For also knowledge itself is power.'
***Francis Bacon, Meditationes Sacrae* (1597)**

Once you have identified your competitors, you must find out all you can about them in order to understand where they are and where they are heading. The more traditional and less DisOrganized a company is, the easier it will be to understand and predict its movements. Yet another advantage for DisOrganization: your competitors won't have a clue what you are doing.

It's out there, somewhere

Before we start looking specifically at identifying competitors and dissecting them, a bold statement about information. If you want it badly enough, it is out there, somewhere. Even if you do not try too hard, but work systematically, you will find more than you believed possible.

This is an issue of mind-set. If you start knowing how hard information will be to find, then your prediction will come true. If you start knowing that the information you need is available, it will be. This is not wishful thinking. We have seen time and time again how effectively people can uncover information when they are told in advance that it is available (even when the person telling them that has no idea where or how it can be found).

Identifying competitors

It sounds ridiculous to say that you must be careful to identify who your competitors are, but think about the changes that are taking place in the world, particularly if companies start to DisOrganize left, right and centre. There will be mini companies out there that were once part of a competitor that could usefully become a supplier. Even if they do not supply to you, they are not necessarily going to compete with you. There will be companies in sectors that you have never even looked at that will step into your marketplace and take your customers. How will you know who they are and who they are going to be?

Many times you will not. Rapid shifts in the marketplace will catch you unawares and will leave you puzzling over what to do. This will happen more and more often in the future. The DisOrganized company is in a better position to cope with this future than is a traditional company because it is fleeter of foot and responds faster than a traditional company. Still, the sudden shifts will cause problems.

A good starting point for the basic set of competitors is looking at how your customers get to you. Do they use *Yellow Pages* or a reservation system? Do they use the Internet or find you by looking at newspaper advertising? Look in the same places (and a few different places, too).

Sometimes you will be able to anticipate these changes. Begin by understanding your relationship with your customers in terms of the utility you provide rather than the more traditional view of your product. You must then try to see this utility from as many directions as possible in order to see who else might be in good shape to meet their needs.

To explain what we mean, a few years ago one of us was in a lecture where the lecturer asked whether or not we had ever bought a drill bit. I, like most of the audience, put up my hand. 'No you haven't', he said, 'None of you has ever bought a drill. What you bought was holes.' His point was that (with the rare exception of drill bit collectors) our interest as consumers was not in the drill itself, but in the holes we needed to make. He went on to say that he could envisage a future where competition for drill manufacturers would come, not from higher quality steel or tungsten-carbide, but from lasers or ultrasonics. If someone built a machine capable of producing a hole of known diameter and known depth at a reasonable price, few, if any of us, would buy a drill bit again.

As another example, those who work in utilities, such as water, electricity or gas, tend to view their product in terms of the distribution network, the pipelines or power grids that bring the product to the point of use. Imagine a future where the bulk of our water was recycled within our homes or local community or where electricity was generated on demand where it was needed using sunlight or nuclear fusion.

In this world, the distribution technology that has been the backbone of the utilities, work becomes redundant and the new competition is from the recycling plant manufacturers or the power generator manufacturers. Unless they are already seeing their customers in terms of the end use of the product rather than the limitations of current technology, they will fold when this world happens.

Obviously the first people you need to speak to are your customers. Find out how and why they use your product. Break this down to the lowest level of utility. Simplify your understanding and separate yourself from any notion of the way things are done today. Do not treat this as a desk research exercise. You do not know your customers nearly as well as you think you do.

CRYSTAL BALL

Consider your prime product or service. Project yourself forwards ten years. Imagine that what you produce has been banned. How would your customers cope? Who would they turn to? Is this a possible source of competition? What would a product that was a whole order of magnitude better be like? Who is most likely to make it, whatever their current markets?

Next, take a look at the way the world is going as far as the utility derived from your product or service is concerned. You might employ a physical scientist or even a science fiction writer to look into their own brand of crystal ball and imagine what might happen in the next 10 or 20 years. After this you can be sure of one of two things. The future predicted will happen much faster than predicted or it will happen much more slowly. OK, that isn't what you want to hear when you are looking for certainty, but it is the way of the world.

Once you have done this, you ought to be in pretty good shape to go back to looking at your competitors and imagining how well placed they might be to steal your customers. You might also be in good shape to look at other industries and see how they might step into your current market.

What do you want to know

Time to look at some basic analysis tools, applying a creative approach to your need for information. The first of these is to identify what you want to know about your competitors.

There are some potential pitfalls here. You are likely to limit what you want to know by what you think you are able to find out. Don't. Spend some time thinking about the information that you would like to know in an ideal world and with no limitations. It is there somewhere.

Also, you are likely to limit your questions to history because most data is historic. Don't. Ask yourself what your competitors are doing today and what they are going to do tomorrow. You may not get answers to these questions in the form of hard, quantifiable data, but you will get answers.

Finally, as we suggested in the last section, you are likely to limit your hunt to your current competitor set. Don't. If you have gone through the process of thinking about the real problems you solve for your customers, you will be in a really good position to add a whole load of potential competitors to the pot and to look at them, too.

Build a skeleton

Next, build the skeleton of the Frankenstein's monster you are setting out to create. You have a series of questions and wishes from the 'What do you want to know?' stage; start answering those questions from the information you already have in your head. This is also a good time to be listing further avenues that you can go down in order to find more information.

Flesh it out

The next stage is to build the monster in full. For this, you need to do a fair amount of research that will provide the data for the mental and paper model you are creating. We cover some of the sources of data that you might decide to use in the next few sections, but you will know of industry-specific sources that will supply more detailed information. One word of warning: do not rely too heavily on the industry-specific sources. This is what the rest of your competitors are doing and the objective is to be better than them, not merely as good.

Igor, it lives!

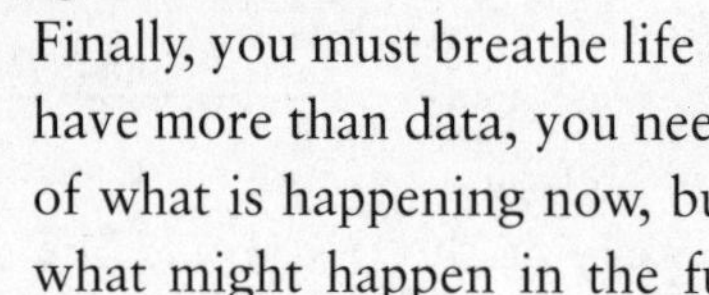

Finally, you must breathe life into your monster. To do this you must have more than data, you need stories. The stories will be anecdotes of what is happening now, but will, most significantly, be stories of what might happen in the future. There is nothing as convincing when it comes to crystal ball gazing, as a well-told story. All the data and all the trends in the world are useless unless you find a way of connecting with your emotions (and the emotions of the rest of your company). Tell the stories and see how the possibilities come to life.

STORIES

See what Mark Adams of PR company Text 100 has to say about stories in Chapter 19, page 213.

Avoid boiling the oceans

Having looked at the stages that your competitor analysis could go through, it is useful to remember some common mistakes. The first is that of boiling the ocean when all you want is a cup of tea. That is, many people, when trying to answer a question, will attempt to gather all of the data available from everywhere and then sort through it to find what is relevant. The gathering of data takes time, so why would you want to collect more than you need to answer the questions you have set yourself? Address yourself to each question and gather the data that would answer that. By all means collect up any interesting snippets you stumble upon, but do not set out to gather anything and everything. You only have to spend a few hours meandering the almost limitless span of the World Wide Web to appreciate just how much information there is out there – and how much of it is useless. If you've never used the World Wide Web, make sure you get access to it in the next month. Don't bother with excuses about having difficulties with technology; you need it, and when did you last hear anyone complain about the technical difficulties of reading a newspaper? This is easier.

OBJECTIVITY

'For what a man had rather were true he more readily believes. Therefore he rejects difficult things from impatience of research ... numberless in short are the ways, and sometimes imperceptible, in which the affections colour and infect the understanding.'

***Francis Bacon, Novum Organon*, 1620**

Avoid eating the tea leaves

If one common mistake is to boil the oceans in order to simply make a cup of tea, another is to end up eating the tea leaves because you can't see the water. Many people will set themselves a question and then will consider it answered without having collected any data or affirmed any of their beliefs, but a collection of prejudices does not amount to an analysis of a question. Until you have tested your own answers and provided some support for them, you are still at the skeletal stage we described earlier. Go out and find some flesh to put on the bones.

Be prepared to estimate

Analysis does not have to be data to ten significant figures and backed up by a dozen independent sources. It is possible to answer a question by estimating.

Let us say that you have set yourself the question 'How many gallons of fuel are consumed by cars in the United States in a year?' It is probable that there is a source somewhere that will provide this information. It is also probable that an approximate answer would do. If so, you could start by taking a guess at the proportion of the population who own a car – say two thirds, allowing for multiple ownership. Now we have no idea how accurate this is, but it feels OK. If you wanted a better estimate, you could use the Delphi technique. Gather a group together and ask them to estimate. Show them the estimates of the group and ask them to have another go. Zero in on an agreed answer.

So, if two thirds of the population own a car and there are 250 million people in the USA, that means that there are about 167 million cars in the USA. How far does a car drive in a year? Well, again, we don't know, but our guess would be about 15,000 miles (24,140 km). How many miles to the gallon (4.5 litres) does a typical car do? Again we don't know but we would guess at about 18 miles (29 km) to the gallon. This gives you 167 million cars, each using 833 gallons (3787 litres) in a year – a total of just under 140 billion gallons (632.5 billion litres) used by cars in the USA each year.

This answer is wrong. It is bound to be. If you need an accurate answer, it is no good to you. However, if all you need is an order of magnitude, finding it this way will have saved you a significant amount of time.

For something slightly better, you could refine the inputs. Find out how many cars there are in the USA or how many miles to the gallon (or kilometres to a litre) a typical car does.

The main point here is to have an idea of how important accuracy is in advance and answer the question accordingly.

Where do I look?

The first question you are likely to ask when trying to find data is

'Where is it?' There is no simple answer. Much of it is probably already in your company. Once you have thought through the questions you wish to ask, the first stage should be to ask around your colleagues. They may well be able to help. If not, here are some other places to look.

The Internet

It was inevitable that we would suggest searching the Internet for information – it is becoming an unparalleled source. It is still an unstructured, rag-bag of data and is likely to stay that way. Having said that, it will offer answers if you take the right approach.

The first thing to do is to look at the web sites of your competitors. If you don't know these already, shame on you. When you look at them, you will often be surprised at how much people say about themselves. Even, in some instances, their intentions for the future. They will certainly give you an idea of the types of customers they are targeting and the methods they are using to do this.

HALF HOUR INTERNET

Take your most important competitor. Check out its web site. Don't know what it is? Shame on you. Try http://www.companyname.com or http://www.companyname.co.xx – 'xx' being your country identifier (for example, 'uk'). If the name has more than one word, try it run together or hyphenated. Either way, enter the company's name in a couple of search engines. Your goal is to find out three important things you didn't know about the company in half an hour.

The next thing to do is to use some search engines to look for less structured information. Using search engines on the Web is becoming easier, but is still more of an art than a science. In general, you will start with a simple query, find that you have an enormous number of matches and gradually make that query more specific until you have a manageable number of responses. If you have not used a search engine before, ones you may want to start with are Alta Vista and Yahoo! Giving specific web addresses is dangerous in a book – the Internet changes faster than the printed word ever can. If these changes mean that the following addresses are out of date when you come to use them, then we apologize. You are on your own. At the time of publication, Alta Vista can be found at:

http://www.altavista.digital.com

and Yahoo! at:

http://www.yahoo.com

Governments

Governments can be a great source of information in many countries. They often compile industry statistics and also require companies to provide a minimum set of information that they then make available to the public. In the UK, this is provided through Companies House. In other countries there are similar central sources.

Libraries

This is often a long shot if you are looking for company-specific data, but is good for the more general questions that will arise as you are pulling together a picture of your competitors and your industry.

Press clippings

An online press service is an invaluable source of data. You will find that many companies court publicity and much will be written about them. Those that do not court publicity tend to have as much written about them because of the perverse sense of justice of the average business journalist.

Your suppliers

A great source of information can be to talk to your suppliers. They may be loath to give specific data about their other customers, but will often be willing to tell you what they are supplying to whom. They will also be well aware of changes in usage of particular raw materials across the industry. If you are seeing a shift in your sales, talking to your suppliers may give you a chance to verify whether this is something that is just affecting you or is an industry-wide phenomenon.

While you are talking to suppliers, you should also take the time to find out how easy you are to deal with relative to your competitors. In the past, there has been a tendency to believe that dealing with your company is a privilege and so suppliers should be grateful for your business. In the world we are proposing, suppliers are your partners. The easier you are to deal with, the more accommodating they are likely to be. Establishing a strong and lasting relationship with suppliers can be a powerful way of beating the competition. This process starts by being easy to deal with. The chances are that you are not. While we aren't suggesting that your suppliers will break business confidences, if you manage to become easy to deal with before your competitors do, you may well find that mutual suppliers are prepared to gossip about them, because now it's 'us' and 'them'.

Your partners

Talking to those businesses you are in partnership with will also give you a fuller picture of the state of the industry. Partnership can be a wide term in this context. For instance, if you belong to an industry body, it is likely that it collects data about that industry. Tap into this. The chances are you've paid for it already, so use it.

Your customers

Your customers are also a great source of information about your competitors. If you have lost customers recently, where have they gone and why? Don't tell us that you can't find the answers to these questions because you've lost the customers – use your imagination. Find a way of asking them. Even if you can track down a small number and the result is statistically insignificant, it doesn't matter. It is still an indication.

What about new customers? Where have they come from? Why have they switched to you? How can you persuade more to do the same?

Yourself

We have already suggested that you search your company for answers to the questions you have set yourself. Now we are saying it again. Do not underestimate the amount of information that is available within your company if you only talk to the right people.

Silver bullets

Some companies use 'silver bullets' – documents about competitors and competitive products that say why the other people's products are much worse than their own. Silver bullets are great, but there are some provisos that are rarely thought about.

Silver bullets are only of value if they're accessible to everyone in the company. Partly because everyone's a salesperson, but also because that way it's more likely to reach the people who really know the competitors' products. If you have silver bullets, you must also have a mechanism for feeding back inaccuracies. An inaccurate silver bullet can blow up in your face. Finally, and most importantly, silver bullets must include the advantages of the competitors' products as well as the disadvantages. It's not enough to know what's wrong with the opposition, you have to know what's better, too.

There's also one very genuine concern about this process. These documents will occasionally fall into the wrong hands. Do you really want to be caught saying that the opposition is better? Yes, if that's what it takes. But make sure that the reason you can say it and be untroubled is because you're doing something about it.

And so?

You might well be reading this chapter and saying to yourself that there is nothing particularly mindblowing or startling here; it is all fairly straightforward. That is true. Competitor analysis is not rocket science. We would be willing to bet, though, that those of you who are most strongly critical of the fact that this is common sense are among the worst culprits in terms of not doing it.

Like a lot of business, there is no magic wand that will take away all of your problems and make life easy for you. If you are looking for one, perhaps you should be reading a spell book rather than a business book.

Success often comes down to applied common sense, a dose of luck and a good idea or two that your competitors haven't yet had. We can provide some of the common sense and a few good ideas. The luck is down to you.

So, you have decided what you want to know, you have answered all of your self-imposed questions by means of analysis, anecdotes or guesswork and you have a strong picture of what your competitors have done, are doing and are likely to do. What now?

You can bet that while you have been doing this there is at least one competitor who has been doing the same thing to you. How do you beat this approach?

The DisOrganized company has an advantage because it is harder to track and inherently more flexible than a traditional company. The only real way to confound the competition is to build unpredictability into your processes. As somebody from one company said recently (and neither of us can remember who it was or where we heard it), 'Our philosophy is to run like hell and then change direction.'

19

Communication: targets and vehicles

- Communication in its own right
- It's too important to leave entirely to an agency
- Why the Internet matters
- Making communications simple
- Setting objectives for communication

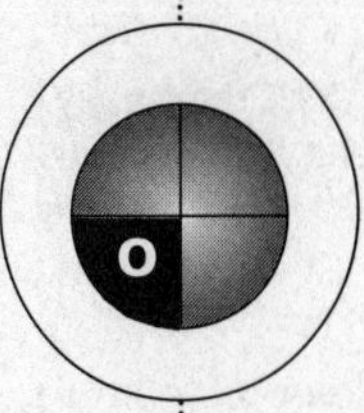

Is there more?

It's tempting to think that we've said everything that has to be said about communications already. After all, we've looked at our staff, customers, products and the systems to make communication work in the hypercompany. What more is there? There's a special aspect of communications that haven't been covered. It's like the difference between a TV broadcast and a letter. Each is a way of communicating, but the approach has to be very different, because a broadcast is not aimed at a single individual. Whether you are narrowcasting to a small segment or truly broadcasting, there's an extra layer of communication that isn't covered adequately by the other channels.

I'm just a simple business person

That's all right, though. There's nothing for you to worry about. You've got an advertising agency handling your ads, a PR company handling the press and an Internet specialist building and managing your web site. No worries – or is that dinosaur thinking? There isn't a straight answer. If you can say with your hand on your heart that your agency, PR company and web designers are true parts of your hypercompany, fine. If not, worry.

We certainly aren't saying that expertise in these areas is unnecessary, but the way that these agencies work with your mini companies is liable to be drastically different to the way they interact with the old dinosaur. Mini companies will expect to have more freedom in the way that they advertise and deal with the press. The DisOrganized company will also expect to have more creative input than has traditionally been the case. Remember, creativity is an essential part of the DisOrganization armoury. If your staff are trained in creativity, should they really be handing over creative control of advertising to an outside agency that knows about as much about your product as the average American knows about the game of cricket?

ADVERTISING

'Half the money I spend on advertising is wasted, and the trouble is I don't know which half.'

Viscount Leverhulme (William Hesketh Lever)

Yes, the advertising agency has some expertise you won't have. In advertising production, in placement and so on. But what makes you (or them) think that they have a monopoly on bright ideas? In fact, if you are creativity trained and they aren't (ask your advertising people today: what training have they got in scientific creativity techniques), maybe you ought to be thinking of reducing their fees. And certainly having a lot more of an input. Being creativity trained won't make you a graphics designer or a film director, but it will give you more original ideas than the copycat advertising that you often see.

As for the PR company, try it out from the journalist's point of view. Even if you regularly test your own customer service, how often have you tried out your service to journalists – some of your most important (if not paying) customers. PR companies vary hugely in how much support they give a journalist and how proactive they are. They vary in how much they use a whole range of communication channels themselves (some seem to think there hasn't been anything new since the fax). Some will really deliver, searching out the right information, getting the right contacts to call the journalist direct. Others think it's enough to pass on a telephone number – a directory would do a similar job and be much cheaper. Next time you're asked to give an interview, establish a dialogue with the journalist. How was it for them?

If you have in-house PR and use an agency, think hard about how the relationship is split. In a DisOrganized company, do you really need both? After all, an in-house PR mini company is no different to an external PR agency. Are they doing the job? If so, why use someone else? If not, why use them?

Web site design is the most tempting job of all to parcel out, giving little input yourself. It's all far too technical. Grow up – that's like saying you can't cope with a pen and paper because you don't know how ballpoint pens work.

If you are dealing with web business, you ought to ensure you have a basic familiarity with web design. Use a friendly package (there are plenty about now) to build a personal web page. Understand the basics of what you are doing, and what the web site can do for you. Then, go to your web developer with all the same considerations you would take to your advertising agency. You might not be able to program in Java, but you can certainly have some excellent creative ideas about what you want to put across on your site and how it might feel – it's down to the developer to make it reality. If you are using your web site to sell, not just to advertise, you need to take to it all the consideration you put into customer service in any other medium. The Web will be like a shop for you – make sure it's as attractive and as business-driven as an actual, physical shop.

Mark Adams is Director of international PR group Text 100 Group PLC. Mark has over 20 years' experience in the PR industry and cofounded Text 100 with his partner Tom Lewis. He has worked to build the company from a two-man operation in 1981 to the largest technology PR company in Europe. Mark is renowned as an innovator of PR methodology and creative thinking. This is applied to both existing campaigns and the industry in general. Using PR as an effective part of the marketing mix and as a tool for brand support are his key areas of interest.

Has organizational structure any impact on communications?

'Organizational structure' is an outdated term. Does a building have structure? Yes. A statue? Yes. Does a tree have structure? No – it has form. Does a newt have structure? No, it has shape. Future-changing organizations, as opposed to old-fashioned organizations, are not structured. They have form and shape. They evolve and change that shape or form in the wind, as they grow, as they move.

So the question should be: 'Has organizational form or shape any impact on communications?' Yes – structured companies communicate in a structured way – they talk when they want to, they summon meetings, they make announcements.

Modern organizations with shape and form communicate differently – informally, *ad hoc*, frequently and little rather than much and seldom. They are in their environments, not above them and so their communication is always interpreted and fed back to them. Their communication is much more two-way then it ever was for the structured company.

Are conventional media doomed?

No, no, no, no, no. They have grown in importance. The paperless office is a myth – consumption of print media is growing. It is fragmenting, but it's more plentiful than ever. TV and radio are conventional and they're fine. The real conventional media is talking (really old-fashioned), but it is the one which the organization of the future will use more and more – Internet will grow, paper will grow and talking will grow – there will be more communication.

What PR problems can an international marketplace raise that don't appear in a purely domestic business?

None. Well, that's wrong – many, but they are more in the mind of communicating companies than in the reality. Example: if you want maximum market penetration in the UK (say, for telephone companies – BT versus Mercury), you target groups – both telephone companies going for expatriates from Australia and the Asian population to get them to make long-distance calls. This is fragmented marketing. The company that does good fragmented marketing will have no problem doing international marketing – it's one and the same (I've been running a German PR company for five years by the way).

When content can be changed as frequently as the Internet allows, should advertising be handled differently?
No – advertising is a mood/fashion form of communication which changes frequently anyway. It needs to change more, like daily newspapers, but it's already well-prepared to do that. Advertising is a performance. The Internet is a stage. A poster site is a stage.

Why should a corporation not handle PR internally?
We are a PR company. We have two PR agencies working for us. Why? Because they bring an outside perspective. A company that does its own PR will be good at doing messages which say 'We are great' and 'We are wonderful'. A company which uses an outside agency will be able to build these into stories which mean something to audiences, which move audiences and which generate reaction from audiences. Companies are far too close to themselves to be capable of ever being really close to their audiences.

Also – is PR a core competency? It may well be for some companies of the future, but at the moment it's not. So, outsource it – every company these days is focusing on core skills and outsourcing other stuff.

How do you organize a PR agency for most effective results?
Like a growing bag. Lots of fertilizer and a few well-chosen seeds. The seeds grow if the fertilizer creates the environment for them to thrive in. The PR company is as organized as it is disorganized because people who communicate (communicate is the wrong word for PR – we 'build relationships') are creative and challenging, as well as managed and measured. We have small groups – clear goals and lots of freedom to do it 'your way'.

'We're not a computer company – the Internet doesn't matter to us'

Of course. Can't you just picture it? Caxton comes around with his new, exciting product – the printed book. 'It's not really for us', says Town Cryer Limited. 'The church might be interested, they're into books, but to be honest, the monks can turn out as many handwritten jobs as they need. As for us, we're just not into paper technology. Our job is transmitting the news to the masses, paper and print is nothing to do with us.'

We've already said that you ought to have a hand in any use you make of the Internet, but too often companies feel that there's no need for them to be there at all. It's not entirely surprising, given the early history of the medium. Many companies felt they had to have a site 'because everyone else is getting one', but without any good commercial reason or any business strategy in doing so.

The trouble with the Internet is that it is both a tremendous opportunity and a nightmare. The opportunity is that of reaching millions upon millions of people worldwide. Only a tiny percentage of them need to get to you through your site to make it a rich source of income. The nightmare is that the Internet – or, rather, the World Wide Web, the glitzy part of the Internet you are liable to use – is an immense morass of information. There are search systems and indexes, but a lot of them are incomplete or out of date. There could be customers out there dying to get to you who will never even know you exist.

Yet, just because the Internet is problematic, it doesn't mean that you can afford to ignore it. The investment required to become involved is fairly small. Provided you use it well – and many firms don't to begin with – you will get an impressive long-term return. Most of all, though, forget the idea that the Internet is about computers. It's a communications medium, just like TV or radio or newspapers. It has its own special characteristics that mean it has to be treated quite differently, but the computing part is incidental. You don't need to worry about the immensely complicated technology underlying modern television to get something out of it, so don't worry about computers either. The Internet is an information medium: as far as you are concerned, it is a sales and marketing opportunity.

Entranet's Managing Director Nick Spooner emphasizes how the Internet will come into business, like it or not:

> 'For the current generation, it's not part of their consciousness. For the next generation, it won't be a problem. The Internet's kind of like the wheel. After all, it took the telephone 25 or 30 years to get going. The Internet has gone from static sites to applications in three. People *will* begin to exploit it. We are breeding Internet-literate people. It'll develop like the wheel.'

Micro-franchising

The Internet has provided the environment in which entirely new ways of doing business can develop. A classic example is the micro-franchise. This brings together three groups of people in an unusual win–win–win business example.

The most mature example of micro-franchising is the Internet bookshop business. General bookshops can't have in-depth expertise in every subject they cover. At the same time, there are enthusiasts on the Web who are steeped in knowledge in their particular subject, but have no outlet for their expertise. A micro-franchise combines the two. The expert can recommend books in a particular subject and put a button on their site that lets a browser go to a bookshop and buy the book. So, the shop benefits. The expert benefits because they get a small commission and because it gives their web site more utility. The third party to benefit is the customer, who gets much better-informed opinions than would be possible in any other form of bookshop.

There will be much more micro-franchising, and other new web business models developing rapidly over the next few years.

MICRO-FRANCHISE

For an example of a micro-franchise, see the business/creativity bookshop at: http://www.cul.co.uk.books

Who are you reaching, how?

You can imagine a continuum of vehicles along an axis with 'direct means' at one end and 'indirect means' at the other – from the face-to-face sales call, through point-of-purchase contact, telephone, e-mail, fax, letter, customer service support, Internet site, advertising and promotion to company image. For any individual sender, the direct channels are likely to be available at a higher cost than the indirect ones for a given audience size. For any individual recipient of communication, the direct channels are likely to be more compelling and convincing than the indirect ones. (See Figure 19.1 for a summary of the target and vehicle options.)

Figure 19.1
Target/vehicle options matrix

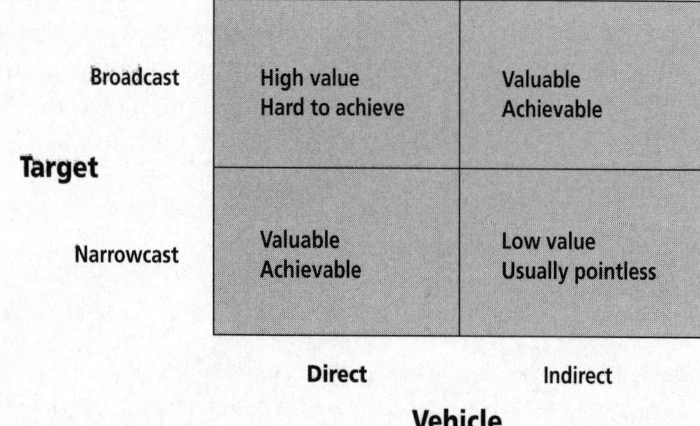

In general, there will be a path from narrowcast and direct to broadcast and indirect, but there will be some high-value items that *feel* direct despite being broadcast. Carefully targeted direct mail might be an example of this. If it is done well, the recipient feels that you are talking directly to them, but the sender's costs are kept low. This is not the same as a 'You, MR JONES, are the lucky recipient of ...'. Such letters look and feel broadcast. The indirect narrowcast is likely to be of low value at all times. The value of the items on the trend line will depend on the context, but the best at each position are likely to be of similar value in relation to cost.

How to ...

- make communications simple;
- set objectives for communications;
- make use of the Internet;
- deal with the Internet's worldwide market.

Making communications simple

As we have seen, communications are the lifeblood of any company, but doubly so when you are DisOrganized. The mini company structure and the leadership approach both demand excellent communications, yet there's something more – simplicity. Software publishers spend millions on making their products more usable, yet, frighteningly, few of them are simple. The humble VCR, a very everyday product, still proves a problem for many customers when it comes to programming the timer. It's not just a matter of making communications available, the DisOrganized company has to make them *simple*.

USABILITY

The usability (or lack of it) of everyday products is a great lesson for business as a whole.
See D. A. Norman's *The Psychology of Everyday Things* (Basic Books, 1988).

Take e-mail. E-mail is an absolute essential of the DisOrganized company. Not necessarily within the mini company, because the mini company's size often makes it easier to use informal, face-to-face communication, but all the time across the hypercompany. In a small way, this book is the product of a hypercompany. Each of the authors runs an independent consultancy. Our mini companies are collaborating on the book. Because we are located 70 miles apart, face-to-face interaction is not always practical, so chapters and thoughts are constantly flying back and forth.

What does making e-mail simple entail? First, putting e-mail in its proper place. It isn't trivial. It isn't a nice-to-have item. It is an essential part of the workings of the company and should be treated as such – from top to bottom of the organization. That means giving it enough resources. It also means e-mail being taken seriously by the whole organization, from the top down. Listen to John Ruscoe, an employee of UK computer firm ICL who teleworks from a sheep farm in the remote Orkney Islands: 'I have access to everyone in ICL by e-mail. It's considered my right to mail the Chief Executive if I need to – and to get a reply. That mutual respect is what's needed more than anything else.' Treating e-mail right actually influences corporate culture.

Then there's *doing* e-mail right. There's no excuse for still having mainframe-based e-mail. There's no excuse for an e-mail system that doesn't connect to the Internet or can't send attached files. There's no excuse for e-mail that can't simply be cut and pasted into and out of documents or that can't send the whole document. E-mail should be capable of handling simple things like routing a message around a chain of people, picking up their comments. It should do what you need, without causing you trouble.

All of this is possible with off-the-shelf products available today. There's room for improvement, particularly in terms of simplicity, but there is hardly a company that couldn't vastly improve its e-mail if making it simple was considered mission-critical.

Once you've got e-mail sorted out, there's your intranet. The Internet is great; a company with more than a handful of people needs an internal equivalent for sharing the information that is needed to make DisOrganization work. Remember that the World Wide Web was devised by the people working in laboratories at CERN in Geneva with the sharing of information in mind. It's an ideal vehicle for making access to information simple. Alongside your e-mail, in the mission-critical slot, should sit your intranet.

Setting objectives for communications

In simple terms, the process for working through communication vehicles and targets looks something like Figure 19.2.

The final objectives lead on to buying decisions, creative input, tailored events, informational broadcasts, placed press items, customer service strategy and so forth.

An important consideration when deciding why you are communicating depends on the company versus product and tactical versus strategic dimensions. Company versus product describes whether you communicate at a company or a more specific level. Tactical versus strategic is about whether you are communicating in order to place yourself in the general thinking of the targets or have a specific, tactical objective in mind. For instance, letting people know of an event or sale.

One deciding factor (by no means the only one) for the communications spend is your share of voice. In other words, how loud and

Figure 19.2
Generating communications objectives

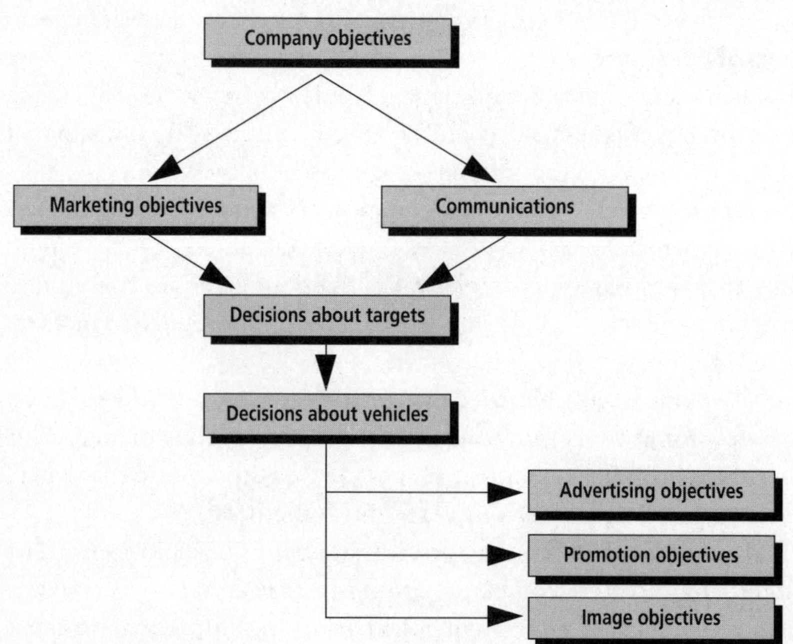

how frequently you communicate in comparison to your competitors. Actually, it might be better to say how well you are heard because share of voice is more about what is received than what is broadcast – despite its description.

All in all, the more we look into advertising and promotion, the more we believe that there are few clear, guiding rules and that those that do exist are there to be broken. You must use your judgement. If you don't trust your judgement, find someone whose judgement you do trust.

Making use of the Internet

As the Internet is just another medium, how are you going to make the best use of it? First, we need to qualify that word 'just'. For most users, the Internet is a 'pay as you view' medium, involving a considerable outlay per minute compared with TV. For that reason, avoid pure advertising. No one likes to pay money just to see an advertisement. Advertise, certainly, but do it as a minor part of a desirable service. Remember the old 'message from our sponsors' – fine, but you have to sponsor something.

You can do that in three ways. The simplest option is to buy advertising space on an existing popular site, such as one of the big search engines. Second, you can provide a free service that people will want anyway – it needn't have anything to do with your business, but should be attractive, usable information, such as airline timetables or TV schedules. Third, you can advertise by providing easy access to your product range – your *whole* product range. In the early days of commerce on the Internet, many companies dabbled, sticking a toe into the water by putting a small subset of their range on the Web. Then not many people were biting, so they concluded that the Internet was not a good sales channel. Rubbish. Who wants to go into a shop that only sells half a dozen products? The whole advantage of Web shopping should be easy access to a bigger than usual range.

Do all this, and you can still fail. Remember the problems of visibility. Nick Spooner, Managing Director of the UK electronic commerce firm Entranet, is clear about the importance of being seen, whether it's coming top of the list on a search engine or via conventional marketing. Don't underplay conventional marketing. When Entranet produced a site for insurance company Eagle Star, it got over 130 articles into the media, including front-page coverage in *The Sunday Times* newspaper. People aren't necessarily going to trawl the Web on the off chance that there's a site selling leather goods or business consultancy, but if they're looking for your products and services and see your site address in the newspapers, they're going to take notice. As Internet commerce becomes more and more common, this approach will become harder. Having a Web site won't be news in itself: you will have to use your creativity to come up with new and exciting reasons why you can make the news.

For the DisOrganized firm, the Internet is a natural vehicle. Part of the communications linking the mini companies is liable to be an intranet, so everyday familiarity with the possibilities of the Internet is liable to be greater than in a conventional firm. The creativity inherent in a DisOrganized firm will come in useful all along the line.

Dealing with the Internet's worldwide market

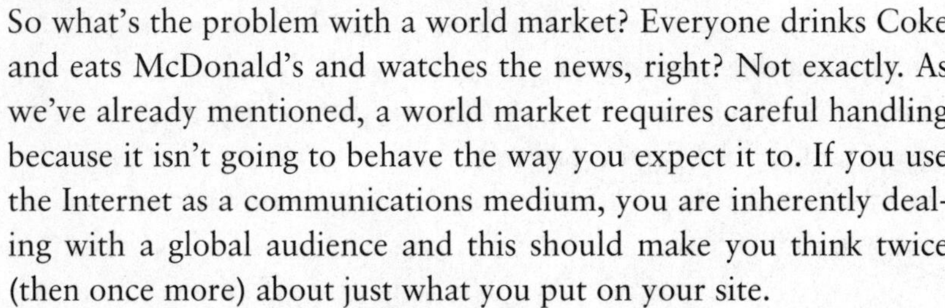

LOCAL DIFFICULTIES

In the early days of personal recommendation, Coca-Cola had a film star of Italian extraction eulogize about the product. To paraphrase, she said, 'We always drink Coke at home, only in Italy we call it Pepsi.' Oops.

So what's the problem with a world market? Everyone drinks Coke and eats McDonald's and watches the news, right? Not exactly. As we've already mentioned, a world market requires careful handling because it isn't going to behave the way you expect it to. If you use the Internet as a communications medium, you are inherently dealing with a global audience and this should make you think twice (then once more) about just what you put on your site.

If you have contact numbers or addresses, make sure they are usable outside your own country. Monitor where your business is coming from. There are plenty of Internet businesses that trade more outside their own country than they do within it. The UK's Internet bookshops, for instance, have found that around 75 per cent of their business is from overseas – and not all from the US either; in fact, continental Europe is the largest market segment. If you can pin a big customer base down to a specific country, consider having a set of pages in the appropriate language. It's only polite.

Bearing in mind the diversity of the global market, there is even more need than usual to make everything possible from many different approaches. Whether it's the way you can find a product or the options for payment, the more options you have the better. Remember, also, that the global nature of the market works both ways. The Internet Bookshop has another fine example of this in action. Books in the UK are often considerably more expensive than they are in the US, yet often exactly the same book is available in both countries. Using the database power that gives it the edge over a traditional shop, the Internet Bookshop offers books sourced from the UK or the US. You can choose whichever you prefer – and the savings can be as much as 50 per cent. The customer is happy. The

Internet Bookshop is happy. OK, authors and publishers aren't (we shouldn't really be telling you this – but a cheap sale is better than none at all), still, the lessons for working the global marketplace are clear. Don't be parochial; your own company's sphere probably has similar opportunities to those found by the Internet Bookshop. Grasp them before the competition does.

20

DisOrganization: outward channels

Each major section of *DisOrganization* is summarized in one of these mini chapters.

The bridge

Products and services form a bridge between the inward and outward channels. They are central to a company's communication to the world and so must form a large part of the outward channels, but they also drive the shape and type of activity taking place within the company. In providing your products and services, take away all of the complexity that you can from your customers – make their lives as simple as possible. Continually develop new products, yet, at the same time, be prepared to build on the good ideas that you or your competitors have already had. Learn to kill off existing products. Without someone who is prepared to kill them off, old products will never die, they will only drain resources. Finally, keep the selling process as close as possible to the manufacturing and development process. Keeping it all in the same mini company is ideal if possible. Having a closely linked sales mini company may be a necessary compromise.

Life would be easy without customers

Customers are vital to your business, though. That is such a truism that no one even hears it any more. If they are so vital, why aren't you doing all of the right things for them all of the time? The answer is focus, or lack of it. You keep being distracted by the unimportant but urgent trivia. The focus on customers must also take account of regional variations. The world is *not* a village; different cultures demand different approaches. The bottom line is being prepared to listen to customers and setting up mechanisms that facilitate this.

We are not alone

If customers are vital to you today, in the world of the mini company, partnerships become almost as important. Business must move from the analogy of warfare, rivalry and conflict to one of partnership. The DisOrganization message involves breaking up companies.

Many within current organizations would regard most – or even all – of what they do as core to their business. Our contention is that this is untrue and that almost everything you do could be done more effectively by small, focused partners. The benefits of partnership are support, production and product focus, synergy, global focus and networking.

The bad guys?

Despite the importance of partnership, competition is, and will remain, a reality of business life. To compete effectively you need to know a great deal about your competitors. That information is available to you if you are clear about what you want and set about searching for it systematically. Build the skeleton of the information you want, flesh out the skeleton and then make it live by adding stories and anecdotes. Gather only the data that will make a difference; do not be tempted to boil the ocean for a cup of tea. Similarly, do not rely on your own existing prejudices. Good information is supported by data, not supposition. While avoiding supposition, remember that estimates may well be OK for your needs. There is a wide range of sources of the data you need. Learn about those sources that are most useful to your industry. Finally, in order to avoid becoming transparent to your competitors, work at building unpredictability into your processes.

Pure communications

Many of the outward channels have focused on communication, but there are some aspects of communication – advertising, PR and, increasingly, the Internet – that need special handling. At the heart of communication is a need to make it simple and appealing to the audience. This may mean a local focus for a local message, but, with a DisOrganized company, this should not be too rigid.

The wheel

We have now covered all of the elements that make up the centre of the DisOrganization map. We only have the outer circle to go, so stick with it, you're almost there! Monitoring and starting over may not seem the most glamorous aspects of DisOrganization, but they are crucial for continued success.

PART FIVE

The cycle

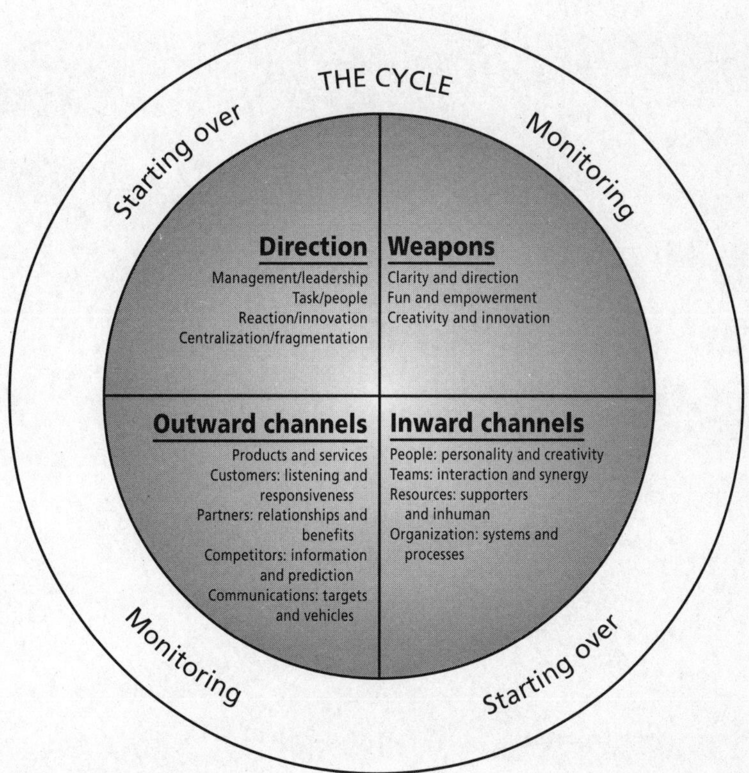

21

Monitoring

- The need for monitoring
- Measurement as an end in itself
- The balanced scorecard
- Considering the environment

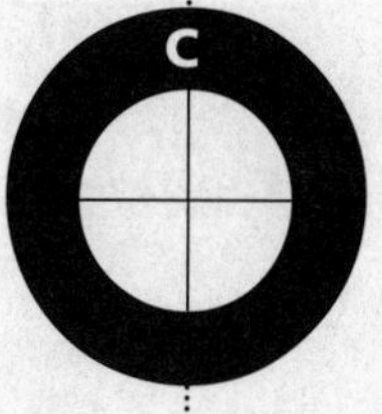

What gets measured gets done

Measurement is essential. It seems to be true that in business what gets measured gets done. If this is the case, how is it that so many measurement systems become corrupted to the point where they seem to work against your company rather than for it?

Take the Management By Objectives movement, through which many of us have lived. This shifted from a great white hope to a huge millstone around the necks of many companies. So many schemes have crashed and burned in similar ways that you have to wonder if it is possible to develop a sensible monitoring system that will last.

Objectives initially mean something – they are genuinely important to the business. Over time, the measurement system becomes an end in itself rather than a means to achieve business success. This happens faster if, as is often the case, responsibility for monitoring business success is put into the hands of the accountants. Their view of what constitutes success is often so monochrome, so single-minded and so lacking in life that it is bound to end in tears. How can profitability be a motivator to the bulk of the people in a company? It doesn't have a direct impact on their everyday lives. Even with a profit-sharing or wide share ownership scheme, the link between action and reward is so separate, so tenuous as to be non-existent. So, how can an objective that is primarily based on money fire people up? It can't.

Worse still, traditional financial measures have a control focus that is a hangover from the industrial age. We measure performance to monitor compliance with systems as much as to measure return. This cannot work with a business that is trying to release the individual, allow innovative action and encourage the offbeat and quirky.

NEEDS SCHMEEDS

A. H. Maslow, *Motivation and Personality* (Harper & Row, 1954).

Most people come to work each day for a whole variety of reasons. A. H. Maslow defined a hierarchy of needs.

Maslow said that individuals are not merely motivated by money. Instead there are five levels of need.

1 *Physiological* This is the money level. It is the basics of food, shelter and so on.

2 *Security* These will only be considered once the physiological needs have been taken care of. These are physical security and ongoing employment security.

3 *Social* To a greater or lesser extent, individuals require acceptance by society. These needs will be considered after the first two.

4 *Esteem* After acceptance, individuals require recognition and authority.

5 *Self-actualization* At this, the highest level, the individual is looking for personal fulfilment. This involves achieving life goals; striving for the limits of personal accomplishment.

People need money, certainly, but once they've got it, what then? If you want your people working with you, you need to offer them more than just pay and even more than security of tenure. For too long the implicit message has been, 'Help us to make a profit and we'll continue to employ you.' It isn't enough any more.

We're not suggesting that you need to find alternative ways to bribe people. The actual approach we advocate is at once far simpler and far more difficult than that. What people will work for is a set of objectives that recognize the range of reasons that motivate them to come to work. Astoundingly, if employees are given these things at work, this also seems to offer a path to business success.

Measurement with action

Finance Director of financial services provider Allied Dunbar, Brian Thomas, is clear that the way to keep measurement valid is to link it to action:

> If you know what you are trying to achieve, it gives you a clear point of reference. What matters is trying to do it in a pragmatic way rather than as bureaucratic overkill. Either you can work together to get results or focus on why someone didn't deliver. Action-oriented reform is so much more constructive.
>
> In finance, we don't issue a report without an action section. You can't just send out data or information. It's a simple rule, but very effective. It says to the financial professional, just stop a minute, you need to make a recommendation to the budget holder. This action orientation alters the relationship. The result is that the finance professional works with the business unit to

make sure what's recommended gets accepted. So, for example, a monthly expenses report actually *does* something.

Size no longer matters

BALANCED SCORECARDS

See Robert S. Kaplan and David P. Norton, 'The Balanced Scorecard: Measures that drive success', *Harvard Business Review*, January–February 1992), 'Putting the Balanced Scorecard to Work', *Harvard Business Review*, September–October 1993, and 'Using the Balanced Scorecard as a Strategic Management System', *Harvard Business Review*, January–February 1996.

The best approach to measurement that we have seen so far is the Balanced Scorecard system developed by Robert Kaplan and David Norton.

Their contention is that this need to change from the traditional focus on profit has been brought about by the information revolution. Perhaps the need has always been there, but the information revolution has made industry dominance harder, and so success based on size is no longer an option.

Before business became as fast-paced, chaotic and downright unpredictable as it is now, it was relatively easy for an industry giant to corner a market to a degree where they were all but untouchable. To be frank, it wouldn't have mattered if measurement systems had been based on the depth of the decorative lake at company headquarters, they would still have been successful.

The inherent inefficiency of large organizations means that economies of scale have never existed in the ways indicated by traditional economists. Large companies have often paid more for their resources, more for their people and achieved a lower unit return than small companies. The reason economies of scale appear to have existed is because of the economies of dominance. It is control of markets, not control of the means of production, that has allowed long-term success for large organizations.

Now it isn't so easy. Success is no longer a given – no matter how well you have stitched up markets. The upheaval in communication and information means that someone will be able to take away some of your customers by means of channels you didn't even know existed. So you had better identify the key indicators for your business and measure them now. If nothing else, at least you'll know you're sinking even if you haven't seen the iceberg. There is even a hope that you won't hit it just yet and may be able to change course before you do.

The Internet doesn't matter

A classic example of the market turning is the development of the Internet in the latter part of the 1990s. Software marketer *par excellence* Microsoft had set up its own communications network and considered the Internet peripheral to the way forward. Then the small start-up company Netscape made Internet browsing easy and, within a ludicrously short time, owned the most popular application software in existence.

It's a measure of Microsoft's skill and ability to monitor the right things that the company was able to turn on a dime and move to a position where the Internet was the core of its development strategy. So successful was the turnabout that, as we write, Microsoft's web browser is about to overtake Netscape's in popularity. An old-fashioned company that assumed its market dominance as a birthright would have foundered.

Microsoft's Chairman Bill Gates has a reputation for pushing his organization and his staff to the limits all the time. This is in part because there is no complacency in Gates' vision. For him, fear is a real motivator. In an interview with the *Wall Street Journal*, Gates said, 'You always have to be thinking about who is coming to get you.'

The Balanced Scorecard

The Balanced Scorecard is a method of monitoring a range of indicators. To keep the accountants happy, one set is financial. There are, however, three other sets that are in no way subordinate to money in importance. These are internal business processes, learning and growth and finally, the customer.

The message is that you should not be choosing between financial measures and operational measures or staff-focused measures and customer-focused measures because they are *all* important. The Balanced Scorecard allows you to pull them together into a single coherent picture. In a few years' time, the Balanced Scorecard will probably go the way of other measurement schemes and fall out of favour. This will not be because it does not work, but because it will be seen to have failed in a few prominent cases. These prominent cases will be businesses that have installed the Balanced Scorecard as

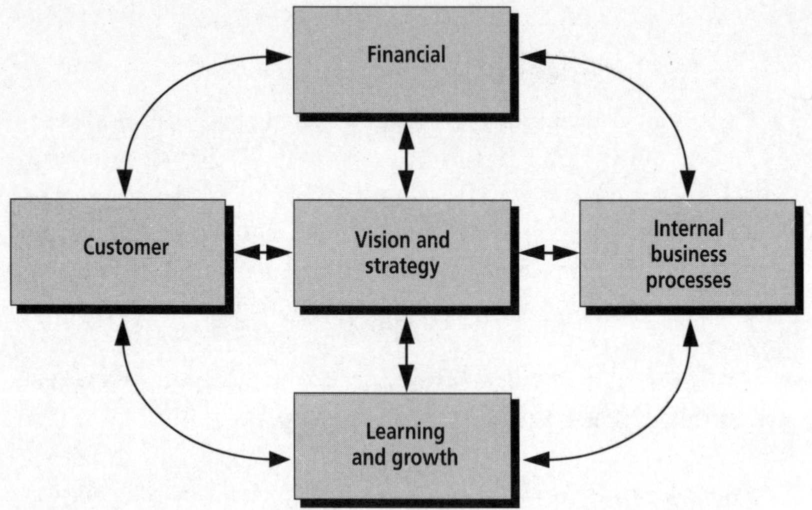

Figure 21.1
The Balanced Scorecard system of monitoring business indicators

a measurement system, but have given dominance to the financial measures and paid lip-service to the rest.

So, what do the measures look like in each box? The glib answer is that they look simple yet crucial. On second thoughts, maybe that isn't so glib. They really must be simple to be easily understood and communicated and they really must be crucial if they are to make a difference. A more useful answer, though, may be to pose the questions that Kaplan and Norton pose for each of the boxes.

- *Financial* 'To succeed financially, how should we appear to our shareholders?' So, here there should be a handful of measures that would allow the shareholders to judge the health and wealth of their business.
- *Internal business processes* 'To satisfy our shareholders and customers, what business processes must we excel at?' Here you shift the bias away from the shareholders and give more weight to those processes that support the customer.
- *Learning and growth* 'To achieve our vision, how will we sustain our ability to change and improve?' This set of measures (with some help from the previous ones) will determine how well you support your people in their efforts to support your customers.
- *Customer* 'To achieve our vision, how should we appear to our customers?' These are your most outward-facing measures. These are the ones that let you know how you are succeeding and failing in the eyes of the customer. And remember, success and failure are no longer measured solely in terms of your immediate competitors.

You no longer know who will be taking the next customer away from you. They may not even produce what you produce or offer the service that you offer. You must now measure your customer service against every other business anywhere, in any sector.

'A can of soup and a mortgage, please'

In the UK, banks have traditionally had only one form of competitor – the building society, a mutual organization for savings and house loans. If, five year ago, you had asked the banks where the major threat to them came from, they would probably have said the move of building societies into profit-making banking. This move has taken place, but a potentially more significant threat, which took the banks by surprise, was the move of supermarkets into banking. With a network of shops, good financial strength and increasingly powerful customer loyalty schemes, the supermarkets stand to make significant inroads into banking, provided that they can overcome a customer image that banks have to be staid and solid. UK banks are certainly entering interesting times.

Developing the Balanced Scorecard

There are a few important points about developing the Balanced Scorecard that are relevant to any business or any unit within a business.

First, don't overdo the measures. A few (a very few) indicators within each box will tell you what you need to know if you have picked the right ones.

Second, don't regard any of the boxes as inherently more or less important than others. Once you start doing this you lose the balance and slide back into the eagerly waiting maws of the accountants.

Third, simplify the creation and measurement of items within each box and then simplify again, and then again. The tendency of every business is to move towards lumbering bureaucracy with schemes like this. It is almost as though those at the top of an organization do not care that they are wasting huge amounts of time in the collection and collation of useless data. 'I am important, let them work damn it!' This tendency has not spelled success in the past and is unlikely to do so in the future.

The fourth, and final, point is that you need to involve others in the creation of measures, but remember that, at the end of the day, the person leading is the person being most directly measured. If you are the person leading, you must be the final arbiter. Make unreasonable requests by all means. Stretch people by all means. Never allow your views to limit the scope of the measures and never push them into the unachievable.

The criticism that has been made of the Balanced Scorecard is that it is often values-based rather than results-based. That is, the measures in the scorecard reflect the views and values of the leaders of the business and that everyone else in the business must accept these. However, we would say that they do and they must! Business leaders will continue to act in accord with their beliefs and values regardless of the measurement system in place. Indeed, this could be seen as one of the reasons for the failure of Management by Objectives. Offered a set of measures that did not fully accord with their beliefs and values, the managers of a business did not change what was fundamental to them – they merely fudged the measures.

The fifth box

It is arguable that there is a fifth box that isn't shown in the Kaplan and Norton model. This encloses the other four boxes and is labelled 'Environment'.

It is an unwise company these days that does not consider its attitude to the environment to be an important factor in its success. Even if we ignored the moral imperative to consider the effects our business actions have on the environment, sheer customer pressure would make it a necessity. Not only that, but rightly or wrongly, everyone who has entered the education system since the mid 1970s has been given a dogmatic line that environmental concerns are right with a capital R and business pressures are wrong with a capital W. Whether or not you agree, this public conditioning requires the environment to be part of the scorecard.

The Balanced Scorecard and DisOrganization

The thinking we have discussed so far has been developed with traditional companies in mind, but can we use the scorecard with DisOrganization?

In some ways, the Balanced Scorecard is an ideal measuring tool for the DisOrganized company. It covers a range of measures that work well with individual responsibility and devolution of power. It already has, built in, the concept of high-level scorecards that disaggregate down to successively lower levels. All that is needed is an explanation of how it works for the hypercompany, the net company and the mini company.

At the mini company level, everything is relatively straightforward. The maintenance of the scorecard and any disaggregation within the company would work in the same way as with any small organization.

There is a potential issue about who sets the objectives. Is this done within the mini company or does the net company have a say? Not directly. The mini company has an interest in meeting net company objectives, but only because it regards the net company and other mini companies as customers. Any failure on the part of a mini company to meet the needs of other mini companies or of the net company could result in them losing work in the future. The net company has no role in applying sanctions for failure to set or meet certain targets. Indeed, the very notion of any one net company becoming involved in the internal affairs of a mini company that may work for a range of hypercompanies is somewhat ludicrous. The sanctions come when a mini company loses business because it fails to deliver.

So, what of the net company? Where do its objectives come from? In some ways this is far harder. The net company will need to embody the objectives of the hypercompany as the hypercompany cannot set and monitor its own performance. It is too ephemeral for that. It will also need to set objectives that determine its own performance in managing the network of mini companies. To an extent this is little different to a traditional organization that sets objectives at a high level and then cascades them to lower levels. The crucial difference is that there is no cascade. The requirements of a mini company are defined by other mini companies. The success of the net company is determined by how well it manages to influence, rather than control, interactions in order to achieve the aims of the hypercompany.

What did they say?

There is something about monitoring and measurement that makes it particularly tedious to read about. You have probably, by now, forgotten a lot of what you have just read, so it is time for a brief summary.

What gets measured gets done. What gets rewarded gets done first. Measurement must focus on outputs, not on inputs. Measurement involves far more than mere money. Measurement is about a few objectives well-monitored, rather than thousands of data points. The recording of measures must be simplified to the point that it is invisible; it must never be seen as an overhead. Mini companies must measure obsessively their success at delivering to other mini companies and their end-customers. Net companies must measure the objectives of the hypercompany and their own network management. They may measure the performance of mini companies if this is useful, but they have no sanctions to apply.

So, go out, and start monitoring better.

22

Starting over

- A continuous process of change
- Helping staff deal with a lack of stability
- Problems for old established firms
- Problems for startups

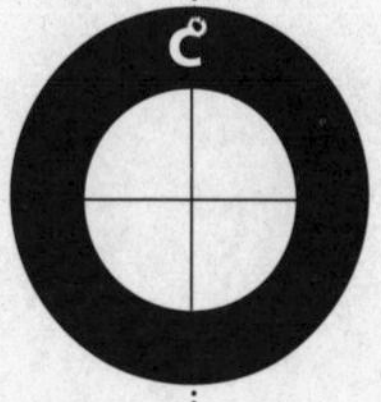

Here we go round the mulberry bush

Change is an uncomfortable bedfellow. We all benefit from having challenge in our lives, but constant change gets in the way of everything. It seems to be generally accepted that if you are going to make a change, you should get it over with as quickly as possible and then reassert stability. How, though, does this fit with a picture of a world where the ground is always shifting? It may be comfortable for us to desire stability, but how realistic is it under such circumstances?

If you aren't lucky enough to be handling a start-up, the DisOrganized company will have gone through a degree of trauma in moving to a DisOrganized state. It is important to overcome any after-effects of the change, but, equally, it's necessary to prepare everyone for more change ahead.

Historically, large companies have enjoyed an illusory stability and safety that small companies lacked. With the move to mini companies, that apparent stability will disappear. What will remain constant – what it's necessary to focus on – is the broad direction and the underlying principles. What will indubitably change are ways of working, types of customers, products, perhaps even the work environment. It's a tough one. Much of the requirement for DisOrganization can be driven principally by the mini company structure itself, backed up by the other vehicles. Here, leadership and creativity will be paramount.

We've just DisOrganized, though, surely that's enough? Sorry, no. By now Lewis Carroll's picture of the White Queen having to run just to stay in the same place has become a cliché, but it doesn't make it less true. Change will continue, and continue to be needed. DisOrganization is often about a major shift in the way a company is run, but then it continues to require change as the environment and product range vary. DisOrganization isn't just a linear process; there's a cyclical element, too, requiring regular revisiting of all the channels to see how they can be improved.

Cosying up to change

The message of change is nothing new. When Tom Peters wrote *Thriving on Chaos*, he was strongly advocating not only coping with change, but actually enjoying and making the most of the frenetic variability that typifies modern life and modern business. This is a brilliant analysis and a wonderful outcome, if you can cope. There are some of us who seem naturally to enjoy change and welcome it. We get restless without it. It's particularly true of a younger set of people, but, whatever the age group, you will find some who like to live on the edge.

THRIVING ON CHAOS

Tom Peters, *Thriving on Chaos* (Pan Books, 1989).

AGE AND CHANGE

'Young men are fitter to invent than to judge, fitter for execution than for counsel, and fitter for new projects than for settled business.'

Francis Bacon, sixteenth-century English philosopher,* Essays *(1625)

The fact remains, though, that most of the members of your workforce probably do not enjoy change. Of course they appreciate some variation, but, equally, they need a sense of stability and consistency. They like things the way they've always been, and aren't about to appreciate anything different. They are experts in all the blockers of creativity, in saying 'It's been tried before, and didn't work', 'It's not my area' or 'It's silly'. You have two main options here. You can sack them or you can help them.

There was a time when Thatcher-style economics implied that it was up to your staff to sort *themselves* out, to get on their bikes and do something. This is not, in itself, a bad concept. As we have already seen with empowerment and fun, you need staff who are prepared to own the problem and get on with it. However, what you can't do is just leave them to it. Neither can you expect the dislike of change to simply fade away – it needs work.

It's inevitable that DisOrganization will result in some staff turnover – some will decide it's not for them, however much effort you put into the transition – but the core of your staff is likely to remain unless you push them out. We believe that you have a moral responsibility to include them in what's happening, to get them on board, because, whatever some may say, a company is not all about the balance sheet and the bottom line. Without people, industry is meaningless, money is meaningless. Does that sound too much like soppy philosophizing? If it does, think about it for a while.

If you are involved in a start-up, it may seem that this is all unnecessary. After all, you've hand-picked staff to fit the company ethos, you've probably got a much younger workforce than the average and you've got a bright bunch. Yet, even excellence can become a habit. Within a couple of years, the 'this is how we've always done it' mind-set will have set in – from Friday afternoon drink and chat sessions to wearing company baseball caps. Start-ups get some valuable lead time in the build-up of resistance to change, but it's still going to come.

The cycle

For a model of how to deal with the difficulties of constant change, we can look to a surprising source. The Church may seem to many a model of reactionary irrelevance and practical ossification, yet the Church has been dealing with a huge organization for more years than any business. When the Church needed to deal with the conflict between people's need to have constancy and the requirement for change to keep things fresh and to focus on the specific targets of the moment, it looked to an even older model – the seasons of the year. Each season brings new challenges, new interests, yet there is the comfortable certainty of year following year in roughly the same pattern.

Similarly, the Church year is effectively divided into seasons, giving constancy to rely on, but wildly changing moods and requirements. This model might be adopted wholesale. It may be practical to have an annual cycle of change, with key times of stability and times for reassessment. It's more likely, though, with the influence that external forces have on the business, that it will be more a metaphorical acceptance. It might not be that there's always a review of communication channels in February or a barbecue in August, but, rather, the knowledge that there will be certain pegs to hang expectation on during the year.

Whether or not it is possible to set review dates ahead of time, it is certainly possible to devise a confidence-building framework. You can't predict when there will be a huge technology shift that makes you totally change strategy or a new competitor that forces you into a totally different business model. What you can do, though, is to provide anchors on humanly acceptable timeframes.

Anchors away

If we accept that change is inevitable and we can't force people to like it, we need to provide conscious support in other ways. Start at the daily level. There should be a degree of daily comfort.

Look at Entranet's Managing Director, Nick Spooner. Each day his company has an 'upper' – a mini milestone that enables staff to feel that they have achieved something. The day we visited, it was an article on Entranet in the *Financial Times*. Other days it might be a new contract, a product milestone, getting a coffee machine – something that makes people feel that there has been achievement.

Spooner combines this with a daily walk round his staff. Managing by walking about might be a cliché, but it still works. Put it into a regular framework and it becomes part of the stability that helps the staff deal with the hectic change. Make it a high priority.

A certain large company had a very effective campaign to change staff values. At the end of practically every day, the chief executive turned up to answer questions. If it wasn't him, the stand-in explained what had taken him away and apologized. The campaign was hugely effective. A few years later, a similar exercise happened, but the closing session wasn't on the CEO's agenda. It flopped. If this approach is to work, it has to be very high on your senior management's list of priorities – and stay there.

Next, there's the weekly framework. There should be at least one fixed point in a week, ideally with a sociable atmosphere. Whether it's a coffee and doughnuts session or an hour at the pub, there should be an opportunity for those in the mini company to get together as a whole and share information. There doesn't need to be a huge amount of structured input – no more than ten minutes, perhaps bringing up the key issues that are facing the mini company or a particular matter that needs addressing. After that, leave it to them.

At least once a year, there should be something more special. Perhaps a half day combining work on major business problems and fun.

All these things are teambuilding exercises for the mini company as well, but the great thing is that they provide stability and the means to become quick at dealing with concerns, to counter the uncomfortable force of change. You can extend the approach into other vehicles as well. E-mail should ideally be available to every employee – via information points if they aren't desk-based workers – and they should be expected to use it to tell management, however senior, what is going right and wrong. Combined with a good information network, again accessible to everyone, this can add to the sense of control.

Old business droop

There are particular problems when dealing with a long-established firm. How do you deal with the manufacturer who has to move from a regime where most workers could expect overtime to one where overtime is the exception, and a four-day week the best that most can expect? How do you cope with bank employees who have spent 20 years seeing themselves as service staff who are there to help customers who are now told that they have to be salespeople and push insurance for all it's worth?

Take the manufacturer. The mini company structure will help. In a smaller company, it's easier to see just what is affecting the bottom line and the ability to put money in their pockets. Next, leadership must be very strong. This is not a time for directives. The staff need to understand what needs to be done and why. Not to enhance profitability, but to ensure they can be paid. Finally, the anchor must be rock solid, providing both comfort and a mechanism for empowerment. Everyone must feel that they have been asked what alternatives there are. The message needs to have come across simply and powerfully.

The bank employees are in a rather different position. If they feel that they are being pressurized to sell, no one benefits. Is it possible to split telephone sales, giving it to those who genuinely enjoy selling? Has there been any attempt to build up enthusiasm for selling? Most importantly, why don't the bank employees like selling? The immediate response is that they didn't join the bank to sell, but to help people with their accounts, but is there an underlying feeling that your products aren't worth selling? If they were so good that the staff really wanted to tell people about them, selling would become a lot easier; after all, you would be doing your customers a favour. Most of all, such change is often undertaken without anchors. There is no feeling of understanding the reasons. There is no feeling of being consulted; it is imposed. If the staff of a branch mini company made the decision together to start selling, things might be very different.

New business hyper

The change cycle may be a problem for old companies, but it's the lifeblood of a start-up, right? It's true to a point. Yet, as we've noted, it's surprising how quickly the new business can settle into a rut – a year is plenty of time. Furthermore, if the business is one where change is the norm from the word go, there could be a counter-problem. You may have recruited staff with the particular intention of having people who enjoy constant change. Now you get a big contract. It means stability for the next two years. All of a sudden, those assets are going to require extra management or they'll get bored and wander off. If you've got a team of change-lovers and are dealing with a static environment, you will have to artificially generate change. Whether it's swapping roles to broaden experience, moving the office furniture around every fortnight or making the creative challenge grow with the job, you will have to engineer change.

Loving change

Are we forced to accept that staff will hate change? Yes and no. There will always be a feeling of discomfort, butterflies in the stomach, but provided that your anchors are strong enough, staff will begin to find that change isn't so frightening. It's a bit like being on a roller-coaster. Normally we would find being on a runaway train terrifying, yet the roller-coaster manages to combine that frightening lack of control with the knowledge that there are checks and safeguards, that it's just a ride, not a disaster. Similarly, if staff can come to believe in your network of anchors, they can see the other changes that they face as being less threatening. It's up to you. As soon as you decrease emphasis on the anchors because you are too busy with other things, they lose all value. It is only by giving solid and consistent support that you can win through.

CHANGE FOR THE GOOD

Marcus Aurelius, a second century Roman emperor gives an optimistic view: 'Observe how constantly all things are being born of change; teach yourself to see that nature's highest happiness lies in changing the things that are, and forming new things after their kind.'

23

DisOrganization: the cycle

The map

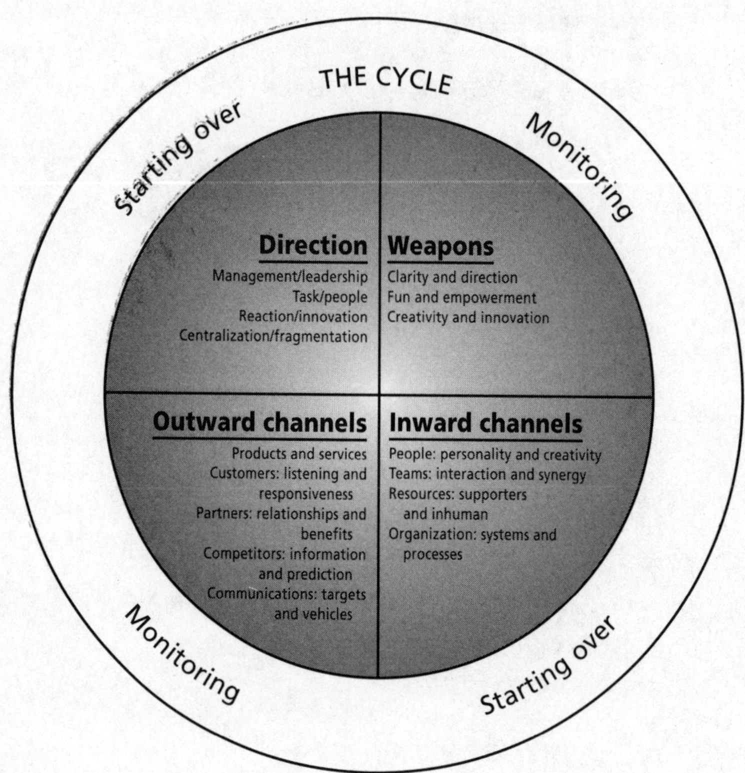

The watched pot

Measurement is a paradoxical activity. It is essential, both to encourage task completion and to spot deviations from the path, but it can become an end in itself, causing more disbenefit than good. Like most of DisOrganization, our message on measurement heads for two extremes. Keep it as simple and as limited as possible, but, at the same time, grow it beyond the traditional financial measures to the expanded view of the Balanced Scorecard.

Constant re-creation

Creativity is at the heart of DisOrganization, and the DisOrganized company will be in a cycle of change. This will be difficult for many of your staff (and managers) who aren't comfortable with change. You may not bring them round enough that they come to love change, but taking the right approach can at least bring an acceptance of it, and may even encourage contributions to the re-creation of the company.

Why DisOrganize?

DisOrganization is about survival and thriving. With a business environment that is rolling away beyond our control, the old ways, the old structures are like prisons rather than greenhouses. They restrain, they don't encourage growth. But don't focus solely on survival. If you accept that work, a sizeable part of most people's lives, should be both enjoyable and fulfilling, DisOrganization is as much about improving your staff and management's quality of life as it is about improving profits. If this sounds wimpish to you, just concentrate on the profits, but what have you got against people?

Will it work?

Without the Chief Executive's backing, no. Without the top team's leadership, no. With these in place, DisOrganization is a life-raft in the sea of business chaos. There's no guarantee of success, and there is risk, but there's a much better chance of keeping alive and happy on the life-raft than there is down in the sea with the sharks.

Index